GARDNER'S THE EPHESIAN GOSPEL

THE
EPHESIAN GOSPEL

BY

PERCY GARDNER, Litt.D., F.B.A.

*Blessed are they that have not seen and
yet have believed*

WIPF & STOCK · Eugene, Oregon

Wipf and Stock Publishers
199 W 8th Ave, Suite 3
Eugene, OR 97401

The Ephesian Gospel
By Gardner, Percy
Softcover ISBN-13: 978-1-7252-9644-2
Hardcover ISBN-13: 978-1-7252-9645-9
eBook ISBN-13: 978-1-7252-9646-6
Publication date 1/5/2021
Previously published by G. P. Putnam's Sons, 1915

This edition is a scanned facsimile of
the original edition published in 1915.

PREFACE

IN 1911 I published a book on *The Religious Experience of St Paul*. This naturally led me on to study more carefully the greatest work of the Pauline School,—greater even than the Epistle to the Romans—the Fourth or Johannine Gospel. I proceeded on the same plan which I had adopted in studying St Paul's works. First, I examined in detail the Gospel itself. Then I wrote a sketch of the results to which that examination led me. Finally, I turned to the modern literature on the subject, and by the aid of it corrected and expanded what I had written. I consider the work of Mr E. F. Scott, *The Fourth Gospel*, as the most valuable of recent works on the subject; and I have usually, though of course not always, found his view in accordance with my own.

I cannot pretend to have studied the literature so carefully as some writers, such as Dr

Sanday or Dr Bacon. My work aims at being suggestive rather than exhaustive. But as my little book on St Paul was in many quarters kindly received, I hope for a similar reception for its successor.

It may seem incongruous, at the present moment of intense stress and anxiety, to publish a work which appeals to quiet thought. It was written before the war broke out; and I can scarcely expect much attention to be paid to it until the war ends. But after all, in spite of all our struggles and anxiety, the saying of St Paul remains true, "The things which are seen are temporal, but the things which are not seen are eternal."

I am indebted to my sister, Miss Alice Gardner, for the Index, and to her and Dr Moffatt for reading the proofs.

PERCY GARDNER.

OXFORD, *April* 1915.

CONTENTS

I

GREEK EPHESUS 1–18

PAGES

Greek and Asiatic elements at Ephesus, 1; the goddess Artemis, 3; strife of East and West, 6; Heracleitus, 9; enlargement of the city by Lysimachus, 11; the Romans, 12; mysticism at Ephesus, 13; raising of men to divine rank, 17.

II

EPHESUS AND ST PAUL . . . 19–33

Followers of John the Baptist at Ephesus, 19; magicians and exorcists, 22; the riot, 24; "fighting with beasts," 26; speech to Ephesian Elders at Miletus, 27; Epistle "to the Ephesians," 31; Ephesus did not greatly influence St Paul, 32.

III

EPHESUS AFTER ST PAUL 34–51

Ephesus in the *Apocalypse*, 34; the Nicolaitans, 36; post-Pauline literature at Ephesus, 38; confusion of Johns, 39; John the Prophet and John the Elder, 40; the *Apocalypse*, 43; Epistle of Ignatius, 47; the Third Council of the Church, 49.

viii   THE EPHESIAN GOSPEL

IV

THE EPHESIAN GOSPEL   .   52–91

PAGES

The literature of the Gospel, 52; the writer and his sources, 53, unessential details either due to symbolism, 57; or to a separate tradition, 60; examples, 61, controversial purpose, 64, comparison with other theories of authorship, 67, corrections of Synoptists, 68, the Johannine source, 69, rivalry with St Peter, 71, date of death of St John, 72; spiritual transposition of tradition, 75; likeness to St Paul, 78, element of materialism, 80; the biography not a mere composition, 83; the conscience of the Church the test of truth, 85; genesis of the Gospel, 86, seeing the invisible, 88; non-natural result, 90.

V

THE WRITER'S IDEA OF BIOGRAPHY   .   .   .   92–123

Differences between ancient and modern writing of history, 92, can we argue from Greek and Roman to Jewish writers? 94; tendencies of Evangelists, 96; parallel case of the two lives of Socrates by Xenophon and Plato, 100, comparison of Platonic and Johannine writing, 109, the last days, 110, artificial construction of discourses, 111; examples, 112, it is not the historic, but the exalted Christ who speaks, 115, this sometimes slips out in the narrative itself, 118.

VI

THE BASIS IN CHRISTIAN EXPERIENCE   124–140

Feeling in ancient times rather civic than individual, 124; the society primary in early Christianity, 126, the Pauline Churches, 127; the common life, 128, the world a hostile medium, 129, after entry into the Church, first forgiveness, 130; then prayer, 132, then power to work marvels, 135; then the bond of love, 136, then eternal life, 138.

VII

THE DOCTRINE OF THE SPIRIT . 141–162

The pneumatic Gospel, 141; origins of the idea of spirit, 142, physical transmission of spirit, 144; the Evangelist uses the word spirit in three senses, 146; first, in a cosmic sense, 146; second, as the inspiration of the Church, 148, comparison with Paul and Luke, 150; the charismata, 153; identification of the Spirit with the exalted Christ, 157, the source of truth and light, as well as of energy, 158; thirdly, the term spirit applied to good and evil demons, 160.

VIII

ESCHATOLOGY ETERNAL LIFE . 163–188

The three questions of eschatology, 163; first, the destiny and meaning of the world, 167, second, the future of the individual soul, 168; how far the Christian doctrine Jewish, 169; third, the relations of the material and spiritual worlds, 170, how Jewish apocalyptic ideas were merged, 171, the Evangelist substitutes present for future, 172, faith confers eternal life, 175; meaning of the latter phrase, 177, in the Synoptics, 178; in St Paul, 180; in the Evangelist, 183; connection with doctrine, 186

IX

THE SACRAMENTS 189–213

Parallelism to pagan mysteries, 189; not seriously disputed, 193; views of the Evangelist, 195; he valued the rites of Baptism and the Lord's Supper, 196, but detached them from history, 198; treatment of John the Baptist, 199, the conversation with Nicodemus, 201; account of the Last Supper, 202; the sixth chapter, 204, spiritualisation of the rite, 206; the miraculous feeding of the multitude, 208; the contagion of the spiritual life, 209; the Incarnation, 211

X

JUDAISM AND THE GOSPEL . . . 214–235

Admission of Gentiles to the Church and Universalism different questions, 214; the racial question in the Synoptics, 215; in St Paul, 218; in the Fourth Gospel, 219; tendency towards universalism, 220; immanent in Christianity, 224; the question of the Sabbath, 226; the Jewish Scriptures, 229, the racial question, 232.

XI

THE CHURCH AND THE WORLD . . . 236–255

Pauline and Johannine doctrine of the Church, 236; differences between them, 239; idea of the Good Shepherd, 240, of the Kingdom, 242; the Evangelist is thinking of the Christ of experience, not of history, 243, the corporate life, 246; opposition to the world, 248; no fixed view as to organisation, 252.

XII

TEACHING AND ETHICS . . . 256–276

The ordinary interpretation of "words and works" inadequate, 256; three kinds of truth (1) scientific, 257; (2) metaphysical, 258; (3) ethical, 259; *truth* in the Psalms, 260; uses in the Fourth Gospel, 261; applied to prophecy of the future, 263; truth not mere truths, 267; rudiments of a creed, 269; truth leads to liberty, 271; it is a touchstone to discern the spiritual, 272; it implies devotion to the Divine will, 274; and leads to love, 274

XIII

MIRACLE . . 277–290

Miracle in the East the sign of a divine mission, 277, the Evangelist looks on miracles as signs, 280; their higher meaning, 281; the raising of Lazarus, 283; the Virgin Birth, 284; the Resurrection, 288.

CONTENTS

XIV

CHRISTOLOGY . . . 291–318

The basis of the Evangelist's Christology the experience of the Church, 292; his special tradition, 292, the claim of Jesus to be Son of God, 294; the Evangelist dwells much on this relation, 298; and on his Master's supernatural powers, 300; but he stops short of Docetism, 302, beginnings of speculative Christology, 308; view of the Atonement, 310; the doctrine of the *logos*, 312, hence superhuman knowledge of Jesus, 316

XV

THE FOURTH GOSPEL AND MODERNITY . 319–358

Summary in relation to modern thought, 319, (1) the spiritual world and eternal life, 321; (2) the history of the Founder, 330; (3) the Sacraments, 340; (4) the Church visible and invisible, 342; (5) the formulation of doctrine, 345; a glance at modern conditions, 355

INDEX . 359–362

THE
EPHESIAN GOSPEL

I

GREEK EPHESUS

THERE are few cities which have a more important place in the history of the ancient world than Ephesus. The main stream of ancient history passes through Ephesus again and again. And I venture to think that in the early history of Christianity, save only Jerusalem, no city has been more influential, not even Tarsus or Antioch or Rome.

In a degree which it is hard to exaggerate, Ephesus was in the ages which preceded Christianity the pivot of civilisation, the crucial meeting place of East and West. Among the great cities founded by the Ionians on the coast of Asia Minor, some were thoroughly Hellenic in type, doors by which the Greek spirit from the seventh century B.C. was constantly penetrating into Asia. Such were notably Miletus and Phocæa. Miletus founded a great trade between Greece and the Black Sea, whence the populous cities of the Ægean derived the corn and fish which were their chief food, and the wood, hemp, and pitch which they needed for shipbuilding. The shore of the Euxine was studded with Greek factories which were the children of Miletus. Phocæa worked westwards: on the shore of Italy, at Velia, and even as far as Marseilles, the Phocæan sailors carried their trade, and their piracy, which was closely allied to trade. With the rise of the wealthy kings of Lydia, there was a reversal of the tide, and the old civilisation of the interior of Asia Minor began to overpower the Greek cities of the coast. When the powerful Persian Empire was organised by Cyrus, Oriental influence grew stronger. The Persians were masters of all Asia down to the coast; and the Ionian aggression was swept back. By the beginning of the fifth century, Phocæa and Miletus were destroyed by the Persians, and did not for centuries recover much power. But Ephesus the Persians never destroyed: rather they cherished it as an outpost against the power of Hellas.

But Ephesus was not a merely Asiatic city. It consisted of two parts. Built on the hills which surrounded the harbour was a Greek city of trade, the city founded by the Athenian

Androclus, and enlarged and fortified at a later time by one of the generals of Alexander, Lysimachus the Macedonian. At some distance inland was the other part of the city, which had grown up round the vast and magnificent temple of the goddess Artemis, and which was not really Greek, but largely inhabited by the peoples of Asia Minor—Phrygians and Leleges.

Such a division was not rare in the case of Greek settlements. When the colonists arrived, they found a great religious community already established. The Artemis of Ephesus was not only the swift huntress, the sister of Apollo, with whom Greek sculpture has made us familiar; she was also the local rendering of the great goddess of nature, who had many shrines in Asia Minor and the East, the deity of the productive powers of nature, source of the overflowing life which wells up with the spring in trees and corn, in animals and in man himself. From a remote antiquity such a mother-goddess had been the chief object of worship among the Syrians and Phrygians and other primitive peoples. The wild places of the land and wild animals were especially sacred to her.

The likeness between the Phrygian goddess and the Greek Artemis lay almost exclusively in this attachment to nature and the animals of nature. Probably, however, the fact that both deities were connected with the moon, and with childbirth, which the religion of many nations has placed under the control of the moon-goddess, formed a further link. But the Asiatic mother-goddess was worshipped in various ways in her different homes. At Babylon and elsewhere her temple was a seat of prostitution. At Ephesus she appears in historic times, owing doubtless to Greek influence, in far less repulsive guise. She was served by a troop of virgin priestesses, called melissæ or bees, under the superintendence of a chief who was an eunuch, and who bore the Persian-sounding title of Megabyzus. These priestesses were supposed to represent the Amazons, who were regarded as having been the original votaries of the deity. They danced sacred dances in her honour at the great festivals. Other servants of the goddess were *Theologi*, who may have recited sacred legends, hymn-makers, and a crowd of slaves or hierodules. Crowds of images were carried in the sacred pomps. Unfortunately, we know but little of the details of the cultus.

Ephesus was not the seat of an oracle: the function of serving as the mouthpiece of the higher powers was left by Artemis to her brother Apollo. But another function of the temple was of great importance. It was a sanctuary: those who had unintentionally committed homicide, and even criminals, were safe from pursuit within a sacred boundary marked out round the shrine. Before justice in a state is organised, while the punishment for offences is left to private vengeance, such sanctuaries serve a necessary purpose. We read of cities of refuge among the Israelites: and in mediæval Europe many sacred places served the same purpose. Mark Antony, with his usual impulsiveness, to please the people, enlarged the limits of the sanctuary, so that it took in part of the town, which, of course, thereupon became a haunt of robbers and assassins, and the dangerous privilege had to be reduced.

The image of the goddess, which was of unknown antiquity, and which, if for a time set aside, had been restored to honour by the time of St Paul, was a mere cone, with human head and hands, and many breasts on the bosom to signify the abundant life of nature. Between this bounteous form and the notion of virginity there seems to be little in common. But the nature-goddess of Western Asia combined many attributes; and in her service the two extremes of sexual relation met. So although at Ephesus the priestesses of Artemis were virgins, yet there were doubtless elements of sexual impurity in her festivals.

How was it that the Ionians, coming at a time when the orderly Olympus of Homer, with a beautiful band of deities presided over by a supreme Father, was fully recognised by the race, were content to regard with veneration this hideous image, and to accept religious customs and institutions full of primitive barbarism, and neither pleasing nor chaste? The answer goes deep. Greek religion, in spite of the æsthetic charm of its ritual, and the beautiful architecture and sculpture and poetry in which it found embodiment, had no proselytising power. It did not satisfy the deep needs of the human heart, the sense of an indwelling spiritual power, the sense of sin and the desire of purity, the longing for a life to reach beyond the bounds of the present. These needs had little to do with the worship of the Greek Artemis, who, except in the important matter of childbirth, had no place in the central tendencies of human life. But they were met in a measure, however crudely and barbarously, by the cult of the great Anatolian nature-goddess, who lived not only in the temple, but in the primeval impulses of her

GREEK EPHESUS

votaries, and aroused in them an enthusiasm which did not suit Hellenic religion, and, indeed, which the more refined and intellectual Greeks were inclined to despise.

Through all the history of Ephesus we see the influences which radiated from the market-place and the harbour, and those which radiated from the temple of Artemis clashing one with the other. The eternal strife of East and West was in no place more strikingly exhibited. As a mart and seaport Ephesus held a very important position. The city was, especially after the fall of Miletus and Phocæa, the natural focus of the trade between Greece and Italy on the one side, and the inland country of Phrygia on the other. Phrygia is a rich country; and through it, by the great Persian road, came the luxurious wares of the further East. Oriental wealth and luxury poured into Ephesus, and with them the ideas of Oriental religion, the chief focus of which in the second millennium before our era was the great city of Babylon.

In prehistoric times Babylon had been to Western Asia and the Levant a sort of religious metropolis, something of what Rome was to mediæval Europe. Then her influence had spread to the coast, and to Cyprus and Crete in the Mediterranean. The Ionians had brought into Asia a wave of fresh air, but their influence at first did not deeply penetrate. When Crœsus, the powerful King of Lydia, came to besiege their city, the people of Ephesus stretched a rope from the commercial city to the temple of Artemis, thus in a literal sense binding the city to its goddess, a goddess whom they expected the king to venerate. And the device succeeded. Crœsus recognised that the Ephesian Artemis was but a variety of the protecting goddess of Sardes, his capital. He became her enthusiastic votary, and helped the Ephesians to build a splendid temple in her honour, on a magnificent scale. Herodotus tells us that he gave to her some golden cows and many columns. And when the English architect, Wood, excavated the site of the great temple, he found and brought to the British Museum many fragments of columns, adorned with reliefs and still bearing fragments of the inscription "Dedicated by King Crœsus." Crœsus soon fell before Cyrus and his hardy Persian soldiery; and doubtless the Persians, in pursuance of their usual policy, cherished the worship of the local deity.

Towards the end of the sixth century B.C., the overflowing vitality of the Greek race acted in all directions. At Ephesus it resulted in the establishment of a remarkable school of philosophy, one of the most important in the days before Socrates. Its chief figure was Heracleitus, whose writings, save for some fragments, have been lost to us, but of whom the ancient historians of philosophy speak in terms of high appreciation. He was said to have belonged to the royal house, but to have given up all worldly ambition and retired into the wilderness like John the Baptist, to live on herbs, and to meditate on nature and man. So far as we can recover his teachings, they seem to maintain that the secret of life and energy in the world is a kind of fire, not the mere visible fire of the furnace, but an energising fluid, which is the cause of life in nature and in man, and which is manifested in the world in the process of becoming, that is, passing from the invisible into the visible or actual. The crude views of the early naturalists of Ionia, such as Thales, who had held moisture to be the ultimate essence of things, were soon surpassed and died away. But Heracleitus founded at Ephesus a school which long survived. It was said of Plato that before he came into contact with Socrates he had been a follower of Heracleitus. Socrates himself professed a great admiration for the writings of the Ephesian philosopher, though he regarded them as hard to understand.

And even as late as the Christian era, admirers of Heracleitus wrote letters in his name, which have come down to our days. Heracleitus seems to have been the first to speak of reason as dominant in the Universe, thus opening a way along which many future thinkers were to travel. I cannot in this place say more as to the philosophy of Heracleitus, but I shall return to the subject when the Johannine *logos* comes up for discussion.

Ephesus took no active part in the Ionian revolt against Persia in B.C. 500; she left the leadership in it to Miletus and Chios, an indication of her closer relations with the East. But when, after the failure of the Persian invasion of Greece Proper by Xerxes, the fleets of Athens were dominant in the Ægean Sea, there can be no doubt that the hearts of the Ephesians turned more to their great mother-city, and Persian preponderance waned. It was, however, in the days of the great Alexander that the West completely turned the tables on the East. Then the Greeks of Hellas and Ionia became the dominant caste as far as India, and the deities of Greece invaded the cities founded by the Macedonian conqueror and his successors in Asia Minor and Syria. But this movement did not decrease the vogue of the Ephesian goddess;

it only laid fresh emphasis on what was Hellenic in her cultus. The great temple built by Crœsus was burned down on the day, it was said, on which Alexander the Great was born. A new and still more splendid edifice rose in its place, the cities and rulers of Asia and Greece making magnificent contributions. Some of the colossal columns of this later edifice also are in the British Museum. Like the earlier columns, they are sculptured in relief, but in the style of the Athenian art of the fourth century.

The coins of Ephesus, about B.C. 287, bear eloquent testimony to the intensification of Greek elements in the religion of the city. At that time Lysimachus, one of Alexander's officers, had acquired the city; he threw a line of walls round the commercial quarter, and renamed the place after his wife, Arsinoe. Up to this time the coinage of Ephesus had been stamped with types of symbolic import, the bee and the stag, both creatures connected with the worship of the local goddess. But under Lysimachus we find on the money beautiful heads of the Greek Artemis. Probably at the same time the primitive Asiatic images which had represented the goddess were superseded in the place of honour by a statue by some great Greek sculptor.

When the Romans succeeded to the heritage of Alexander, and became masters of Asia Minor, they brought great prosperity to Ephesus, which, under them, was the chief port of Ionia. Their rule extended far inland the material features of civilisation, great cities, well built and supplied with water and drainage, roads connecting district with district, and making closer communication possible. The architect, the engineer, and the tax-gatherer spread into Asia, and municipal organisation was much advanced. But as regards the higher aspects of civilisation, the Romans were less successful. The native languages gave way but slowly to Greek and Latin. It was not for the Romans to teach the peoples letters and science and art; they could only make an opening through which the brilliant achievements of the Greeks in these fields might be made familiar to the semi-barbarians of the interior. Greece still produced; Athens and Alexandria and Ephesus still sent out men of science, orators, and philosophers who worked eastwards; so that there arose, at least on the surface, a homogeneous civilisation as far as the confines of the Parthian Empire, and in the great cities, even further, to India and the borders of China.

But what of religion? We have seen how,

GREEK EPHESUS

in the first flush of the victories of Alexander, there was a tendency for Greek religion to gain ground in Asia, and for the deities of the native races to take upon them Hellenic forms. But that movement was neither strong nor lasting. The beautiful religion of Greece, closely allied to art and culture, was not adapted to the rough lives and the untamed emotions of the Lydians and Syrians. The coinage of Ephesus soon marks a retrogression. The beautiful head of Artemis vanishes from it, and the old types of bee and stag come back, to be in turn, before long, ousted by the barbarous, many-breasted image of the great nature-goddess of Asia. This was the image which the people really venerated. There was a story that it had fallen from heaven. The core of it was a rude cone, but it was overlaid, like a modern sacred image, with gold and jewels.

It is well known that in the centuries just before the Christian era there was on all the eastern shores of the Mediterranean a recrudescence of primitive religion. It is a phenomenon familiar to all students of religious history. When the established and received religion of a country grows weak and sapless, there spring from the lower strata of the people fresh shoots of faith and belief, often unlovely in their manifestation, and poor on the intellectual side, but bearing witness to the eternal hunger of the human heart for some medicine which will remove the sense of estrangement between man and the higher powers, and bring the life of the people into some sort of harmony with the spirit which is revealed in the scenes of nature and the events of human life.

Of such a religious revival Ephesus was one of the foci. The Mystery Religions found their richest soil in Phrygia, and most of them, the worships of Sabazius, of Cybele, of Mithras, were full of Phrygian elements. The received religion of Ephesus was of the Phrygian class, with priests who were eunuchs, crowds of virgins dedicated to the goddess, who performed orgiastic dances in her honour, with nightly ceremonies and sacred lore hidden from all but the officials. In the early Roman age there was no cultus more popular than that of the Ephesian Artemis. Pausanias tells us[1] that many people of his time regarded her as the greatest of all the deities, and that almost all cities had temples for her worship; and the latter statement is borne out by numismatic evidence, as there are many cities in Asia in which her effigy appears on the coins.

[1] iv. 31, 8.

GREEK EPHESUS

The mystery religions had a better aspect in that they taught of deliverance from impurity and of a life beyond the tomb, and a worse aspect in that they opened the way to superstition, to materialism, and to magic. This worse side was certainly prominent at Ephesus, since ancient writers tell us of magical formulæ, the *Ephesian sentences*, which were closely related to the temple worship, but were the stock-in-trade of those impostors who tried by means of them to foretell the fortunes of their customers, or to furnish them with spells of great avail for the injury of rivals or the escape from dangers.

Mysticism may be called the protoplasm whence all the higher developments in religion spring. And it is also the source of many of those baser elements in religion which adapt it to popular use, just as the alloy in our gold and silver coins fits them for handling in the market. In every city, as in every nation, there are strata in religion: the stratum of the inspired prophet, of the poet, of the moralist, of the man of the world, of those whose whole energies are absorbed in the battle for daily bread. And yet, in spite of the arrangement in strata and the divergency of schools, each race and district has a tone in religion. The tone in Edinburgh to-day is very different from that in Oxford, and that in Oxford from that in Rome. Centuries of continued influence by the religion of Phrygia, and the proud position of representing the great goddess of nature in the Hellenic world, had prepared the people of Ephesus to give a certain tinge to every school of religion which arose among them. Men of great genius are less open than others to local influence, because they rise above the local level into the air of a higher and more refined humanity. The author of the Fourth Gospel wrote for all Europe and Asia, and for all time. And yet one may venture to say that, humanly speaking, his writings could only have arisen after there had been a fusion of the teaching of Palestine with the tendencies of the mystic cults of Asia.

Sir William Ramsay has shown how Tarsus was the natural and destined birthplace of St Paul. In the same way Ephesus was preordained to be the place which should give birth alike to the writings of John the Prophet, as he calls himself, the author of the *Apocalypse*, and of the great theologian who composed the Fourth Gospel. That John the son of Zebedee settled at Ephesus, and was a venerated figure in the Church there, we have some evidence. His teachings fell on a soil

GREEK EPHESUS

rich alike with the learning of Jewish Hellenists, the wisdom of Greek philosophy, and the enthusiasm of Phrygian mystics, and they bore much fruit for the Church of all future time.

At various periods of her history Ephesus had shown a tendency to raise human beings to divine rank. Plutarch says that Lysander, after his victory over Athens, was the first of the Greeks to receive divine honours. These honours came from the Ionians. As Grote says:[1] "Altars were erected to him; pæans or hymns were composed in his honour; the Ephesians set up his statue in the temple of their goddess Artemis; while the Samians not only erected a statue to him at Olympia, but even altered the name of their great festival—the Heræa—to Lysandria." When Alexander the Great was in Asia, he offered to rebuild the temple of Artemis, then in ruins, if the Ephesians would allow him to inscribe on it his name as dedicator. The Ephesians refused; and the reason which they gave for refusal, if politic, was also characteristic of them: "It is not right for one deity to dedicate a temple to another."

The Seleucid kings of Syria and the Ptolemies of Egypt succeeded one another

[1] Part II. ch. lxv.

in facile deification by the degenerate Ionians. In B.C. 47 Julius Cæsar was deified by the Ephesians with the titles of Saviour and Benefactor.[1] We see, then, that the people of Ephesus were, beyond all peoples, ready to bestow divine honours on generals and kings.

[1] W. W. Fowler, *Roman Ideas of Deity*, p. 144.

II

EPHESUS AND ST PAUL

The importance of Ephesus for Christianity begins with the visit of St Paul, about A.D. 50–55. Every event in the three years' stay of the Apostle which is recorded in *Acts* is characteristic. He found himself in the midst of a society in which religion, good and bad, was the chief interest. His dealings, as always, began with the Jews, who here, as in all the great trading cities, were numerous. But their tendency was very different from that of the conservative Jews of Palestine. They seem to have been eagerly looking out for fresh developments.

Some of these Jews were disciples of John the Baptist, who seem, according to Luke, to have known little of the faith of Jesus, and less of the history of the Church after the Crucifixion. It may well seem extraordinary that news of these doings should not have come to

Ephesus from Palestine; but we moderns are apt to be led astray by the ease and rapidity with which tidings are diffused in our days by newspapers. In a later chapter of *Acts*, Luke tells us that when St. Paul reached Rome, he found that the Jews there had never heard of him: "We neither received letters from Judæa concerning thee, nor did any of the brethren come hither, and report or speak any harm of thee."[1] The testimony of Luke as to Ephesus is not given casually, but he insists on it with iteration. When Priscilla and Aquila were at Ephesus, before Paul's stay in the city, there arrived Apollos, a preacher with a profound knowledge of the Jewish Scriptures, and instructed in the Christian way; yet he had not heard of Christian baptism, but only of that of John. And at a later time, when Paul came himself, he found a small society of twelve men who had received the baptism of John, and been attracted to the Christian society, but did not know of the energising power of the Holy Spirit, which at the time was working so mightily in the Church, inflaming the disciples with zeal, and manifested outwardly in the gift of tongues and spiritual rapture. These gifts came to the men when they had been baptised

[1] *Acts* xxviii. 21.

EPHESUS AND ST PAUL

into the name of Jesus, and when Paul, as we are told, had laid his hands on them. This last statement seems somewhat open to doubt, since in St Paul's own letters[1] we find much about baptism, but nothing as to the rite of the laying on of hands. Since, however, Jesus Himself frequently laid His hands on those whom He would heal, and the rite of the laying on of hands to impart the gifts of the Spirit was practised by the Apostles, it is very natural that Luke should speak of St Paul as conforming to the custom.

The existence at Ephesus, far distant from Palestine, of a set of men who had received the baptism of John, but knew only a stunted Christianity, is remarkable. It does not seem that the Jews who were in this case had themselves been baptised by John in Jordan, but only that they accepted John's call to repentance, and were baptised into the society founded by him, a society which was only gradually merged in the Christian Church. The facts recorded in *Acts* show us, as in a mirror, what an extraordinary change was

---

[1] Excepting, that is, the doubtful letters to Titus and Timothy. In *Acts* xxviii. 8, Paul is said to have healed the father of Publius by the laying on of hands. It is, of course, one thing to heal by touching, and another thing to impart by that means the Christian charismata.

wrought among Jewish disciples outside Palestine by the preaching of Paul and his school. It does not seem that these Ephesian Jews were in any strict sense disciples of John, rather they were disciples of some Christians who had not followed the great change and development which had taken place in the Church in the years A.D. 30–50. They must have accepted Jesus as the Messiah, and probably expected His return in the clouds of heaven; but they did not realise their duties and privileges as part of the body of Christ on earth.

Others of the Jews at Ephesus were magicians and exorcists. Like many Jews in all ages, they had caught the spirit of their surroundings, and carried it further. Ephesus was eminently a city of magic and mysterious spells. The magicians found in the Pauline preaching only material for a further exercise of their arts. The name of "Jesus whom Paul preached" was found to have a greater power in spells and exorcisms than any of the names to which they were accustomed. But when they imagined that they had discovered a new way of bending evil spirits to their will, they were soon undeceived. The touch of St Paul, and even handkerchiefs which had been in contact with him, had a strange power

EPHESUS AND ST PAUL

of healing disease and casting out evil spirits. But when the sons of the Jew Sceva attempted to use the name of Jesus in their incantations, the man in whom was the evil spirit which they were trying to expel "leaped on them and mastered them, and prevailed against them, so that they fled out of that house naked and wounded." They had been indeed playing with fire. The fame of their defeat spread; and by a natural reaction the dealers in spells and charms were ready to confess their impostures, and even to burn their books of magic. These were destroyed in the fire, and the value of them was said to have amounted to 50,000 pieces of silver. It is natural that when books of magic are really believed in their worth is almost beyond price. And nowhere was the literature of magic more plentiful and more in fashion than in Ephesus.

The awakening soon spread beyond the Jewish pale. We learn that some of the Asiarchs were at least interested in St Paul. The Asiarchs were perhaps men of wealth, selected by the Roman Proconsul to organise at their own expense the festival and games in honour of Rome and the Emperor. They would scarcely be Christians; but they were at least so far favourable to St Paul that they advised him to keep away from the theatre at the time of the riot stirred up by Demetrius the silversmith. Everyone knows the story as related in *Acts*. Demetrius represented to others of his craft that the trade by which they lived, the making of silver shrines of the goddess Artemis, was in danger of being spoiled by the preachers of the new religion. With this more sordid motive was mingled a pride in the worship which was the pride of Ephesus. The result was that a great crowd invaded the theatre, dragging with them Gaius and Aristarchus, Paul's companions in travel. The Jews put forward a certain Alexander, apparently offering him to the fury of the crowd; but the excited people refused to listen to his defence, but only cried the more lustily, "Great is Artemis of the Ephesians." The riot was subdued by the town-clerk or treasurer, a wise official, who took the line that the cultus of the goddess was too well founded and universally respected to be hurt by the opposition of a handful of fanatics.

Luke, though full of Christian spirit and an admirable writer, is somewhat prone, as we know from his Gospel, compared with the others, to be dazzled by what is marvellous, picturesque, and striking. This vivid episode has evidently eclipsed for him the other events of St Paul's stay in Ephesus. It is, however, remarkable that St Paul, addressing at a later time the Presbyters of Ephesus, and reminding them of the events of his sojourn among them, does not mention his peril in the theatre, but does speak of dangers incurred from plots of the Jews. We may strongly suspect that in Ephesus, as in Corinth and other cities, the most dangerous opponents of Christianity were really the Jews, and that the doctrine of St Paul found a readier welcome among the Greeks than with them. Of course the pagan mob of the city was devoted to the worship of Artemis; but there were, doubtless, many Greeks of higher religious type, who would welcome the Pauline teaching, and might even find that their pagan beliefs served as guides to bring them to Christianity. The great Pauline teachings of the exalted Christ and salvation by faith in Him were in essence far nearer to the beliefs inculcated in the nobler forms of the Pagan Mysteries than they were to conservative Jewish orthodoxy. We might expect Christianity at Ephesus to move in the direction of Christian mysticism. And we shall find, as a matter of history, that it did grow in that direction.

There is a curious phrase in the *First Epistle*

to the Corinthians (xv. 32), in which the Apostle speaks of fighting with wild beasts at Ephesus. The connection is this: the Apostle is declaring that, apart from hope in Christ, he would never have undergone all the troubles and perils which he had encountered. "I protest," he says, "that I die every day"; and he goes on to mention this fighting with wild beasts as an instance of his sufferings. Is he speaking only figuratively of the fierce opposition of men as savage as beasts; or is he referring to an actual exposure to wild beasts in the theatre? If the latter, it seems strange that Luke should not have mentioned it; and in itself it is extremely unlikely that St Paul, a Roman citizen, should have been subjected to a punishment usually reserved for slaves and those captured in war. Besides, how could he have escaped the jaws of the wild beasts? When, in the second Corinthian Epistle, St Paul is giving a catalogue of his sufferings, he mentions among them no fight with wild beasts. Thus it seems more reasonable to suppose that he is speaking metaphorically of his contests with infuriated enemies.

It is noteworthy that in the Epistles of Ignatius the phrases as to fighting with wild beasts are used both in a literal and in a

EPHESUS AND ST PAUL

figurative way. Ignatius was going to Rome to be thrown to wild beasts, and this form of martyrdom he willingly accepts. But he also speaks of a daily contest with wild beasts in human form, that is, the Roman soldiers who accompanied him.

In any case the wild beasts with whom the Apostle fought cannot be the party of Demetrius the silversmith, as immediately after his encounter with them he left Ephesus, and the first Corinthian Epistle, which was dated from Ephesus, must have been written some time before this.

We hear comparatively little of St Paul's relations with the Ephesian Church after he had left the city. He does not seem to have maintained with it the close relations which united him, for example, with the Church at Corinth. Yet a few rays of light fall on the connection.

We have a very interesting glimpse at these relations, afforded us a little before the Apostle's imprisonment, in his beautiful address to the Presbyters of the Church when he met them at Miletus. None of the speeches attributed by the author of *Acts* to St Paul is so touching as this. The Apostle reminds the Presbyters how he had lived and toiled among them for three years, working with his hands that he might not depend on their charity, and preaching the doctrine of faith in Christ. He mentions the persecutions which he had endured at the hands of the Jews; but, curiously, he does not speak of the dangerous persecution by the votaries of Artemis. He goes on: "I know that after my departing grievous wolves shall enter in among you, not sparing the flock; and from among your own selves shall men arise, speaking perverse things, to draw away disciples after them." Probably the author of *Acts* has slightly changed the character of these sayings, which would be more probably uttered in the way of warning than of prophecy. In any case, they show that before long, after St Paul's farewell, there was a conflict in the Church, and a revolt against the doctrine preached by St Paul. We shall see that this testimony as to inner struggles in the Church of Ephesus is confirmed somewhat later by another witness, the writer of the *Apocalypse*.

Of all the speeches of St Paul given in *Acts*, this one bears by far the clearest marks of authenticity.[1] It is from the *we* narrative, professedly written by an eye-witness; and

---

[1] I have enlarged on this subject in a paper on "The Speeches of St Paul in Acts," in *Cambridge Biblical Essays*, 1909.

EPHESUS AND ST PAUL

while the phrases used by St Paul have close parallels in his recognised Epistles, the whole scheme of the discourse also bears marks of having been written down from memory, after a considerable interval, by an auditor. It is a scene fresh from the life of the early Church, and bearing eloquent testimony to the personal charm of the Apostle, and the love borne to him by his converts.

This fact makes its testimony the more valuable. It shows how slight is the narrative of the Pauline doings in *Acts*, the writer of which work, like ancient historians in general, prefers to narrate in detail one or two striking scenes, painted in vivid colours, rather than to give a complete and balanced history of events. It also throws a light of great value on the early history of Christian church organisation. The representatives of the Church at Ephesus, who are summoned to Miletus, are the Presbyters, who may be a sort of committee of management of the society, or very possibly may have been merely the most important members of it. The picture which is vividly depicted in *2 Corinthians* exhibits the Church at Corinth as a pure democracy, only those being eminent among the disciples who had some special spiritual gift, while the Apostle himself presides over it, rather in virtue of his special endowments and his services as Founder than as having any regular commission. But the Presbyters of Ephesus are addressed by the Apostle as being also Bishops or overseers of the Church. They were such in virtue of the gifts bestowed upon them by the Spirit:[1] " Tend the flock of which the Holy Spirit has made you shepherds." The passage, even if it stood alone, as of course it does not, would be quite conclusive against the truth of the view that St Paul set up in the churches which he founded a single bishop to exercise supreme functions. The Presbyters were not appointed by him, but by the Spirit, as was Matthias, when it was considered necessary to elect an apostle in the place of Judas Iscariot; and none of them had a position of special prerogative.

It is perhaps legitimate to regard the difference between the constitution of the Church at Corinth and that at Ephesus as indicative of the different political conditions of the two cities. Corinth was a Roman colony: the chief magistrates were *duoviri*, many of whose names have been preserved to us on the coins of the city: the municipal organisation was based on that of Rome. But Ephesus, like all the great cities of Ionia, played at being

[1] *Acts* xx. 28.

EPHESUS AND ST PAUL

free, had a senate and a popular assembly, and a variety of magistrates with high-sounding titles, but not much power. The churches of Asia seem to have copied the organisation of the cities in which they dwelt.

The Epistle of St Paul inscribed *To the Ephesians* is of later date than the farewell-scene last mentioned. The subscription says that it was sent from Rome. Whether it is a genuine Epistle of the Apostle is a very difficult question. Certainly its theology is somewhat more developed than that of the other Epistles, and developed in a particular direction. It shows more influence of, or at all events more kinship to, the mystic religions of Asia Minor. A view adopted by some of the best critics, to which I am prepared to adhere, is that it is one copy of a circular letter addressed by St Paul, during his imprisonment at Rome, to several of the great cities of Asia Minor.[1] Its great similarity to the *Epistle to the Colossians*, which is generally regarded as authentic, seems to be in its favour. That it was originally addressed to the Ephesians is more than doubtful. In any case, it does not help us with any facts as to the religious history of Ephesus. There is in it nothing which has reference to the particular history

[1] See Moffatt, *Literature of the N.T.*, p. 392

and circumstances of the Church in that city.

On the other hand, some of the best critics regard the last chapter of the *Epistle to the Romans* as a fragment of a letter to the Ephesians. It is clearly out of place. A number of the persons to whom greetings were sent in it could not well have been at Rome at the time when St Paul was working in Greece and Asia. Prisca and Aquila are clearly the Priscilla and Aquila who are mentioned in *Acts* as having been expelled from Rome, and having met St Paul at Corinth, whence they preceded him to Ephesus; and the whole long list of greetings seems to show that the letter which contained them must have been written to a city where St Paul had long dwelt, and in which he had many friends. This is the latest direct evidence which we have as to the relations of St Paul to the great city of Asia. But we are able to draw, from the Ephesian literature which is discussed in the next chapter, certain inferences as to the conflict of Pauline and other tendencies towards the end of the first and the beginning of the second century.

It is not to be supposed that the religious atmosphere of Ephesus greatly influenced St Paul. He came to Ephesus, as is proved

EPHESUS AND ST PAUL

by the Epistles to the Corinthians sent thence to Greece, with his religious beliefs fully formed. The doctrine of the Exalted Christ, of which he was the great champion, arose early out of the Christian consciousness, and certainly did not first arise on Greek soil. But we can understand how the Pauline doctrine found in the great Ionian city a very fertile soil, where it could speedily take root and grow into a great tree. It would naturally find a far speedier welcome there than in the conservative Jewish soil of Jerusalem. And if there is one thing which is made clear by the history in *Acts*, it is that the Hellenistic Greeks were far more ready to accept and to develop the Pauline teaching than were the Jews, even the Jews of the Dispersion, who had been greatly influenced by their Hellenic neighbours. Everywhere he found friends and disciples among the Greeks, while among the Jews he found a few ardent followers, but numerous and bitter opponents. This was notably the case at Ephesus. On the other hand, some of the later shoots which sprang from the Christian roots, such as the Logos doctrine and the worship of the Virgin Mother, did owe much to the influence of the atmosphere of the Ionian cities of the coast.

III

EPHESUS AFTER ST PAUL

THE message to the Church of Ephesus in the *Apocalypse*, especially if combined with St Paul's address to the Elders of Ephesus in *Acts*, gives us certain data for the history of Ephesus in A.D. 60–90. It is quite clear that in that city the key to the situation is the bitter contest between the narrower or Judaic and the broader or Universalist party. Luke, writing many years after St Paul's speech to the Elders, which took place about A.D. 55, has probably somewhat coloured it, though in the main the report seems historical. I have already called attention [1] to two points in particular. First, whereas, according to *Acts*, St Paul's troubles at Ephesus arose mainly from the opposition of the pagan makers of shrines of the goddess Artemis, in his address he does not mention the pagans,

[1] Above, p 25.

EPHESUS AFTER ST PAUL

but speaks only of the plots of the Jews. And, second, he warns his hearers that they will be in danger from grievous wolves who will enter in, and not spare the flock. We know that the wolves with whom St Paul was all his life contending were the Judaising party.

In the *Apocalypse* we find the reverse, the other side of the same history. There we read that the Church had suffered from the incoming of men who claimed to be Apostles, but were not, and had finally rejected them. Also that there was in the city a sect of Nicolaitans, whom also the Church rejected. Yet the author does not regard the victory over these his enemies as secure: the zeal of the community is growing cooler, and the Church is still in danger. The chief person of whom we know that he claimed to be an Apostle, while that claim was by many rejected, is St Paul. St Paul laboured long in Ephesus, and was the founder of the Church there, but he foresaw that there would come a reaction, and that the Jews who had worked against him in the city would find a footing in the Church, and do it harm. Against them the Apostle tries to arm his friends by pointing out how free he had been from all personal and unworthy motive. Yet it cannot be doubted, considering how completely the

Pauline connection of Ephesus is set aside in the local traditions, that the Judaising party afterwards for a time gained the upper hand. That the writer of the *Apocalypse* was on their side is clear, not only from the strongly Judaic cast of the whole book, but especially from the message to the neighbouring Church at Smyrna, that a plague of that Church is a party which claims to be Jewish, but is not, but is a very synagogue of Satan. It seems no doubt absurd that the followers of St Paul should be spoken of as a party who claimed to be Jewish: such a charge could only be brought against them by one blinded by party zeal. But yet one can understand such a charge, seeing how earnestly St Paul claims for the Church of Christ that it is the true Israel, the spiritual successor of the Jewish nation. A writer like the author of the *Apocalypse* might regard St Paul's spiritual Israel as a worthless and etiolated thing, a ghost without the blood of life. We are not unaccustomed in our days to criticism of this kind. And anyone who converses on the subject with modern Jews will find with what intense antipathy the Pauline views fill them, sometimes even after their conversion to Christianity.

The Nicolaitans are unknown to us except

from the *Apocalypse*. They must have been the followers of one Nicolas. It is a very attractive conjecture that this Nicolas was the proselyte of Antioch, who was, with Philip Stephen and others, named as one of the first set of deacons (*Acts* vi. 5). All these deacons had pure Greek names.[1] Philip and Stephen, as we know, were progressives; and we can scarcely suppose that a proselyte of Antioch would take an opposite line to theirs. Between Antioch and Ephesus at that time relations were close; and it would be by no means strange that a member of the broad and liberal party at Antioch should have founded a party at Ephesus. We can easily understand how hateful such a party would be to the author of the *Apocalypse*. He would regard it much as the hard-and-fast churchmen of our day regard the party which advocates reinterpretation and comprehension.

It is difficult to say what would be the relations between the Nicolaitans and the Pauline party. Certainly we need not identify the two: rather we may suppose that the Nicolaitans were the advanced or liberal wing

[1] It seems very strange that so thoroughly Greek a set of men should have been living at Jerusalem; but it was to attend to the affairs of Hellenist converts that they were appointed

of the Pauline party. We know that several ultra-Pauline parties sprang up in the early Church, the most noted of them being the party of Marcion, which was generally regarded as heretical: Marcion may have carried further the views of the Nicolaitans. At the time when the *Apocalypse* was written, the party of Nicolas seems to have been in an oppressed condition. But, whatever came of it, the liberal or Pauline tendency in the Church was never eclipsed. This is clearly shown by the issue from it of the Fourth Gospel, the author of which goes even beyond St Paul in his ideas of the universality of the faith of Christ. Thus the narrower and the broader parties alternated in their control of the society at Ephesus. The reaction against the exaggerations of Baur has led many recent writers to deny that the contest between the Judaising and the broader party gives us the clue to the early history of the Christian Church; but these writers in turn exaggerate. If we must take one clue as dominant, it can be only that set forth by Baur. Only it is almost always a mistake to confine oneself to one explanation of a complicated history.

There is a considerable post-Pauline Christian literature which is connected with Ephesus. The earliest example of it is the *Apocalypse*.

EPHESUS AFTER ST PAUL

Next come the Second and Third Epistles attributed to John; then the Fourth Gospel, with which goes the First Epistle.

Those who wish to see this literature treated as a whole, with an account of the views of modern theologians as to the date and authorship of the several books, cannot do better than read Dr Moffatt's *Introduction to the Literature of the New Testament*, or the equally lucid *Introduction* of Dr Jülicher, translated into English. Both of these writers are men of great learning and great sobriety of judgment. I shall not attempt to go over the ground which they so admirably occupy: critical questions I only discuss in order to define the position which is taken up in the present work. When I treat of the Gospel, I shall make a statement of my view of its authorship. Here I may premise a few words.

The traditional view which gives all the writings which I have mentioned to one author, and that one John the son of Zebedee, is quite unmaintainable, and is not now maintained by many critics. That it should have arisen in an uncritical age is not surprising. There is a well-known tendency in the world to attribute books, as well as other works of art, such as statues and paintings, to the most noted of the persons with whom they seem to have some connection. The author of the *Apocalypse* gives his name as John, and he wrote before the end of the first century. The Fourth Gospel, except the conclusion, is stated in the Gospel itself to embody the testimony of the Beloved Disciple; and the early Christian commentators had sufficient acumen to see that the Beloved Disciple must be the Apostle John. This identification, it is true, has been denied by many modern critics: some have thought that the Beloved Disciple was Nathanael, who is not mentioned by the Synoptics; some that he is a merely ideal figure; but in my opinion this is a quite unnecessary mystification. The First Epistle is in many respects closely akin to the Gospel. I believe it to be by the same writer; but this again is a point on which critics are not agreed. I shall venture in the following pages to treat the Gospel and the Epistle as by the same man, for if the author of the Epistle is not the Evangelist, he is so closely assimilated to him that he may be used to explain and to enlarge points in the Evangelist's teaching.

To these statements and traditions I would give all the credence which can be reasonably expected for them. The author of the *Apocalypse* was a certain John of Ephesus. At the end of the book (xxii. 9), the angel says to the writer, "I am of thy brethren the prophets." This seems to imply that John was of the order of the prophets or preachers, a distinct class of men in the early Church. Now St. Paul, in his first Corinthian Epistle, classifying the lights of the Church, puts the Apostles in the first place, prophets in the second, teachers in the third.[1] In view of this, it is unreasonable to suppose that the man who calls himself a prophet should really have been an apostle. Thus the Apostle John seems to be excluded from the authorship of the *Apocalypse*. We may add that there is not a single good reason for such an attribution. It is very possible that the Apostle was one of the first Christian martyrs, and dead long before the time of the *Apocalypse*.[2] The tendencies of the book are those of Asia Minor, not those of Palestine; and the name John was so common among Jews that in itself it can prove nothing. The author of the *Apocalypse* thus remains quite unknown to us: we must be content to call him "John the Prophet."

There is far more serious evidence to bring into connection the Apostle John and the Fourth Gospel. In the proper place I shall

[1] 1 *Cor.* xii. 28.   [2] See below, p. 72.

maintain that, though the Apostle did not write the book, there is in it a great deal of tradition which probably came from him. The Fourth Gospel may fairly be called, as it is in our Bibles, the Gospel *according to* John. But the real author was a man of independent genius, who has chosen to remain anonymous. To this same author we attribute the First Epistle; but in writing it he was dependent on no tradition, but followed entirely the bent of his own character. It certainly bears the marks of being a work of the old age of the writer; garrulous and monotonous, though full of the sweetest Christian spirit.

As to the Second and Third Epistles, they are both by one author, who calls himself the Elder. Almost certainly he was not the son of Zebedee; for an apostle would scarcely call himself a presbyter or elder, any more than he would call himself a prophet. There is, in fact, no certain proof that his name was John, for we are compelled to reject the view that he was the John who wrote the *Apocalypse*: and there is little to be said in favour of the view that he was the man who wrote the Gospel. There is, however, considerable evidence of the residence at Ephesus, in the first century, of a certain John called John the Elder, a tradition mounting to the time of Papias. It is, therefore, with considerable probability that we can regard this John as the author of the Second and Third Epistles. These two letters, however, are so simple in their contents, that it is hard to find conclusive arguments either for or against any identification. Nor is the question one which is important for the purposes of the present book. It must have been some unknown circumstance which caused the inclusion of letters so slight and occasional in the New Testament.

To sum up: we find at Ephesus a veritable confusion of Johns. Tradition makes John the Apostle reside there, and it is more than probable that the Fourth Gospel contains traditions which derive from him. John the Elder probably wrote the Second and Third Epistles. John the Prophet wrote the *Apocalypse*. That the actual writer of the Fourth Gospel and the First Epistle was named John there is no evidence; but if this were the case, it would help in a measure to explain the general confusion. In regard to this writer, in view of the untrustworthiness of tradition, we have to fall back on the internal evidence. To this question we return in the next chapter.

The Johannine *Apocalypse* is a document

with which criticism has dealt on the whole very effectively. Its date appears to be in the reign of Domitian, about A.D. 90. However, the person who, in our day, could suppose the Prophet who wrote the *Apocalypse* and the person who wrote the Gospel to be the same would show himself to be destitute of the critical faculty. It is true that there are certain small points of resemblance between the two. Some peculiarities of expression are common to both. And the phrase "Word of God" which figures so prominently in the proem to the Gospel is in the *Apocalypse* applied also to a person, the rider on the white horse (xix. 13), on whose garment was written the title "King of Kings and Lord of Lords." But this only indicates that the two writers belonged to one period and one region. The character and spirit of the two are as different as it is possible to imagine. The Prophet was a devoted Jew, in the succession of the old prophets of Israel, a materialist and a preacher of the coming end of the world. The Evangelist, although of Jewish race, belonged to the extreme wing of those who adapted Christianity to the Gentile world; he was no prophet, but a philosopher and a divine, and entirely pervaded by the love of the spiritual as opposed to the material. He throws aside the apocalyptic notions which so dominate the Prophet, and substitutes a Second Coming and a Heaven of quite another character. To ascribe two writings, one of which is fervently apocalyptic, while the other definitely rejects apocalyptic ideas, to the same writer is a patent absurdity. Even the style of the two authors is quite different: the Evangelist writes in a style which is peculiar, but quite literary; the Prophet in a strange Hebraic dialect, expressive indeed, but quite unclassical.

In spite of the intense Judaism which appears in some passages of the *Apocalypse*, especially in those relating to the New Jerusalem, yet one feels that this nationalism is very different from that of Judæa, more poetical, more imaginative, of wider outlook. And it is largely mixed with ideas taken from other religious sources. As Moffatt well observes, there are in the book elements akin to Zoroastrian, Babylonian, Greek, and Egyptian eschatology and cosmology. This will most clearly appear if we compare the Johannine *Apocalypse* with that very interesting Pagan Apocalypse published by Dieterich under the somewhat misleading title of "A Mithraic liturgy."[1] Cumont has shown that this docu-

[1] *Eine Mithras Liturgie.*

ment is not primarily Mithraic, but composed of Phrygian and Syrian elements; and it is very instructive to place side by side many passages from it with parallel passages from the Johannine work. The Johannine book, though the elements of it are largely Jewish and partly Heathen, is yet a splendid work of early Christian inspiration, containing many passages which are among the choicest treasures of the Christian Church. When it is regarded from the magical side, as a prophecy of the future of the world, it is and has been a source of misleading and of demoralisation. But when it is read as a parable, as a mass of symbolism, it is splendid. If we ask in which of these lights it was likely to be regarded by the people of Ephesus, the answer must be that the Ephesians, like all other communities, contained men spiritual and men carnal, men inclined to the higher forms of Christianity, and men given to spells and magic, and each of these people would interpret the book in his own fashion. All the gifts of God may be used rightly or may be abused. I may mention one or two touches of what I would venture to call Ephesian use in the work; I mean sayings which belong to the atmosphere of the Pagan Mysteries. "I will give him a white stone, and upon the stone a new name written, which no one knoweth save him that receiveth it." The use of amulets inscribed with mystic words was quite familiar to those who used "Ephesian letters." Again, the way in which numbers are used is very suggestive of Neo-Pythagorean speculations. "He that hath understanding, let him count the number of the beast; his number is six hundred and sixty and six." Similar passages occur all through. Of course one could not say that they could only be written at Ephesus. They would be almost as appropriate to Laodicea or Antioch; but yet we may say that no city lay more in the full current of mystic lore than Ephesus.

To discuss the *Apocalypse* in the light of comparative religion, to trace its sources and its interpretation, would be a fascinating task. That task, however, is in the hands of very able scholars, and I must not turn aside to it, but must confine myself to the great investigation to which this book is devoted—the analysis and exposition of the Fourth Gospel.

Another glimpse at Ephesian affairs at the beginning of the second century is afforded us by the Epistle addressed by the venerable Ignatius to the Ephesian Church, when he was going to martyrdom at Rome. The testimony of this Epistle must be used with caution, since it seems, even in its more authentic and shorter form, to have suffered from interpolation. We may, however, note one or two points. The letter mentions as Bishop of Ephesus a certain Onesimus, whom it is very tempting to identify with the young friend of St Paul mentioned in the Epistle to Philemon. That St Paul should have appointed him as Bishop is in the last degree unlikely: at that time the Bishops were selected by some form of lottery, as in the case of Matthias, or elected by the community. It is also noteworthy that the letter dwells on the connection of St Paul with Ephesus, but says nothing of any connection with Ephesus of St John or any of his school.

During the second century, a period of great ferment in Christianity, Ephesus was one of the chief foci of thought. Our knowledge of that century is unfortunately very fragmentary. It was at Ephesus, according to his own account, that Justin the Christian philosopher held his colloquies with his rivals and with the Jews. When Montanism, that revolt against the growing secularity of the Church, arose in Phrygia, its influence was strong at Ephesus, as had been for ages the influence of the Phrygian religiosity. Polycarp, Bishop of the sister-city of Smyrna, claimed to have been an auditor of "John and others who had seen the Lord," though whether he means the Apostle John has been a matter of much dispute. He clearly carried on a Johannine tradition which belonged to that region of Ionia, and which was inherited by Irenæus. Cerinthus, the earliest of the Gnostics, lived at Ephesus, and a tradition makes him an opponent of the son of Zebedee, while an opposed tradition even makes Cerinthus the author of the Fourth Gospel. To find the facts in these matters is almost hopeless: but one cannot doubt that Gnosticism, like Montanism, found a fertile field in the soil which had once belonged to the great goddess of Ephesus.

Ephesus, four hundred years after the death on the cross, was destined to be the seat of another Christian movement which has been of scarcely less importance to the history of the world than was the Fourth Gospel. In Ephesus, in A.D. 431, was held the memorable Third Council of the Church, in which the doctrines of Nestorius, or at least what at the time were supposed to be his doctrines, were condemned, and himself deposed from his bishopric and sent into exile. The doctrine that Christ united two natures in one person was finally established in the Church. These decisions had no particular relation to the place of the Council: they represent the working out of certain impulses of the Church on the lines of the accepted Greek philosophy. But one doctrine which had been in a measure opposed by Nestorius, and which was asserted by the Council, seems to have deeply interested the people of Ephesus. It is the so-called θεοτόκος doctrine, that Mary was the Mother of God. When we learn that the people of Ephesus greeted this doctrine with bonfires and rejoicings, we cannot help remembering that the Virgin Mary, thus finally apotheosised, in a way succeeded to the honours of the local mother-goddess. Some authorities who are well acquainted with the peasantry of Greece and Asia Minor think that there is much in common between the veneration paid by the people of ancient Phrygia to their Artemis or Cybele, and the peasant worship of the local Madonnas, to whom, rather than to God, the people resort in trouble and perplexity.

Of course I cannot say anything as to the effects, enormous both for good and for evil, of the final exaltation of the Mother of Christ. These effects are written large over the history of chivalry in the West and on the Christianity of Greece and Rome. The historian observes the wonderful power of continuity in religious history. He sees how the virgin huntress of the Greeks became merged in the Phrygian deity of nature ; and how, at a later time, in the same region, the Phrygian enthusiasm modified the Christianity preached by St Paul. It is not the business of the historian as such to estimate the values of these phases of religion : that is a matter which must be settled by the instincts of the living Church : the question of value is quite apart from the question of origin.

IV

THE EPHESIAN GOSPEL

By far the highest claim to a great place in the history of religion which Ephesus possesses rests upon its function as the soil which produced the Fourth Gospel. But while all would concede the greatness of the Gospel, there is, as we know, an immense mass of controversial writing centring in it. The date, the authorship, the composition, the tendencies, have been discussed at length by a multitude of able writers, many of whom have given their best years to the study of these problems. No one has a right to publish a book about the Gospel who has not in a measure surveyed this mass of literature. I say "in a measure," for to master it completely would be the work of many years, if not of a lifetime.[1] But the English reader who carefully considers B. W.

[1] A complete bibliography will be found in Moffatt, *Introduction*, pp 515–519.

THE EPHESIAN GOSPEL

Bacon's *Fourth Gospel in Research and Debate*, Canon Sanday's *Criticism of the Fourth Gospel*, the Introduction to Loisy's *Quatrième Évangile*, or the chapters on the subject in Professor Moffatt's *Introduction to the Literature of the New Testament*, will find at least clear and dispassionate statements of the questions involved and the views about them held by modern writers.

If I here entered upon this sea of research, I should violate the plan of this work, which is intended not for scholars, who can consult the great specialists, but for ordinary persons of good education. All that I can attempt is to state the views which commend themselves to me, and which are assumed in the chapters which follow. But I would ask the reader to believe that these views have not been formed hastily, or with a view to support ready-made theories, but have grown out of my studies in literary and religious history.

If we except the episode of the woman taken in adultery, which is of doubtful authenticity, the whole book is of uniform character, and is the literary creation of a single author, including the last chapter, which is of the nature of a supplement. Who he was will never be determined with certainty. But that he was John the son of Zebedee is so improbable, that we may regard this view as set aside. It is not asserted even in the heading of the Gospel, which only says that it is the Gospel *according to* John, not that it is the Gospel written by John. It bears something of the same relation to the Apostle John as the Gospel according to Matthew bears to the Apostle Matthew. As I shall presently maintain, there is in it a Johannine element. But as a literary composition it is quite beyond the powers of the fisherman of Galilee. The true author was a highly educated Jewish Christian, one of the second generation of Christians, who may have listened to some of the Apostles, and certainly came in contact with historic traditions of the Master's life. He was in most ways a follower of St Paul, a Jew of the Dispersion, resident at Ephesus. His work shows him to have been acquainted with the Synoptic tradition in something like its present form. But he seems to have been dissatisfied with it on two grounds. First, he thought it in some points inconsistent with the statements of a teacher or teachers with whom he had conversed, and who had in his opinion truer views as to certain events of the great biography. And, second, he thought that the Synoptists had imperfectly appreciated the

THE EPHESIAN GOSPEL 55

higher and more spiritual side of the Master's teaching. They had been too literal, and not seen far enough beneath the surface. Hence his writing is in a measure controversial, though behind the controversy lay the great impulse of his inspiration, the deep need which he felt of giving utterance to the profound religious ideas with which he was inspired.

Such is the view here taken. To establish it in detail would be impossible without long argument and the sifting of evidence which has already been weighed and sifted a score of times by highly competent scholars. My object will be rather to illustrate and amplify the view than to establish it. If in the treatment of the Gospel it works out in a consistent way, that will be all that I could expect. On one point only a few words are needed. I have called the Gospel the Ephesian Gospel, and I certainly lay a certain amount of stress on its relation to the religion and thought of the most important of the Greek cities of Asia Minor. On this point the evidence of tradition is very strong, since the Ephesian source of the Gospel was accepted by Christian writers from the second century onwards. There is no rival view of any importance. And the internal evidence is quite consistent with the local attribution.

Every critic remarks in the Gospel a number of details which do not seem in themselves important, but which give to the narrative an air, which is in fact somewhat delusive, of being a very exact narrative. These details sometimes specify time or place. Such and such an event took place at the sixth hour, or the ninth hour, or the tenth hour; such and such a journey or discourse took place on the next day, or on the third day. John was baptising at Ænon near to Salim: where the mention of the place seems immaterial. Jesus came to a Samaritan town called Sychar, and there sat by a well. A careful description is given of the pool of Bethesda, which had five porches. And so forth. In a modern narrative such exactness in unimportant and unexplained detail would be natural and expected, and would be regarded as a proof that the writer had access to a diary, or some contemporary record. In some of the narratives of the New Testament, such as the account of St Paul's shipwreck, we have a wealth of detail which convinces most readers of the exactness of the account. But in the Fourth Gospel the details do not help the narrative: very often they seem quite superfluous; and one feels that to construct an exact and chronological narrative is a notion quite foreign to the mind

THE EPHESIAN GOSPEL 57

of the Evangelist. The names of places which I have mentioned sometimes are not to be identified in ancient geography, though every candid critic must allow that it does not follow that they never existed.

There are two ways, and only two ways, in which this particularity in unessential detail can be reasonably accounted for. The first way is to suppose that they have some hidden and allegoric meaning. In the mind of the writer, it is said, everything was a type and symbol, even the hour of the day and the names of places. Critics have tried with great learning and ingenuity thus to explain details. And in the notion there is nothing unreasonable. We know that Philo in the same age interpreted in mystic and allegoric fashion all the narratives of the Old Testament. And St Paul, a far more practical and level-headed man than Philo, regards the Fall of Adam, the journeyings of the Israelites in the Wilderness, the birth of Jacob and Esau, as events of deep meaning not merely in their literal acceptance, but as symbolically interpreted. It is most natural that the Evangelist also should allegorise. And few people would deny that in places he does so. When, for example, he lays special stress on the statement that when the side of Jesus was pierced with the spear, not blood only issued, but blood and water, and when he speaks of this fact as a prop of faith, one cannot doubt that he regarded it in a symbolic light. For him, as for the writer of *Hebrews*, the sacrifice of the Paschal lamb was typical of the death on the cross; and so in other cases, some of which will be mentioned in the course of this work.

Those especially who have studied the writings of that most difficult and elusive author, Philo, are apt to see symbolical meanings in the narratives of the Evangelist. Whether he was actually acquainted with the works of Philo has long been a disputed point. Dr Moffatt is convinced that he was. He writes of the Evangelist:[1] "Symbolic or semi-allegorical meanings are not to be expected or detected in every phrase or touch: generally, however, the reader of the Gospel is surrounded by allusions which are not always obvious upon the surface. There is often a blend of subtlety and simplicity, in which the significance of some expression is apt to be missed, unless the reader is upon the outlook. The brooding fulness of thought and the inner unity of religious purpose which fill the book demand for its interpretation a constant sensitiveness, especially to the deeper meaning

[1] *Introduction*, p. 523.

THE EPHESIAN GOSPEL 59

which prompted the methods of contemporary religious speculation along the lines of the Alexandrian Jewish philosophy, as represented by Philo." Mr Scott also [1] mentions a number of points in which the Evangelist shows so close a likeness to the works of Alexandrian philosophy that we must needs suppose that he was influenced by it. But Mr Scott adds, with his usual insight: " Nevertheless the Alexandrian influence is not to be recognised as primary, like that of the Synoptics or Paul. It does not affect the substance of the Johannine thought so much as the forms under which it is presented." To which I would add that, if the Ephesian philosophical works of the time had come down to us, it is extremely likely that we should have found in them far more points of contact with the Evangelist than we find in Philo. We are apt to forget that Alexandria was but one of the great cities of the Hellenistic world, and that other cities also produced a literature which has unfortunately perished.

The allegorical method of interpretation can seldom lead to results which are certain. Unless one were in very close contact with the mind of the writer, one could seldom be sure of the point of his allegory, unless he stated it

[1] *The Fourth Gospel*, p. 60

himself. We find that modern critics diverge considerably in their attempts to read as symbolic the details of time, of place, and of number which are frequent in the Gospel. There may be a deeper meaning in the six water-pots of the miracle at Cana, in the five porches of the pool of Bethesda, in the hundred and fifty-three fishes drawn from the lake. But I am quite content to leave the search for that meaning to others. A simpler explanation seems more to be trusted.

Sometimes it may readily be found in the desire to conform to the words of the great prophets of Israel. Those words dwelt, to a degree which it is hard for us to realise, in the minds of all the Evangelists, and guided their pens constantly. For example, the curious statement that the soldiers by the cross of Jesus divided His garments into four parts, and then cast lots for the seamless chiton or shirt, can scarcely be taken as literal fact, since it implies a plurality of garments not customary. Some critics have tried to find a symbolic meaning in the "seamless robe." But here, if we turn to the words of the Psalm as quoted by the Evangelist, "They parted my garments among them, and upon my vesture did they cast lots," we have at once an almost undeniable explanation of

THE EPHESIAN GOSPEL

the story. So it was destined to be, and so it must have been.

Another probable and defensible view of the reasons for the insertion of details is that the Evangelist had heard tales of the doings of Jesus from an eye-witness, or the disciple of an eye-witness. We know that to tales thus told long after the event, and especially if told by old men, little details of time and place and circumstance naturally cling. Very often they become altered with time; but something of them still adheres, just as a few patches of colour often remain on a wall after the fresco which had been painted on it has mostly disappeared. This is the view on which, in general, I am disposed to rely.

We will take an example. When Nathanael in the Fourth Gospel comes to Jesus,[1] the Master says of him, "Behold an Israelite indeed, in whom is no guile." Considering the way in which the Evangelist always speaks of the Jews, it is difficult to regard this saying otherwise than as one actually handed down by tradition. The same applies to what follows. Jesus says to the new-comer, "Before Philip called thee, when thou wast under the fig-tree, I saw thee." Nathanael is so

[1] *John* 1 47

much struck by this saying that he becomes a disciple on the spot. No explanation is given of the reason why the saying went so straight to the mark. The attempts of critics to find symbolical meaning in this narrative have not been happy; and the most natural supposition is that it happened to be preserved in the memory of one of the Apostles who was present, as a little piece of wreckage.

Bishop Lightfoot laid some stress on a particular passage as a proof of detailed tradition. The Evangelist represents the Jews as saying of the temple, "Forty and six years was this temple in building." The temple appears to have been begun in B.C. 20 or 19. Forty-six years from that date would fall in A.D. 27 or 28, that is, in the time when Jesus was teaching; and at that time the temple seems to have been incomplete.[1] This report of the Evangelist fits in well with the theory I am maintaining. The number forty-six adhered to his memory, and was preserved as a fly is preserved in amber.

In the same way, it is more than probable that some actual sayings of the historic Jesus are set down in the Gospel. But in allowing this, we must proceed very cautiously. That the long and wonderful discourses in the

[1] See Drummond, *The Fourth Gospel*, p. 371.

THE EPHESIAN GOSPEL 63

Gospel are an accurate record of the speeches of Jesus no one with any sense of literary style would allow. If we compare them on one side with the speeches in the Synoptic Gospels, and on the other side with the Johannine Epistle, it will be at once obvious how much more in them belongs to the Evangelist than to his Master, and I may add, how evidently they belong to the end and not to the first half of the century. I have sometimes tried to find in them sentences which may be the original word of the Saviour which was the germ of the speeches. But such an attempt has usually broken down, for the germ turns out to belong to post-crucifixion times, as well as its amplification. Nevertheless, here and there one finds sayings which have the air of authenticity, and which commonly the Evangelist has somewhat transposed. We may take, as an example, the saying which comes twice over in the Gospel[1] as to the lifting up or exaltation of the Son of Man. The words vary; but some such speech may well have come to the writer from his Apostolic authority. It is interesting to see that he interprets them in two ways: first literally and then more broadly. In one place he regards the saying as a mere prophecy

[1] III 14; XII 32-34

of the lifting up on the cross; but in another he adds a thoroughly Johannine interpretation: "So must the Son of Man be lifted up, that whosoever believeth may in him have eternal life." This is the voice of Christian experience.

Nowhere is the possession by the Evangelist of a definite tradition more clear than in that passage in the supplement (ch. xxi. 22) in which the rumour current among the Christians that the beloved disciple should not die before the second coming of his Lord is controverted. "This saying therefore went forth among the brethren, that that disciple should not die: yet Jesus said not unto him that he should not die; but, If I will that he tarry till I come, what is that to thee?" It is difficult to resist the impression that on some occasion, perhaps not that mentioned in the context, Jesus did utter these very words in regard to the Apostle, and that an auditor repeated them to the Evangelist. If any reader has confidence in his power of discerning beneath other words of the Evangelist actual sayings of the historic Jesus, he engages in a most legitimate task, in which success will be very valuable.

Another motive which is usually attributed to the Evangelist is a controversial one.

THE EPHESIAN GOSPEL 65

Here we are on surer ground, and less likely to be warped by mere subjective tendencies —those tendencies which make us all more disposed to regard as actual words of the Founder the sayings which we most highly value. Every book of the New Testament contains a certain amount of controversy. It was impossible for the writers to set forth their views as to the Person and work of their Master without at the same time attacking the views of those who felt differently. In Matthew's Gospel there is much controversy with those who denied that Jesus was the Messiah. In *Acts* there is much controversy with those who taught that Gentile converts must keep the Law of Moses. The Fourth Evangelist has strong opinions as to the Person of his Master, and in setting them forth, he naturally attacks the teaching of those of opposite opinions. In the *First Epistle of John*, almost certainly written by the Evangelist, he breaks out into open controversy : " Who is the liar, but he that denieth that Jesus is the Christ ? This is the antichrist, even he that denieth the Father and the Son."

But though it is fair and natural to examine every chapter of the Gospel in order to see not only what doctrines the writer supports, but also what doctrines he denies, yet it is possible to apply this useful key to locks which it does not fit. In particular, I think the notion that the Evangelist had before him, as he wrote, the texts of the three earlier Gospels, and that he endeavours at every point to correct and supplement them, has been carried too far. Such a course would be natural in a modern writer, who would have the earlier texts lying open on his desk, and would refer to them every minute. But such a course would not be natural to an ancient writer, save he were a literary man like Plutarch or Pliny. The Evangelist is primarily positive, not negative: he writes from the abundance of the heart, not in a critical vein. In many of the cases in which he is supposed to be correcting Matthew or Luke, I think he is only transposing into his own key the traditional narrative. It is likely that, when he wrote, the Gospels were current at Ephesus. He had doubtless often heard parts of them read. He was not satisfied with them, because he thought that the view which they took of the Person and sayings of Jesus was literal and materialist. Sometimes he was able to correct or supplement them in detail, by the help of oral tradition which had come down to him from a particular source. More

THE EPHESIAN GOSPEL 67

often he preferred to narrate tales which they had omitted. But in every case, he transmuted everything in the light which came to him from the experience of the Church, and from the personal revelation which he, like St Paul, supposed himself to have received from the exalted Head of the Church.

My view on the whole nearly coincides with that of one of the most judicious as well as learned of recent writers, Dr Moffatt:[1] "The least objectionable hypothesis lies among those which postulate . . . a certain oral tradition upon the life of Jesus which had hitherto flowed apart from the ordinary channels of evangelic composition." In a word, the Evangelist had a source of information derived from the teaching of one of the Apostles, whether he had himself listened to him, or had only been a hearer of some of those who repeated his words. This view may in fact be regarded as the most natural one; and to it many of the best critics incline. It may be held in a variety of forms, from that of H. Holtzmann, who holds that elements in the narrative look like reminiscences without regard to dogma, to that of H. H. Wendt, who thinks that it is the speeches in the Gospel which are derived from an earlier written source, while the

[1] *Introduction*, p. 562.

narrative is a freer composition. A. Harnack also thinks that in some way or other John the son of Zebedee stands behind the Evangelist. The view of Wendt seems to me a precise transposition of the truth: yet it is curious that I could accept his concluding chapter with small modifications.[1]

Some of the statements in the Synoptic Gospels the Evangelist does certainly seem intentionally to correct. The date at which Jesus carried out the cleansing of the Temple at Jerusalem and the date of the imprisonment of John the Baptist are altered by him. In these cases there is no visible reason of symbolism or doctrine for the correction: it seems to be the result of a variety in the tradition. He states that Jesus bore his own cross to Golgotha.[2] Mark had written that the cross was borne by Simon of Cyrene; and as Mark adds, "the father of Alexander and Rufus," we can scarcely doubt the correctness of his assertion. It is possible that, in this case, the Fourth Evangelist altered the statement of Mark, because he thought it beneath the divine dignity of Jesus that He should accept the aid of a man on such an occasion. Or it may be that at the start Jesus bore His

---

[1] Wendt, *The Gospel according to St John*, Eng. trans., p. 254   [2] xix. 17

THE EPHESIAN GOSPEL 69

own cross; and that the Evangelist, knowing this, desired to correct the current tradition. In all such conjectures it is hard to say when we can reach certainty, or even strong probability.

Of course the most natural view would be that this witness who repeated, probably in Ephesus, the events of the life of Jesus was the Apostle John, the son of Zebedee. This is the readiest way of accounting for the persistent early tradition which regarded the Gospel as the Gospel according to John. And it seems to be definitely stated in the appendix to the Gospel: "This is the disciple who bears witness of these things and wrote these things." This is of course said not of John by name, but of the "beloved disciple." who has been by most commentators, and in my view rightly, taken as John the son of Zebedee. The words "and wrote these things" certainly give us some pause, as it would seem far more probable that the source of the Apostolic tradition was oral rather than written. But people in those days did not use their words with the pedantic accuracy to which modern scholars are accustomed. Any fragmentary piece of writing left by the Apostle might justify the vague phrase of the text.

It is indeed very doubtful whether John

the fisherman of Galilee would have had sufficient literary training to write any continuous composition, above all a composition in a language so little familiar to the Galilean peasants as Greek. But if he did leave any writing which could be used as biographical matter, it would probably be an account of the trial and death of his Master. The phrase "who wrote these things" is immediately in connection with the details of the Crucifixion, which perhaps John alone of the disciples witnessed. The account of the last days is in the Gospel so very much more ample and detailed than any other part of the biography, while at the same time it has not at all the air of mere invention, that one is compelled to think that the Evangelist regarded this part of his work as in a special degree founded upon the testimony of an eye-witness. But whether he was merely incorporating details which he had learned orally through frequent repetition, or whether he was using a written document, we cannot doubt that he would feel justified in proceeding with perfect freedom. That part of his narrative is in the same style, and shows the same tendencies as the rest. However much of actual tradition it may include, it is essentially a part of the new, more spiritual Gospel.

THE EPHESIAN GOSPEL

It seems quite incredible that if the Apostle John were the actual writer of the Gospel, he should have designated himself in it by the phrase "the disciple whom Jesus loved." But if the Gospel were written by a follower of his who held him in high esteem, nothing could be more natural than such a designation. Such a follower would remember how the Apostle dwelt lovingly on the various occasions on which his Master had treated him with confidence and affection, and reverted gladly to such incidents again and again; and the phrase "the disciple whom Jesus loved" would naturally form itself in his mind. Details and circumstances not exactly given in the ordinary tradition, but repeated by the Apostolic teacher, would especially dwell in his memory, and he would naturally incorporate them in his narrative.

It has often been observed that there appear traces in the Gospel of a rivalry between St Peter and the Beloved Disciple, and that the Evangelist is on the side of the latter. At the Last Supper the Disciple has a place next to Jesus Himself, and Peter can only ask a question of the Lord through him. It is through the influence of the Disciple that Peter is admitted into the court of the High Priest. When Peter and the Disciple ran together to the sepulchre, the Disciple arrived first. And whereas Peter denied his Lord, the Disciple was standing by the cross, and received a charge to take care of the mother of Jesus. Some critics have supposed that these touches prove that St John, when writing the Gospel, took occasion to put Peter in the second place. It is surely a far more satisfactory view to hold that the depreciation of Peter when he comes into rivalry with the Beloved Disciple is a result of the honest love and partisanship of one of the followers of that Disciple, rather than of his own jealousy or self-assertion.

The objections to the belief that we have in the Fourth Gospel a strain belonging to the son of Zebedee are two. They are serious, but not, as I think, conclusive.

One is that several good authorities have in recent works maintained that John the son of Zebedee was martyred, like his brother James, early in the Christian history, and that the traditions which bring him to Ephesus and represent him as living to an advanced age arose out of a confusion between him and another John—John the Elder or Presbyter, who was the author of the second and third of the Epistles which go by the name of John, and of whom we find traces in the tradition of Papias. As Dr Latimer

THE EPHESIAN GOSPEL 73

Jackson puts it:[1] "There is but one John of Asia Minor to be reckoned with. Going down, the old man full of years, to his Ephesian grave in peace, he was, it may be conjectured, that enigmatical but real personage who somehow refuses identification with the son of Zebedee, the 'beloved disciple.' As for the Apostle John, it is within the bounds of probability that, whatever the locality and date, he died a martyr's death."

A further objection is that the Gospel does not in tone and character correspond to what we learn in the Synoptic Gospels about the son of Zebedee. Hot and fiery in temper, he was for calling down fire from heaven on the village of the Samaritans which would not receive his Master; and it was he who forbade the man who cast out devils in the name of Jesus. He deeply offended the Apostles by allowing his mother to claim for him the highest place of honour in the coming Kingdom. Although he was one of three disciples admitted to the closest intimacy of his Master, he does not seem to have shown the power to fully appreciate His spirit and purposes. These facts do certainly furnish a very strong, perhaps a conclusive, argument

[1] *Proceedings of the Society of Historical Theology*, 1912, p 35

against assigning to the Apostle the writing of the Gospel. But they are not at all valid against such an association with the writer as I have suggested. For it is in the very nature of the actual author of the Gospel, whoever he may have been, to transform every fact and every statement with which he came in contact by the power of a sort of spiritual magnetism.

The arguments for the death of the Apostle by martyrdom do not appear to me to be so strong as they seem to Dr Latimer Jackson. But I think that the question of the Johns of Ephesus is so obscure that it will never be finally solved. There is John the Apostle, whom early tradition takes to Ephesus, and whose grave was shown there. There is John the Prophet, who wrote the *Apocalypse*. There is John the Elder, author of two Epistles. In my opinion we have much reason for thinking that the Gospel was written by a disciple of John the Apostle.

In whatever way the tangled skein be unwound, it does not greatly matter to the purpose of this book. I may fairly confine myself to the statement, not based on untrustworthy traditions, but derived from a study of the Gospel itself, that the writer had in his mind an oral tradition of the life of

THE EPHESIAN GOSPEL 75

Jesus which had hitherto flowed apart from the ordinary channels of evangelic composition.

But I have yet to speak of the second and more dominant element in the mind of the Evangelist. To such a nature as his, though he is always in a sense striving to be exact, facts appear in so changed a form that their mere outward and physical side matters but little. St Paul speaks of looking not on the things which are seen, but on the things which are invisible. But the Fourth Evangelist carries that habit of mind much further than even St Paul. Every event for him is translated from a temporal and spacial setting into one which is ideal and spiritual; it has a meaning in relation to the great purposes of God. And this higher aspect of deeds and words so overshadows their mere physical side that the latter almost ceases to exist. " It is the spirit that giveth life," he writes; "the flesh profiteth nothing." These words might well be printed at the head of the Gospel, as the text on which all the rest is but commentary. I shall have continually in the present work to recur to them.

This manner of looking at tradition is quite characteristic of the mentality of the sages of Alexandria and other Hellenistic centres. It is best illustrated for us in the commentaries of Origen, which set forth, with an abundance of instances,[1] how the Scriptures, under which name he includes not only the Hebrew Scriptures but the Gospels and the Pauline Epistles, have ordinarily not only a material or literal, but also an inner or spiritual meaning. And of these the spiritual meaning is the more important and to be preferred when there is a clashing between them. He is even ready to allow that some events narrated in Scripture did not as a matter of fact take place, but are to be regarded as symbolic only.

Almost the only case in which the authority of the Apostolic teacher is expressly cited is when the Evangelist records that when the soldiers after the Crucifixion came to Jesus and saw that he was dead already, they contented themselves with thrusting a spear into his side, " and straightway there came out blood and water. And he that hath seen hath borne witness, and his witness is true." This statement has greatly perplexed the literalists; for when a dead body is pierced, blood mixed with water does not come out, unless indeed there be some local disorder, some blister on the surface or cyst within, which might hold water. But the statement can scarcely be pressed as evidence which would satisfy a physician. It

[1] *De Principiis*, iv chaps. xi.–xvi.

THE EPHESIAN GOSPEL

is sufficient to prove that in the eyes of the witness standing by there was some appearance which seemed to resemble blood mixed with water. But the Evangelist looks on the testimony with very different eyes. To him it is a mere parable, a symbol to show that the death on the cross was a sacrifice of cleansing in both the ways in which such cleansing took place according to the religious views of the time. It was by the water of baptism or sprinkling, and by the blood of animal sacrifices, that men were cleansed from impurity, and made fit to approach the Divine presence. The Evangelist delights in the fact and emphasises the testimony for it, because it has a high significance and shows how the death on the cross is a part of the eternal purpose of God for the salvation of men.

Another example may be taken of a somewhat different kind, in which the Evangelist still more clearly shows the working of his mind. The high priest Caiaphas "was he who gave counsel to the Jews that one man should die for the people."[1] And the Evangelist comments on this counsel: "This he said, not of himself; but being high priest that year, he prophesied that Jesus should die for the nation, and not for the nation only, but

[1] *John* xviii 14; compare xi. 50.

that he might also gather together into one the children of God that are scattered abroad." The obvious fact was the callous utilitarianism of the high priest, who, careless of justice, was ready to destroy a reformer who brought the nation into peril. But the Evangelist sees beneath the words of unprincipled expediency the utterance of a magnificent spiritual prophecy, which God spoke by the mouth of a high priest, however unworthy.

St Paul and the Fourth Evangelist have in the main the same conception of Christianity. They are both inspired by the same great ideas. St Paul comes first, and opens the way; and it is obvious that without his preaching and influence the Fourth Gospel would not have been written. It is the result, setting aside the special divine inspiration of the writer, of the working of the Pauline teaching in the rich religious soil of Ephesus. But though the informing ideas in Pauline Epistles and Johannine Gospel are much the same, yet their manifestation in the two is astonishingly different. We cannot hope wholly to explain that difference, since it is impossible ever fully to explain the path of divine inspiration. "The wind bloweth where it listeth: so is everyone that is born of the Spirit." But it is our duty to explain and to understand it as far as we can. We have duties to history, as well as duties to religion.

In a previous work[1] I have tried to show that the divine ideas working in the world may alternatively find expression in history marked with a strong ethical tinge, and in doctrine. In the Pauline Epistles, which are mainly doctrinal, there is a certain admixture of what may be called history. The writer has notions as to the character of Adam's fall, the calling of Abraham, and the like. But it is so filled with, and transposed by, doctrine that historic fact, or fact at the time supposed to be historic, is overlaid and almost lost. The writer of *Hebrews* is almost entirely doctrinal, but he brings in a touch of history in quoting the meeting of Abraham and Melchizedek. In the Fourth Gospel, history takes a very different place. The Gospel is professedly historical; and is, as I believe, in parts full of genuine historic tradition. But in the amalgamation of history and doctrine the writer goes far beyond St Paul and the writer of *Hebrews*.

The Evangelist felt that the life lived on earth by Jesus was a real life, conditioned not only by time and space, but by real humanity.

[1] *Exploratio Evangelica*, chaps. ix. x.

His body was no illusion, but a solid fact. The Evangelist not only ascribes humanity to the Divine Word, but even says, "The word was made flesh," the term flesh indicating the complete materiality of the body of Jesus. He was born of human parents; for the story of the virgin birth, already current in the Church, is not repeated by the Evangelist, nor alluded to by him. The Evangelist had a loftier doctrine of the Incarnation. Jesus, he knew, had suffered from weariness and thirst; he had wept for sorrow, and when his side was pierced blood had flowed from it.

We come here on one side, and a very important side, of the Evangelist's mind and teaching. Spiritual as he was, there was in him also a certain vein of materialism, as there must be in every man who is fitted for life on this world of ours. When we come to speak of the Christian sacraments, we shall find that he regarded them on their literal and ritual side as of great importance. There can be little doubt as to the current which drove the Evangelist in a direction with which he had little real sympathy. Already Gnostic notions, such as those of Cerinthus, were a danger to the Church. There seemed a possibility that those who carried further the Pauline line of the spirit being everything and the flesh wholly unprofitable might not only dispense with the sacraments of Christianity, but even regard the life of the Founder as a matter of indifference. We know that before long there arose the Docetic tendency to maintain that the life of Jesus on earth was a mere apparition or delusion; that it was only a simulacrum which suffered on the cross. They denied that the Word of God could really be human, though for a time He might inhabit a human body. Against the rise of this tendency even St Paul, who was in a sense its author, protested. And it is infinitely creditable to the wisdom of the Fourth Evangelist—I should prefer to say a proof of the reality of his divine inspiration—that he set himself rigidly against the Gnostic aberrations He saw the danger, which was a real danger, that Christianity might be emptied of positive contents, and become a mere form of theosophic speculation. Like all great teachers of men, he was able to draw the line against the excess of his own tendencies. Some writers have said that Socrates, who spent his life in warring against the Sophists, was the greatest of the Sophists. And some have said that the Fourth Evangelist, who protested against Gnosticism, was the greatest of Gnostic thinkers. That is a superficial view: the wise mean is always regarded by each extreme as on the side of the other. The Evangelist tried to hold the scales even. He thought, however, that material and visible conditions had blinded the eyes of the disciples to the manifestations of the spirit which showed through corporeal conditions. Hidden under the veil of the flesh was no human spirit, but the eternal Word of God, who had been working in the world since it was formed from chaos, and was now revealed in form as a man, but with wisdom and powers more than human.

According to St Paul, the Spirit who dwelt in the earthly Jesus had dwelt with the Divine Father before the world was made, and after the death on the cross returned to sit on the right hand of God, while at the same time He guided and inspired the Church. But St Paul had dwelt on the suffering, the humiliation, and the death of Jesus Christ, not on His life. He held that in coming to earth He had emptied Himself of divine prerogative, and that His divine nature had, as it were, for a time suffered eclipse. But the Evangelist believed that, in all the steps of that life, those who had spiritual discernment might see the indwelling Word, that even on earth He showed a glory as of the only-begotten Son of the Father, which shone out in works such as

THE EPHESIAN GOSPEL

no other man did, and in words which no other could speak.

Some critics have held that, filled with such purposes, the Evangelist freely composed a life of his Lord, making occasions in which he could work in the higher spiritual teaching with which he was imbued. But I regard such a view as not merely in itself unsatisfactory, but as contrary to the evidence. It seems quite clear that he was conscious of possessing knowledge as to the biography of Jesus, which previous writers did not possess. He often clearly intends to correct current historic statements. Of the last days before Calvary he gives a minute and detailed history, which seems to many unprejudiced critics to be more precise and accurate in its sequence of events than the account in other evangelists. He brings in many statements as to geographic and personal fact which appear to be exact. So far as events go, he tries not to write a romance, but to narrate a life. That he is careless as to the succession of events is but natural to so highly idealist a writer, writing under conditions quite different from those of the modern world.

It appears to be quite clear that he regards himself as commissioned to give to the Church the testimony of an eye-witness of the events which he records. To take a single instance: he says that when the beloved disciple, running with Peter, came to the tomb, he did not content himself with looking in from outside, but "entered into the tomb; and he beholdeth the linen cloths lying, and the napkin which was upon His (Jesus') head, not lying with the cloths, but rolled up in a place by itself." This detail must either be an invention, for which some origin in symbolism may be suggested, or a piece of testimony handed down by a witness. I have no doubt that it is the latter; and in this and other cases it is made clear that the witness on whom the Evangelist relies is the beloved disciple, who, as I have already observed, must be the Apostle John. It seems perfectly clear, then, that the Evangelist had been an attentive and admiring hearer either of John the son of Zebedee, or of one of his immediate disciples and followers.

It is, however, not legitimate to leap, as so many writers do, from this conclusion to the conviction that the narrative in the Fourth Gospel, reproducing the testimony of a deeply interested eye-witness, is of equal or superior value as regards historic fact to the Gospel of Mark, which is on good grounds regarded as giving a summary of the preaching of St Peter. People who proceed thus can have no notion how far, to such a writer as our Evangelist, idea is more important than historical fact, and edification than intellectual instruction. St Luke, writing as a Greek, does give it as his purpose that his readers may know facts, although his notion of history is very different from that of modern days. But the Fourth Evangelist writes: "These things are written that ye may believe that Jesus is the Christ the Son of God; and that, believing, ye may have life in His name." He writes primarily to build up the Church of Ephesus, and only secondarily to correct some of the mistaken views of his predecessors. The element of Christian experience tells far more in his writings than the element of tradition. In his Epistle he repeats this notice:[1] "The anointing which ye received of Him abideth in you, and ye need not that anyone should teach you." It was the conscience of the Church which was the test of all truth, even truth in regard to the life of the Founder of Christianity. The scientific historian, of course, cannot take this view. But so modern a writer as Dr Dale of Birmingham accepts it in his very suggestive work, *The Living Christ*. This writer thinks that converse with the exalted Christ will enable a Christian to

[1] 1 *Epistle* ii. 27.

judge of the historicity of events recorded by the Evangelists. From the point of view of historic science this of course could not be allowed. But it is a notion far more excusable in the first century than in the nineteenth.

It is all but impossible that one who had been an actual companion of Jesus should have had all his recollections so transmuted in course of time that the Jesus reflected in the Synoptic Gospels should have become transformed into the Jesus of the Fourth Gospel. I say "all but impossible," not "impossible," because the early history of Christianity is so full of the utterly unexpected, of events which a historian finds it very difficult to account for, that one can scarcely venture to say what is and what is not impossible. The inspiration of the Church worked in ways so strange that we can only follow it with open minds and bated breath. But when the choice lies between two views, one of which is in the highest degree unnatural and unlikely, and the other by no means outside our experience and the bounds of probability, we are bound to accept the latter.

By far the most probable and reasonable view is that the Fourth Evangelist, a man of philosophic mind and profound genius, had been as a young man converted by the preaching of St Paul, which teaching he never did more than modify, never gave up. Afterwards coming under the strong influence of St John or one of his immediate followers, he heard many details of the life of Jesus, listening with ears still full of the Pauline teaching, and a heart full of the spiritual presence of the Christ of the Church. The simple narrative of the eye-witness took in his mind a new and exalted character. He was convinced that the Apostles, even the most favoured of them, did not fully comprehend the life which was unrolled before them, and accepted the teaching only as it lay on the surface, not understanding the depths which lay beneath. Often between the words of his teacher he would see an opening into great spiritual vistas. At the same time, he clearly had a deep love and profound admiration for the son of Zebedee: he realised that the relation in which he had stood to his Master consecrated him for ever. Only, his eyes had been dazzled by seeing: those who had not seen, like St Paul and himself, were in a sense more blessed; because to the vision of faith only, and not to the eyes of the body, could the true majesty of Jesus Christ become clear.

It has further been suggested that in early life the Evangelist may have belonged to the Society founded by John the Baptist. This theory has so much in its favour that it is almost more than a theory. We know that at Ephesus, in the time of St Paul, there were followers of the Baptist. Mr Scott[1] has pointed out that in the Clementine Recognitions (probably of the third century) mention is made of some of the followers of the Baptist who maintained their master to be the Christ: this proves that the sect was not early merged in Christianity. The account of the Baptist at the beginning of the Fourth Gospel is very appreciative; but emphasis is laid on his position as a mere herald, not as "he that should come." And further, the rather remarkable emphasis laid on the rite of Baptism by the Evangelist may be held to show that belief in the rite had at one time taken an important place in his scheme of religion. All this would be most natural in one who passed from the religion of the Baptist to that of St Paul.

The Evangelist makes it quite clear that he prefers the faith which sees the invisible to the mere bodily seeing. Indeed, he expresses this clearly in the words addressed to Thomas: "Because thou hast seen thou hast believed: blessed are they that have not seen, and yet have believed."

These words remind us of the very similar

[1] *The Fourth Gospel*, p. 80.

utterance of St Paul: "We look not at the things which are seen, but at the things which are not seen: for the things which are seen are temporal, but the things which are not seen are eternal." But in fact this way of thinking goes back far beyond St Paul. These two great lights of the Church baptised into Christianity a mode of regarding things which can be felt and seen—the mystic way, which has been prevalent as far back as history will take us in India and other Asiatic countries, and which was brought into Greek philosophy by the genius of Plato.

To the sage of India, now and in the past, sight has been a mere source of illusion: his great object, pursued through fasting and self-denial, through meditation and prayer, is to pass beyond the material and the sensible, and to dwell in the world of pure thought or pure being. Pleasure and pain, earthly enjoyments and ambitions are merely illusion, impediments which hinder men from approach to the Divine: to rise beyond them, to annihilate them, is the end of his asceticism. In coming westward, among people of more practical and energetic temper, this tendency has been greatly modified. But as regards thought and knowledge it is fairly embodied in the system of Plato. For Plato taught that all visible and material things are but shows and images, reflections in the world of sense and time of the divine ideas, which alone have true being. The well-known simile of the *Republic* which compares mankind to prisoners chained in the depths of a cave, and seeing only the shadows of things which pass before them, but supposing those shadows to be realities, became a commonplace in the schools which followed. We see reflections of the Platonic ideality not only in the works of the philosophers, but in the epitaphs of tombs, the rise of mystic cults, the gradual dissolution of the simple naturalist religion of Homer and Pindar.

It must be confessed that the picture drawn by the Evangelist is as a whole a non-natural one. The greatest contrast exists between the Jesus of the Synoptists, who is exquisitely and touchingly human, and the figure who says, " I am the light of the world, the door of the sheepfold, the true vine," " Ye are from beneath, I am from above," and so on. We see that such a figure could not historically have existed. This figure is halfway to the Gnostic Jesus whose life on earth was that of a phantasm. But, on the other hand, we must consider two facts. In the first place, we must allow that in his procedure there was nothing in disaccord with the notion of historic truth prevalent at the time. And, in the second place, we must discern of what infinite value the spiritual teaching of the Evangelist has been to the Church in every age of her history. In rewriting the life of the Saviour in the light of His exaltation, he has shown that Divine inspiration of which the clearest indication is the adaptation of the words of a prophet to the promotion of the good of generations to come.

V

THE WRITER'S IDEA OF BIOGRAPHY

IT is very hard for a modern mind, and especially for those unversed in Greek and Roman literature, to understand how the ancient world regarded history and biography. With us, if an author writes a professedly historic work, or a biography, he is expected to adhere closely to document and evidence. If he writes a historic romance, he may invent to his heart's content, but no one would think of taking his book as a serious historic document. Either he professes to narrate the facts, or he does not, but, if he does, any kind of deliberate invention is remorselessly condemned. In the Hellenistic world this clear line of distinction did not exist.

The change of view between ancient and modern literature is especially noteworthy in the way in which speeches are inserted. No modern biographer would think of inserting a speech and attributing it to his hero, unless he had the authority of some written or printed report of that speech. The custom of ancient biographers was quite different. It was quite a recognised and legitimate thing to compose a speech, and put it in the mouth of the hero, if it was convenient in that way to give the outlines of a situation, or to express the views which the biographer supposed his subject to entertain. Of course, if he was inserting a speech made in his own hearing, he would naturally repeat such points of it as had struck him. But he would see no possible objection to omitting any parts which he regarded as inappropriate, or, on the other hand, to adding any words of his own which made the discourse more telling. If he had not heard the speech, he might make inquiries of those who had been present, or again, he might not; and, in any case, if he was satisfied that he had produced something appropriate to the occasion and characteristic of the person who spoke, his conscience would be at rest. I cannot here give examples, or go into details; but the realisation of the change of view which I have mentioned is a sort of *pons asinorum* over which everyone who wishes to attain any sound knowledge of the ancient world must pass—or else fall through into the gulf.

It will, however, naturally occur to the reader that there is danger in passing from the literary customs of historians like Tacitus and Plutarch to the early biographers of Christianity. Tacitus was making a literary history, and none of the Emperors of whom he writes was his master and hero. The Evangelist was recording the deeds and the words of one whom he regarded as the Saviour, to whom he looked up as divine, as the Son of God, and the light of the world. How would he dare to ascribe to him words or works for which there was not the clearest authority? I am anxious to give to this objection as much weight as I possibly can; and, therefore, I will say the most I can in its favour. "The words which I have spoken unto you," says Jesus in the Fourth Gospel, "they are spirit and they are life." Would any biographer, not insane, put forth words of his own composition as spirit and life? In the Jewish Talmud the greatest care is shown in the repetition of the sayings of great Rabbis: how much more care would the Evangelists show in the preservation of the very words of Him who spoke as never man spoke. Moreover, it will be said, if the Fourth Evangelist composed speeches

THE WRITER'S IDEA OF BIOGRAPHY

for his Master, why should not the others have done the same, so that we have no speeches of Jesus which can be shown to be indubitably authentic? Yet the picture of the Master in the Synoptic Gospels is far too vivid and too original to be a mere creation of the disciples.

The argument is strong, and I should be glad, were it possible, to regard it as conclusive. But it is overthrown, not by reasoning, but by clear and undoubted fact. We have three Synoptic Gospels; and all critics are agreed that Matthew and Luke had the written text of Mark, or of a document which lies behind Mark, before them, which they used as a basis. Did they then regard the words which came to them with written, and probably with Apostolic authority, as too sacred to be altered? Everyone knows that they did not. We can place a diatessaron before us, and study at leisure the way in which they modified the text before them. Did they venture to do so because they were in possession of what they regarded as a better tradition of the exact words of the Master? Perhaps this may be the case in some instances. But there cannot be any doubt whatever, in the mind of anyone who considers the evidence, that the reason for their alterations was in many cases subjective. They thought the sayings reported in *Mark* inconsistent with some quality which they thought inherent in their Master, and altered them to bring them nearer to what they considered it fitting that he should say. Luke often alters the text of *Mark* to turn it into better and more literary Greek: Matthew more often in the interests of what he considers a higher truth.

The nearest we can approach, from the strictly historic point of view, to the actual facts of the life of Jesus is given us in the Gospel of Mark. The nearest we can approach to His teaching is given us in the document now called Q, which is much the same as that formerly called the Logia, a document which lies behind the sayings reported in *Matthew* and *Luke*. *Mark* we cannot very effectually criticise, as we have no other biography of equal value to set beside it. But critics now generally recognise that, for all its apparent simplicity, and its inestimable historic value, it is really, as Dr Westcott says, the result rather than the foundation of the Apostolic teaching. There is worked into it a great deal of theory: it is written primarily for the edification rather than for the information of the Church. As to Q, it cannot be with any certainty reconstituted, for the critics all differ as to its contents. But if we take a few well-known passages, such as the Sermon on the Mount or the Lord's Prayer, and compare the versions of them which we find in *Matthew* and *Luke* respectively, we shall see how very variously this primitive document is repeated or re-presented in our Gospels. Matthew and Luke had very different tendencies of mind. Matthew, as a pious Jew, wrote for Jews, and he requires, above all things, a conformity between the life of his Master and the prophecies of the great prophets of Israel. Luke wrote rather for the Jews of the Dispersion and the Gentile converts; but his great sympathy for the weak, the fallen, the poor, and especially for women, leads him to lay most stress on the humanitarian side of the Master's teaching, while Matthew dwells more on its aspect of lofty spirituality.

To us moderns it seems almost miraculous that in a place so far from literary influences as Palestine there should be produced works of such admirable beauty as the First and Third Gospels. It could only be possible through the influence of an unique personality living on earth, and the continued working of Divine inspiration after the death of that personality. And if those who are accustomed to take the Synoptic Gospels as literal history are shocked at the notion that the subjective tendencies of the writers have a great part in them, that the light which passes through them is not white, but coloured as by "a dome of many coloured glass," that feeling will pass on further reflection. If we had an exact and infallible record of the words and deeds of the Founder, or even such a history of them as a Polybius or an Arrian might have written, we should be forever bound by the tyranny of authority, and Christian freedom and character would have no chance of developing. We should have been in a position similar to that of the Mohammedans, to whom the authentic writings of their Prophet supply a law which may not be altered, so that all progress becomes identified with heresy. As it is, the search into the Christian origins has become a vast branch of historic research, requiring as complete devotion and as complicated investigations as do any of the physical sciences. And, meantime, ordinary Christians, free from the trammels of literalism, may read into the Gospels the facts of their own spiritual experience, drawing their life from them as plants draw life from the moist soil, by transmuting the bare fact into something suited to their own growth in religion.

The Fourth Evangelist was not satisfied with the three Gospels, all of which he may have known. In his time the sources of inspiration were still freely flowing, and he did not think that the three channels already cut were sufficient to convey it. There was an overflow, a side of the life of the Church which had indeed found expression in the Epistles of St Paul, but which was not connected closely enough with the earthly life of Jesus. St Paul had said little as to that life; the intensity of his conviction of a personal inspiration had filled him, and his genius moved rather in the two directions of missionary enterprise and ethical instruction. There was a danger that the recorded life of Jesus, and the Pauline enthusiasm for the living Christ, might drift apart, and leave between them a gap. The Gnostics were trying to throw a bridge of fanciful theory across that gap, to treat the historic human life as a sort of mirage. The Evangelist hoped to build a bridge which might be a lasting possession of the Church. And he succeeded.

When we set side by side the character and teaching of Jesus as set forth in the First and the Fourth Gospels respectively, most readers feel baffled. How can it be, we think, that a historic personality should be so differently apprehended by two of his disciples in the century following his death. It is not strange that certain hasty and superficial writers of our time should have come to the conclusion that there was no historic Jesus at all; that the Christian Messiah was evolved out of the Jewish hope of a Messiah, when reflected in a variety of national and cultural groups of minds. I call this view hasty and superficial, because, as I think, it could not have arisen in the mind of anyone accustomed to weighing historic evidence and the formation of the fabric of ancient history. It is essentially a caricature of historic procedure. I shall not attempt to disprove it: indeed, it is sufficient to refer to refutations already published.[1] But the best of all refutations is to consider the parallel case of Socrates. No one doubts the historic existence of Socrates; yet in his case, as in that of the Founder of Christianity, we have widely divergent accounts of his teaching. We owe to Schleiermacher a comparison of the two cases, of the lives of the Founder of modern religion and the Founder of modern philosophy. Though it would distort the plan of the present work to treat of the matter quite adequately, I propose to speak of it at some length.

[1] The best short account of this controversy will be found in Loofs' *What is the Truth about Jesus Christ?* 1913.

There are extant two biographical accounts of Socrates. One is in the *Memorabilia* (memoirs), the *Symposium*, and other works of Xenophon, a soldier and a gentleman, who was among the hearers of Socrates, and wrote, after his death, an account based on his memory of what he had heard. The other is contained in the wonderful dialogues of Plato, in which the figure of the great master stands enshrined, painted by the hand of a consummate artist. Both of these biographies were written early in the fourth century, a considerable time after the death of Socrates, but while a multitude of his friends and auditors still lived. The biography of Xenophon is that of a simple-minded man, of no great imaginative or constructive power. It may fairly be compared with the Gospel of Mark. The biography of Plato is incomparably superior from the literary point of view: sometimes it may be as near to the actual fact as the writing of Xenophon; but, generally speaking, we find in it rather a working out of the thought of Socrates by one who was a profounder thinker, but of far less striking character. There is much in Plato which reminds us of the Fourth Gospel.

Of course in many respects all comparison between the biographies of Jesus and the biographies of Socrates breaks down. Socrates was not regarded by any of his followers as a divine being. He is not credited with any miracles. After his death he did not become the life of any Church. Our parallel is only historical and literary, not in the least religious. Yet it is valuable as showing us how minds worked and how biography was written in the ages when Greece was the controller and director of the thought of the world. Palestine, it may be said, was never dominated by the intellectual customs of Athens. That is only in a measure true: Alexandria was a meeting point of Jewish and Greek thought. Rome was intellectually still more the mere follower of Greece. And Ephesus, a colony of Athens, was through all her history largely dependent upon her mother-city for all that raised her intellectually above the level of the barbarous Lydians and Phrygians who dwelt about her.

When we read the *Memorabilia*, we find ourselves in contact with a character far more than with a thinker. Xenophon was himself a very practical man, who by conducting the Ten Thousand Greeks right through the heart of Asia Minor proved himself one of the great leaders of men. He was devoted to the management of estates, to horsemanship, to hunting. So it is natural that the practical side of the personality of Socrates should impress him far more than the speculative side. His Socrates is a being of infinite courage and splendid manliness, whom no threat and no bribery can turn from the pursuit of the one object which he has set before himself. That object is the search for truth, which he follows by the way of dialectic, by questioning all whom he meets and testing their replies, by following every clue and working through all analogies. His trust in reasoning might have led a smaller nature, as in fact it did lead many of the Sophists, his contemporaries, into pedantry. But in Socrates there was little fear of such a decline. He possessed an astonishing clearness of insight, which enabled him to see all events and all phenomena in the whitest of lights. And he had complete faith in God: he claimed that in all his actions he was led by a Divine purpose and monition, which warned him when he was verging towards what was evil, and opened for him a way towards what was best.

All who conversed with Socrates, says Xenophon, became both wiser and better. Statesmen learned to see the pitfalls which lay in their path; artists were stimulated to attempt a higher line; soldiers saw the way of their duty more clearly. Children, brothers, friends, gained a nobler view of their ties to relatives and associates. If some of the pupils of Socrates, like Critias and Alcibiades, were not reformed, it was because, being of corrupt nature, they only sought the society of the master in order to learn a more effective style of speaking. Socrates was thoroughly pragmatist in his notions about education: he thought of all education as a training for a particular manner of life; and he was convinced that for every kind of action, political, military, financial, training was necessary. But though pragmatist, he was not sordid: he held that cultivation of intellect and formation of character were, after all, the great and only foundation for a noble career; skill in this or that matter might be easily acquired by one who was, so to speak, a trained intellectual athlete.

We find Socrates in the *Memorabilia* maintaining, what in a Greek shows extreme originality, that the beautiful and the useful are really the same. He often uses the language of the Utilitarians: but such language is only base when the notion of utility is low and degraded. He rates *sophrosyne*, self-control, as the greatest of the virtues, and in fact as including them all. His insight looks beyond the worship of the Greek deities, though to this as a good citizen he would

THE WRITER'S IDEA OF BIOGRAPHY

carefully conform, to a Deity who has provided in the world for the wants of man, and has adapted man to the frame and order of the world.

But the feature which again and again impresses us, as we read Xenophon's work, is the complete unity in Socrates of thought and deed; how he never reveals a conviction for which he is not prepared to die; how he never hesitates in his certainty of the Divine purpose of life, and the Divine care of those who listen to the inner voice. He is like an embodied conscience walking among men, a glass in whom all may see their weakness reflected, a voice which calls to what is best, and which may be silenced but can never be turned aside.

In all this there is probably little that is not historic. Xenophon gives us a truthful portrait. But he does so not on principle, for his purely fanciful life of Cyrus (the *Cyropædia*) proves that he was quite capable of turning a biography into a romance. He depicts things as they were merely because the reality had so deeply impressed him that his mind could not be diverted into another channel. And yet sometimes we see clearly the mind of the biographer rather than that of the master. For example, in one place,[1] after Socrates has

[1] *Memorabilia,* III., ch. v.

spoken in his usual strain to the son of Pericles as to the necessity of severe study of military matters for one who would conduct a campaign, he makes suggestions as to the actual military situation which can scarcely come from any but a practical soldier like Xenophon, especially since he speaks of the military situation of the Mysians and Pisidians of Asia Minor, tribes well known to the leader of the Ten Thousand, but probably unknown to Socrates. In another place,[1] Xenophon makes Socrates disclaim the identity of knowledge and virtue which was probably a doctrine of Socrates, and to him appropriate, but one not suited to the very practical turn of mind which marks Xenophon.

The manner of speaking of the Socrates of Xenophon is strongly marked. He does not discourse, but contents himself with dialogue of brief question and answer. He shows no subtlety, lays no traps, but goes straight into the matter in hand. Almost the only fable or myth which he narrates is professedly taken from Prodicus of Ceos: it is a moral apologue of the choice of Hercules between Virtue and Pleasure, strictly ethical, and quite free from intellectual speculation.

When we turn from the memoirs of

[1] *Memorabilia*, III., ch. ix., and IV., ch. vi.

Xenophon to the dialogues of Plato we find ourselves in a very different intellectual atmosphere. Plato is infinitely superior to his fellow disciple in intellectual force, in dramatic skill, in literary accomplishment. He has made of Socrates a far more striking and impressive figure than could Xenophon. In him the biographical interest and purpose is strong; but it has to make terms with another interest which is even stronger, the power of systematic thought, and the desire to build on a Socratic foundation an ideal and spiritual view of the universe. When Plato, in his *Crito, Phædo* and *Apology of Socrates*, treats of the last days of his master, the poignant interest of the facts and the sublime courage of the hero overpower him. His account of these days, apart from the subtle theories discussed, is probably almost as accurate as that of Xenophon, while it is at the same time much more detailed and at a loftier tragic level. The picture which Plato draws of the daily life of Socrates, his scanty clothing, his bare feet, his immovable temper, his kindly humour, is drawn by a consummate artist. But when we come to Plato's account of the talk of his master, we see at once how strongly refracting is the atmosphere. Socrates both loses and gains. He loses the simple directness, the intense ethical purpose, the consistent determination to see only what really exists, which are so conspicuous in Xenophon's memoirs. But he also gains. With consummate skill he leads his interlocutors from point to point; with delicate irony he professes to be only anxious to learn, and to have no pretension to teach. And after long discussion he sometimes breaks out into a discourse of a more constructive character. When he does not feel capable of clearly tracing the outline of his creed on some deep subject, he falls back on a tale or myth, in which he explains by symbolism what cannot well be set forth by system.

But the most striking parts of the teaching of the dialogues, the doctrine of the immortality of the soul, the nature of justice in an individual and in the state, the careful devices for training the young, and more particularly the doctrine of ideas, are not the views of Socrates but of Plato.[1] The Socrates of Xenophon must have worked in the city of Athens as an intellectual and moral tonic, and must have made hundreds

---

[1] I must ask pardon if I state dogmatically what I cannot here prove. I am aware that Professor John Burnet has in an able recent work (*From Thales to Plato*) taken the opposite view; but he has not convinced me.

feel that a life of search for truth and of devotion to the will of God revealed within was the only noble life. But he would never, as did Plato, lay a foundation on which systems of ideal and spiritual philosophy could be built up through all ages. The Cynics, those Friars of the Pagan world, may represent a side of Socrates in exaggeration. But the other ancient schools—the Academics, the Peripatetics, the Stoics, and at a later time the Neo-Platonists and Mystics —owe their existence in a great measure to the thought of Plato, whether by following him, or by reacting against him. The doctrine of ideas in particular, the view that the visible world is a mere copy and manifestation of realities hidden in the spiritual realm, has, ever since the time of Plato, been the great corrective to the natural materialism of mankind, and helped them to look beyond the things which can be seen to the things which cannot be seen, but which exist eternally in the world of the ideal. But this doctrine seems to have been foreign to the mind of the historic Socrates. It seems, indeed, to belong only to the latter years of Plato.

It is, of course, with the memoirs of Socrates by Xenophon that we would compare the

Synoptic writers or the authorities whom they follow, and with the dialogues of Plato we would compare the discourses in the Fourth Gospel. Doubtless the comparison will not hold in all respects, though it is sufficiently close to be illuminating. Both writers re-interpret the simple teaching of tradition in the light of a spiritual mysticism. In particular we may dwell on two points — the account of the death of Jesus in the Fourth Gospel, and the careful and artificial construction of the dialogues there reported.

It is noteworthy that the Fourth Evangelist, just like Plato, is far more detailed, and probably more strictly historic, when he gives an account of the last days of his hero. In the general narrative we find no consistent sketch of time and place. "After these things" and "not many days" are the vague phrases sometimes used in regard to time; while the scene shifts from place to place, and is indeed of no great importance, and its appearance of exactness is to a great extent an illusion. The Evangelist is careful to attach some of the discourses to particular scenes: and here there is very probably some foundation in tradition; but he does not produce anything like a consecutive biography. We find no gradual development of a situation. But when he comes to the end, he is far fuller of detail, and far more vivid. And the reason is, no doubt, the same as that which we have conjectured in the case of Plato. The Apostolic tradition naturally dwelt more fully on the sufferings and the death of the Master; and on the mind of the Evangelist they were more vividly stamped, in proportion to the frequency with which he had heard of them, and their natural intense pathos. Whether, nevertheless, he consciously transposed them in deference to a theological interest is a further question.

In the memoirs of Xenophon the talk is comparatively simple and artless. Socrates goes straight to the point, and those who converse with him make objections which seem to us natural. But Plato's dialogues are carefully constructed, and the course of them thought out from the beginning. With great skill the writer uses the replies of the hearers of Socrates to bring out point after point of his argument. These hearers grow angry at the right point; they reflect the attitudes assumed by different classes of men in the city; they give way and retire when the stage is suitable to a more detailed and elaborate exposition by the great protagonist. A parallel, if not quite a similar contrast, may be observed between the discourses of Jesus in the Synoptists and those in the Fourth Gospel. In the former Jesus does not argue, he teaches with authority. Sometimes, indeed, a question put by a bystander, such as that as to giving tribute to Cæsar, and that as to the non-observance of the Sabbath by the Apostles, gives occasion for an admirable saying. But here the questions are such as would naturally be asked; and both question and answer are probably historic; they are sayings exactly of the kind which linger in the memory of the hearer. But when we turn to the Johannine dialogues between Jesus and the Jews, we find a far more elaborate construction.

Let us briefly analyse three of the most characteristic Johannine discourses: (1) that with Nicodemus (ch. iii.), (2) that with the woman of Samaria (ch. iv.), and (3) that with the Jews at Capernaum (ch. vi.). In each of these we shall distinguish (*a*) the occasion, (*b*) the thesis, (*c*) the misunderstanding, (*d*) the development.

(1*a*) The occasion of this discourse is the visit of Nicodemus to Jesus by night. The appropriateness of this occasion lies in the fact that a highly educated Jew ought to have known the doctrine of the higher life, the life of the Spirit; but he does not: "Art thou a teacher in Israel and understandest not these things?" (1*b*) The thesis is that man must be born again of the Spirit before he can enter into life. (1*c*) Nicodemus falls into a vulgar and materialist error of interpretation: "How can a man be born when he is old? Can he enter a second time into his mother's womb?" And (1*d*) this crassness acts as a foil to the exposition which follows as to the action of the Spirit, which is like that of the wind, unseen and unexpected, breathing now here and now there, and bestowing the gift of spiritual birth.

(2*a*) The occasion at Sychar is the thirst of Jesus, which prompts Him to ask a draught of the woman of Samaria. It emphasises the essential unity of mankind, as a thirsty man does not ask whether the person who has water to give him is of his own or of an alien race. (2*b*) The thesis is that there is a stream of living water, of which a man may drink to satisfy a higher craving. (2*c*) The Samaritan woman thinks that this living water is an actual fluid, the magic effect of which is to prevent the feeling of thirst in the future. (2*d*) Thence arises the discourse of Jesus as to the fountain open to all mankind who call upon God in spirit and sincerity: open, that is, to all of mankind who receive the Divine Word, and believe on the Saviour.

(3*a*) The occasion at Capernaum is that some of the Jews, having had their hunger miraculously satisfied, follow Jesus as one who can easily supply their material wants. (3*b*) The thesis is that there is a heavenly bread which abides unto eternal life, a bread which comes down from heaven and gives life to the world. This bread is the flesh of the Son of Man. (3*c*) The Jews, with their customary materialist crassness, ask a question exactly parallel to the question of Nicodemus and the Samaritan woman: " How can this man give us his flesh to eat? How can he say that he came down from heaven? Is he not the son of Joseph?" (3*d*) Not in so orderly a fashion as in the other cases, but clearly enough for any careful reader, Jesus turns the discourse in a spiritual direction. He that eats of the spiritual bread shall live for ever, not like those who ate in the wilderness the manna which fell from the sky, and yet died. Jesus is the bread of life, and of spiritual origin; He came down from heaven because He came not to do His own will, but the will of Him that sent Him.

I do not pretend here to develop the full

meaning of these sayings. There are elements in them of which I am not now speaking, but to which I shall return when I treat of the Johannine doctrine of the Sacraments. At present I only wish to direct attention to the form of these discourses, and to insist on their artistic scheme. In manner they are totally different from the discourses reported by the Synoptists. And the view has spread, and become almost axiomatic with most trained critics, that this form belongs altogether to the Fourth Evangelist. Materialism has been a besetting fault of the common people among the Jews in all ages; though, on the other hand, it would be difficult to find a nobler spiritualism than is to be traced in such books as *Isaiah* and the *Psalter*. But this particular kind of materialist misinterpretation seems too crass to represent the tone of any people. When the Fourth Evangelist says "the Jews," he means the enemies of the Christian Church, and he takes them on the lowest and most ignorant level.

In the Johannine discourses of Jesus, and more especially in the long monologue towards the end of the Gospel, we feel that it is not the visible and audible Jesus who is speaking, but the Christ who is the life of the Church, and who is revealing Himself in the spirit. No doubt this is a view which will be very repugnant to many Christians, who have been accustomed to find in the wonderful words of these discourses a message heard by an eye-witness, and preserved for the encouragement of the Church. If they do not come from the very lips of the Master, they seem to lose their unique authority. They have been for ages a main source and a strong stay of the spiritual life. And if a Christian does not take up the historic question, but reads only for edification, he may well think of the Johannine sayings as coming from his Lord during His lifetime, just as he may think of the Ten Commandments as given to Moses by Jehovah engraved upon tables of stone. People whose whole tone of thought is literal must literally interpret the inspired Scriptures. But they may still remember the saying of a notable modern Christian, Cardinal Newman, that to the Christian religion a figurative interpretation of the Bible is a necessary condition.

But for those whose minds are cast in a historic mould, who want to know what really took place at the time of the Christian origins, it is quite impossible to regard the speeches given to Jesus by the Fourth Evangelist as

THE WRITER'S IDEA OF BIOGRAPHY

actually so uttered. If Jesus had been in the habit of thus openly proclaiming Himself as the Son of God, the light of the world, the trial before Pilate must have taken a very different turn. We read in *Mark* that there was a great difficulty in finding evidence that Jesus had claimed a divine origin; and the most definite point brought forward against Him was that He had said that if the temple were destroyed He could build it again in three days, a very obvious materialist distortion of Jesus' teaching as to the unimportance of mere places and rites. Even in the Johannine account of the trial, the main accusation brought against Jesus is that He claimed to be a king of a spiritual realm, a claim which Pilate does not regard as punishable. Had Jesus openly made the claims which He is said in the Fourth Gospel to have made, His life would much earlier have been sacrificed. In the Synoptic writings we can see how the notion that Jesus was the promised Messiah slowly penetrated the minds of the Apostles; but in the Fourth Gospel Jesus is proclaimed by the Baptist as born to take away the sins of the world. And throughout Jesus speaks of Himself as the light of the world and the life of men, as the Head of a great spiritual society and a direct revelation of God. His way of speaking, as we know from abundant evidence, was on a quite different plane.

No! It was not Jesus of Nazareth who spoke thus, but the exalted Christ who came to inspire the Apostles after the death on the cross, who arrested St Paul in his career of persecution, who was the life and spirit of the Church, in whom alike individuals and the community lived with a new and spiritual life.

Sometimes the Evangelist, by a natural inconsistency, reveals his plan of writing. For he puts into the mouth of Jesus utterances which imply that His life on earth was at an end. He slips from the present into the past tense. Thus in iii. 13, Jesus is represented as speaking of His descent from heaven and His ascending thither, and adds, "the Son of Man who is in heaven." The authenticity of these words is, however, doubtful; and if they are genuine it may be maintained that they are really the words of the Evangelist, and that the sayings of Jesus end with the previous verse: if so, it proves how little the writer cares to separate the words which he attributes to his Master from those which he speaks in his own person. A better example can be found in chapters xvi. and xvii. In xvi. 4 we read, "These things I said not unto you

THE WRITER'S IDEA OF BIOGRAPHY 119

from the beginning, because I was with you." And in xvii. 12 we read, "While I was with them I kept them in Thy name which Thou hast given Me, and I guarded them." Here again it may be maintained that these words, spoken on the last evening, refer to a life virtually, though not actually, ended; but it is simpler to suppose that the writer is thinking of the life of Jesus on earth as in the past.

There are other passages with a similar bearing. In the last great discourse of Jesus we read, "The hour cometh when I shall no more speak unto you in parables, but shall tell you plainly of the Father." Every reader of the First Gospel knows how plainly in the Sermon on the Mount and elsewhere Jesus speaks of the Father in Heaven. The Evangelist must be thinking of further revelations of God made to the Church after the Crucifixion. Later on, in the same discourse, Jesus says, in His prayer, "I finished the work which Thou hast given Me to do." How incongruous and unnatural such words must seem, if spoken before that suffering which was near at hand, even before the scene in the Garden of Gethsemane! They can only be natural when applied, from the point of view of the Church, to the whole life and death of its Founder. We must accept one of two views. Either Jesus was continually speaking to His disciples in a way which they could not understand, in virtue of a superhuman knowledge peculiar to Himself, or else the Fourth Evangelist has put into His mouth words which belong not to the visible, but to the exalted Christ.

A passage which throws light on the Evangelist's way of working, and the method in which he adapts the traditional teaching of Jesus to his own point of view, is to be found in that remarkable saying in the seventh chapter, "He that believeth on Me, as the Scripture hath said, out of his body shall flow rivers of living water." The commentators are unable to find this phrase (or rather the latter part of it, for it is the latter part which is important) in the books of the Old Testament. But Jesus is said to have uttered the phrase during the Feast of Tabernacles, one ceremony of which was that a priest daily brought water in a golden vessel from the pool of Siloam in procession, and poured it out on the altar; and this gives a natural occasion for the exclamation. We are told that this ceremony was by some Rabbis interpreted as a symbol of the outpouring of the Spirit as spoken of by Isaiah (xii. 3).

THE WRITER'S IDEA OF BIOGRAPHY

That the Evangelist was repeating some traditional saying of Jesus, which he had heard repeated, is by far most probable, though he is mistaken as to its being a quotation from Scripture, and it is almost certain that the words have been modified, and the original sense somewhat changed. But when the Evangelist has written them, he sees that, taken in the sense in which he takes them, they are not suitable to the lifetime of Jesus. So he adds, "This spake He of the Spirit, which they that believed on Him were to receive: for the Spirit was not yet given." To his mode of thinking, which was entirely unhistoric, it does not seem incongruous that his Master should have uttered words which would be unintelligible to the disciples, and only full of meaning to their successors many years later.

To this we may add that sometimes, even in the midst of words attributed to Jesus Himself, the Evangelist forgets himself, and breaks out into words of assertion or controversy quite unsuitable to the connection, and only fit for the synagogue or the church assembly. One of the most remarkable of these lapses is in the discourse to Nicodemus.[1] Jesus has been uttering lofty truths, and when

[1] *John* iii 11.

Nicodemus fails to understand them, tells him that as one of the teachers of Israel he ought already to have been acquainted with them. Then comes the extraordinary verse, "We speak that we do know and bear witness of that we have seen; and ye receive not our witness." In a dialogue between two persons the *we* and the *ye* are quite unintelligible. But if we turn to the last verse of the Gospel we find a parallel. "This is the disciple which beareth witness of these things, . . . and we know that his witness is true." In the Epistle the phrase "we know" occurs nearly twenty times: it has evidently slipped into the discourse to Nicodemus by mistake.

Thus the Gospel, in spite of its majesty of style and high unity of thought, is from a critical point of view a tangled skein. We have the greatest difficulty in separating in it what came from tradition, what belongs to the experience of the Church, and what is added in the way of comment and background by the Evangelist himself. That the Gospel is divinely inspired I strongly hold, and especially inspired in being adapted to further high Christian thought in ways which the writer only dimly foresaw. It is a fruit of the Christian tree of life. But inspiration does not work by giving the inspired man a direct knowledge of events which have happened in the world: that is not the character of inspiration. He may be careless of fact, or misled by incorrect information, nor is he in any way infallible; but he is an exponent of the life of the Spirit under the forms of his own age.

VI

THE BASIS IN CHRISTIAN EXPERIENCE

THE first, and the most important, of the strands whereof this Gospel is made up is that of Christian Experience. The phrase in modern days of over-individualism has a subjective sound: to us it means in the first place the secret realities of the converse of the spirit with God. To one accustomed to the far less individual life of early Christian days, this would not be the primary significance. The days of the city-state, when every man merged his existence in a great degree in the life of the community, were passing away. But much of the common feeling which it had fostered survived. And even in our age, which has seen so marked, and in many ways so disastrous, a growth of national and racial passion, it is hard to realise the place taken by patriotism and racial feeling in ancient days. A

THE BASIS IN CHRISTIAN EXPERIENCE 125

reading of some of Plutarch's *Lives* helps one in this matter as much as anything can. Probably none of the races of the ancient world had a more strongly developed sense of the corporate life than the Jews. The stories of Jael and Sisera and of Judith show how, in the opinion of the people, no act of treachery or cruelty was wrong, if it tended to the preservation of Israel.

The Roman peace had, it is true, in the case of most peoples, except the Jews, somewhat blunted the edge of this general patriotism. Religious feeling, also, was turning away from the merely patriotic cults to those which gave more scope for personal reliance on the unseen and spiritual. But it takes many generations before feelings deeply impressed upon the minds of men are effaced. And still, in Western Asia, men's minds were largely dominated by the racial and civic ideal.

Thus to thinkers of the time experience would be collective rather than individual. The Christian Church had taken, in the minds of all the followers of Christ, the place of city and nation, and to it the shoots which arose from the ground of collectivism naturally clung. It is the experience of the Christian Church, rather than his own private spiritual history, on which the Fourth Evangelist bases his Christology.

This transference of social consciousness from a city or a state to a religious society was no new thing in the history of mankind. The Jews of the Dispersion, who in the Hellenistic age were scattered abroad over all lands from Rome to Babylon, found their unity in their religion, in their relation to the God of Israel, and through Him to one another, much more than in any mere racial feeling. They freely proselytised and welcomed to their community all who would accept Jehovah as their God, and would keep the law given by Him to His people. There had also arisen, in the region of the Eastern Mediterranean, a variety of mystic sects, the votaries of Isis of Sabazius or of Mithras, to whose adherents the relation to their patron deity and their fellow sectaries was the closest and most sacred bond which they recognised. If we rank these societies with the Fellowship of Christ, we no doubt judge superficially, as did the Roman authorities, who put all these new cults on the same footing, and saw in them all a danger to extreme patriotism. What is true is that they belonged to the same genus as Christianity, but were infinitely inferior species of the genus. And they certainly tended, perhaps even more than the Jewish Dispersion had tended, to prepare the way for Christianity, and to incline the hearts of men to accept it. Thus St Paul found that on his missionary journeys it was precisely the cities most affected by the new tendencies of religion, such cities as Antioch, Corinth, Ephesus, and Colossæ, which were most ready to receive the word.

St Paul was the preacher of a mystic communion, which in the time of the Fourth Evangelist had already struck deep roots, and was bearing in the Churches of Asia the fruits of a redeemed and exalted life.

The Christian consciousness of the Evangelist, on the whole, moves on lines much like those on which St Paul's moved. It is almost certain that he was a convert of St Paul, or at all events that he belonged to a society moulded on the Pauline ideas. There were three Christian Churches in particular which looked up to St Paul as their founder: those of Galatia, Corinth, and Ephesus. The Epistles to the Galatians and Corinthians show us with what intense love St Paul regarded those Churches, and how no mere bodily absence prevented him from keeping up with them a close spiritual sympathy. With regard to the Church at Ephesus we know much less, but the address to the Ephesian Presbyters at Miletus shows a very close union in love and in doctrine between the Apostle and them. The Pauline view was that the Christian Church was the earthly body of Christ, that every member of it was in direct union with Christ as his Head and his Saviour, that one spiritual life ran through the Head and the limbs, and that to the common life the individual Christian owed his ability to live a Christ-life on earth, and his hope of a blessed life hereafter. This was the root of all the Pauline theology. And it could scarcely be called a doctrine, for it had in it no reasoning, no theory, little of the intellectual element; rather it was a mere throwing into words of the daily experience of the infant Society.

This experience, and this doctrine, if doctrine it may be called, is the most conspicuous feature of the Fourth Gospel. That it could not belong to the lifetime of the Founder is evident; the kind of communion involved in it was spiritual, and not possible while the disciples saw and conversed with their Master day by day. The Evangelist himself expresses this in several passages: "It is expedient for you that I go away"; "Blessed are those that have not seen, and yet have believed." His plan, whether it was a right or a wrong one, to work

THE BASIS IN CHRISTIAN EXPERIENCE 129

out this Christian experience in the form of a biography, necessarily involved, as we see clearly, the production of a non-natural, a scarcely human Jesus; but the transposition does not prevent him from setting forth the realities of the converse between the Church and her Lord in a series of sayings and similitudes which are of imperishable power and divine beauty. Let us turn to some aspects of that converse.

The first point to notice is that the Society is an exclusive one, apart from the world, which is described as a hostile medium. "If ye were of the world, the world would love its own; but because ye are not of the world, but I chose you out of the world, therefore the world hateth you." In many other passages the world is thus spoken of as an enemy and a persecutor; but it cannot destroy the Society. "In the world ye shall have tribulation; but be of good cheer, I have overcome the world." To the Evangelist in most of his moods, as to St Paul, the Church is the only way of salvation. "No man cometh to the Father but by Me." And this view is insisted on in the well-known parable in which Christ is spoken of as the door of the sheepfold, by passing through which only, the sheep can be safe. In a slightly varied image Christ is spoken of as the only true shepherd of the sheep, others who claim to be shepherds being only robbers.

The first-fruits of an entry into the Society is a consciousness that the union with the indwelling Christ results in the forgiveness of sins. Both St Paul and the Evangelist throw the forgiveness of sins into a quasi-historic setting. St Paul[1] speaks of redemption through the blood of Christ; and the Evangelist in his Epistle writes, "The blood of Jesus, His Son, cleanseth us from all sin." Later writers work out this theme in a systematic way, and represent the death on the cross as a full and sufficient sacrifice to do away the sins of all those who have faith in Christ. At first this teaching is implicit rather than expressed. The Evangelist writes, "God so loved the world that He gave His only-begotten Son, that whosoever believeth in Him should not perish but have eternal life"; and it is noteworthy that he does not in this passage mean only the death on the cross; it is the life rather than the death, and especially the exalted life after death, of the Saviour of which he is thinking. Again, both St Paul and the Evangelist connect the forgiveness of sins especially with the rite of baptism.

[1] *Eph* 1. 7; *Col.* 1. 14.

THE BASIS IN CHRISTIAN EXPERIENCE 131

Here again it is later writers who fully carry out the idea. In a later chapter I shall treat in more detail of the teaching of the Evangelist in regard to the Sacraments.

Though there is no great difference between the doctrine of sin and its forgiveness held by St Paul and that preached by the Fourth Evangelist, yet in the writings of the latter this doctrine does not hold anything like so large a place as it does in the Pauline Epistles. This may well be accounted for on the grounds of experience. St Paul's conversion was the result of a bitter inward conflict; he was driven to Christ by the conviction that so, and so only, he could escape from the thraldom of sin. The escape from that servitude loomed so large in his mind that he constantly recurs to it; and he seems to expect his converts to pass through the same terrible conflict. The Fourth Evangelist had never been a persecutor of the Church; he had never fought hard against the influence of the Divine Spirit. He had not therefore the same intense feeling in regard to sin. Rather he must have been one of those whom Christianity from the first attracted. It is probable that he passed into the Christian Society from the ranks of the followers of the Baptist. When he writes, " Everyone that is of the truth heareth My voice,"[1] and "He that doeth the truth, cometh to the light,"[2] he expresses the natural attraction which led to Christianity all men in whom the spiritual life was strongly developed. Sin does not appear here as a deep shadow thrown over all life, but as a perversion to which one who is born of God is not attracted. In the same way the doctrine of election, which stands out in the Pauline teaching with such rigid severity, is greatly softened, though it is not entirely abandoned, in the Fourth Gospel. Election there is not the work of an arbitrary potter, who makes some vessels for honour and some for destruction, but the result of a natural difference in men, some of whom are born children of the light, and some children of darkness. "I manifested Thy name," Jesus says,[3] "unto the men whom Thou gavest Me out of the world; Thine they were, and Thou gavest them to Me." The words of Jesus naturally attracted to the Church those who had in them the seeds of eternal life.

The first steps from the threshold of religion towards the spiritual life were accomplished by the help of prayer. This also is one of the simplest and most usual phenomena of spiritual awakening. Of course the Evangelist speaks of prayer, and the way in which he does so is

[1] xviii. 37   [2] iii. 21.   [3] xvii. 6.

THE BASIS IN CHRISTIAN EXPERIENCE 133

of singular interest. It tells of a transition through which the Church was passing. We must pass in review the chief passages in which prayer is spoken of. "This is the boldness which we have toward Him (God), that, if we ask anything according to His will, He heareth us."[1] This saying is in exactly the same key as the statements about prayer in the Sermon on the Mount. "How much more shall your Father which is in heaven give good things to them that ask Him?" But in other passages the special nature of the prayer which is Christian, which belongs to the Society, is insisted upon. "That whatsoever ye shall ask of the Father in My name, He may give it to you."[2] Still more explicit is another phrase,[3] "Verily, verily, I say unto you, if ye shall ask anything of the Father, He will give it you in My name." It is prayer in the name of Christ, prayer which belongs distinctively to the Society which is in constant communion with Christ, which is sure of a Divine answer.

There is one passage in the Gospel which seems to be of a somewhat different complexion.[4] "If ye shall ask Me anything in My name, that will I do." It seems at first sight that the writer is here speaking of direct

[1] *Epistle* v. 14.
[2] xv. 16
[3] xvi 23.
[4] xiv. 14.

prayer to Christ. But, as the Revisers point out, the word *me* is omitted in many ancient authorities, and the phrase "ask Me in My name" is obviously unsatisfactory. The only prayer of which the Evangelist speaks is prayer to God in the name and in the spirit of Christ. St Paul also does not speak of prayer to Christ, but to the Father. "I bow my knees unto the Father . . . that Christ may dwell in your hearts through faith."[1] Harnack observes,[2] "As the Mediator and High Priest, Christ is, of course, always and everywhere invoked by the Christians; but such invocations are one thing, and formal prayer another." Such cries as that of Stephen, "Lord Jesus, receive my spirit," do not show that the custom which arose in the second century of addressing Christ in prayer was in use in the Apostolic age.

Historically it is important thus to trace the gradual development in the early Church of prayer to Christ, out of prayer in the name of Christ. But to all who think on the lines of pragmatism the importance of the distinction is not great. The Evangelist would have held that Christian prayer was unique in kind, but that its wording was less important. What is important in prayer is not the name

[1] *Eph.* iii 15 [2] *History of Dogma*, i. 184.

THE BASIS IN CHRISTIAN EXPERIENCE 135

to which it is addressed, but its spirit and purpose, whether it represents the best feeling of the Society, and whether it is in accord with the Divine will.

Not only is the Christian Society united in spirit with its Lord, but it also derives thence a power to accomplish mighty works in the world. One of the most remarkable passages in the Gospel is that which speaks of this power as resting in the Church. "He that believeth on Me, the works that I do shall he do also; and greater works than these shall he do; because I go unto the Father."[1] And again,[2] "The glory which thou hast given Me I have given unto them." In another chapter I shall have to show that, with all his spirituality, the Evangelist does attach great importance to the miracles wrought by Jesus, though he is fond of regarding them not only in a literal but also in a symbolic way. And he here plainly says that the supernatural power which rested on Jesus rested also on the Church, enabling its Apostles to work signs and wonders. *Acts* records a number of remarkable miracles wrought by St Peter and St Paul, miracles of healing, of escape from prison, and the like, which are quite as striking as those recorded

[1] xiv 12   [2] xvii 22

of Jesus Himself, and which, like prayer, are wrought in the name of Christ. We cannot, however, be sure that Luke's account of these wonders is accurate.

But the great miracle of all is that which is implied in the very nature of the Society, in the character which comes upon those who join it, however low the level from which they start. This character is that set forth in one of the most noteworthy of the sayings of Jesus, "Thou shalt love the Lord thy God with all thy heart and with all thy soul and with all thy mind," and "Thou shalt love thy neighbour as thyself." The love of man to God is preached with an energy and iteration which passes description in the Hebrew Psalms. The love for man as man, the "enthusiasm of humanity," is the main text of the Synoptic Gospels, and is set forth with unsurpassable force in the tale of the Good Samaritan in *Luke*, and the sublime Vision of Judgment in *Matthew*. What is most prominent in the Fourth Evangelist, as in St Paul, is a love which lies between the two, a love for the brethren, an intense sense of Christian charity or brotherhood. "A new commandment I give unto you, that ye love one another, even as I have loved you, that ye also love one another." The Epistle of

THE BASIS IN CHRISTIAN EXPERIENCE

the Evangelist is, as we all know, so filled with the expression of this love that it has long passed, together with St Paul's hymn of charity, as the highest expression of the Christian spirit. It is to be observed that though the Evangelist sometimes gives utterance to the wider enthusiasm of humanity, he regards the love of Christian for Christian as something quite characteristic and unique. It is primarily the bond of a society, a bond stronger than any tie of blood, of family, or of nationality. It is, in fact, a blend of love to God and love to man, being inspired alike by what is divine and what is human in the Church. The Evangelist sums up the matter in his usual way in pregnant phrases, "He that loveth not, knoweth not God, for God is love"; "He that abideth in love abideth in God, and God abideth in him."

That such love could be felt for those outside the Society would naturally seem to the Evangelist impossible. The attitude of the world towards the Church is one of hatred and persecution. And it was only natural that the Society should dislike the world. "Love not the world, neither the things that are in the world. If any man love the world, the love of the Father is not in him."[1] Of course I do not

[1] *Epistle* ii. 15

mean that the Evangelist preaches hatred of those outside the Church: his character is far too sweet for that. In other places he writes, "God so loved the world." He uses the term world (kosmos) in a variety of senses without careful distinction. But certainly he holds that the love of one member of the Church for another must be wholly different in character from the love of a Christian for one outside the community.

The fruit of repentance, prayer, and love in the Church is eternal life. This phrase is so fundamental with the Evangelist that though I devote a later chapter to the idea, I must here say a few words in regard to it. The meaning which the Evangelist attaches to the phrase shines out with such luminosity that no careful reader can miss it. It is by partaking of the Spirit of Christ, doing the will of God as revealed in Jesus Christ, becoming a member of His earthly body, that a man attains to a new birth, and thenceforth lives a life which is eternal, because it has in it nothing of the fleshly elements which have in them the seeds of decay and death.

When he speaks of "eternal life," the Evangelist moves altogether on Pauline lines, though he never borrows from the writings of St Paul. But there is one notable difference between the two writers. Paul, as we might expect from his practical genius and his missionary life, has a far more ethical complexion than the more meditative Evangelist. Paul is never tired of speaking of the fruits of the Spirit as manifested in the life of the Church, of the uprightness, gentleness, and kindness which must mark the members, alike in their dealings with one another and in the relations with the outer world. It is true that in his hymn of charity he represents love as the sum and the root of all the Christian virtues. But yet he dwells, as a founder of churches was bound to dwell, on the necessity of conforming to the rules laid down by society for its own preservation: obedience to authority, a quiet and gentle behaviour, absence of a litigious spirit. Actual deeds of sensuality done by a Christian, move him to such indignation that he can scarcely find words to express it. The Evangelist takes morality much more for granted, for an obvious corollary of the relation of the Church to Christ. In the Gospel, perhaps, he has no great opportunity for insisting on moral teaching. But in the Epistle also he says very little of duty and of conduct; but a great deal about love. He bids the converts "walk in the light"; and he insists that "whosoever is born of God doth not commit sin." But he seems to think that sin is almost inconceivable in one who is a member of Christ. Herein, no doubt, he takes a line too lofty for this world of ours. Love for the brethren may easily lead to injustice to those who are not brethren. To be independent of the rules of morality is an unsafe position for any man, however spiritual by nature. It is strange that the charge of antinomianism, so often unjustly brought against St Paul, should have been less often brought against a follower who more unguardedly exposes himself to it. But, after all, from his own point of view, the writer is justified. It is not the task of an inspired teacher to make a balanced scheme of virtues, or to guard himself against misunderstanding; but to say boldly what it is given him to say. When he sums up his teaching in three words, " God is love," he utters a truth so vast and so difficult, that if all his writings help us but in some measure to grasp it, they will place him among the immortals.

VII

THE DOCTRINE OF THE SPIRIT

THE account of the nature and purpose of the Fourth Gospel which we find in Eusebius[1] characterises it better than all the theories of modern critics. He is quoting, or giving the substance of, a passage in the *Outlines* of Clement of Alexandria, which Clement himself had derived from earlier authorities. "Last of all," he writes, "John, perceiving that the material (or external) facts had been set forth in the (other) Gospels, at the instance of his disciples, and with the inspiration of the Spirit, composed a spiritual (pneumatic) Gospel." That John, the son of Zebedee, was the actual writer of the Gospel is, as we have seen, if not quite impossible, at least exceedingly improbable. But that the author, whoever he may have been, was dissatisfied with the earlier Gospels as being too much confined

[1] *H E*, vi 14, 7

to the setting forth of the mere audible words and visible acts of the Master, and as often missing their higher significance, is clear. So, as a supplement to them, he wrote a Gospel which should in some cases supply omissions and correct errors of detail, but which should above all show the true and higher meaning of the teaching of Jesus, and the place of His life and death in the spiritual sphere. Compared with that higher meaning, the truth to fact appeared to him indifferent. This, indeed, would be essentially the view of all the great teachers of Christianity at the time, and especially of those who had a leaning towards mysticism. Very enlightening is the saying of Origen on the subject, that the Fourth Evangelist often preserved spiritual truth in what might be called material inaccuracy.

When we come to the question of spirit (pneuma) and the spiritual, we are obliged to hark back for a minute to the origin of the notion among the most primitive men. This has been set forth by Tylor in his admirable *Primitive Culture*, a work which in its main views will scarcely be superseded. The primitive man, whether it be from the experience of the phenomena of trance and dream, or from any other source, acquires the notion that to every man visible in the flesh there corresponds a semi-material shadow or ghost, a duplicate of the visible and active human creature, who dwells in the body, but occasionally leaves it in order to roam about, and who after death often hovers about the place where he had lived, and has relations with his descendants, whom he helps in return for the offerings which they bring him. Out of such beliefs grows, on one side, a strong conviction of the survival of death by human personalities. This side of the doctrine of spirit does not concern us in the present chapter; we shall have to return to it when treating of the subject of eschatological belief in another chapter. But there is a growth on another side of which we must here treat. With the notion that all men are ghosts or have ghosts, soon arises a general animistic way of regarding the universe. Not only men, but also animals and plants, the forces of nature, sun, moon, and stars, are all regarded as having something like a personality, and being powerful for good and evil in the world. Over against the visible and material world there is set a realm of ghostly or spiritual being, which is always reacting upon the human world. This is the root, the deep-lying root, of the tree of which all spiritual beliefs and philosophies are branches.

It is not easy to say exactly what views of the nature of spirit were held in Palestine and Greece at the beginning of our era. No doubt such views varied greatly, in proportion to the education and intellectual tendencies of various persons. But such refined notions of spiritual personality as we find in Greek philosophers or among well-educated people at the present time were not widespread. To the notion of spirit there still clung many views which we should regard as barbarous.

It is, of course, not exact to say that the Greeks and Jews regarded spirit as material. But they regarded it as having some qualities which we might consider material. Pneuma is properly breath or wind; and spirits were regarded as having some likeness to breath or air. Besides the spirit, the breath of life, which each man received at birth, he might at any time be invaded by a pneuma from without, which came into the body. It might be a good spirit or a bad one; but in either case it acted strongly in the body of which it thus took possession. If the pneuma were bad, it was necessary to exorcise it and cast it out. If it were good, it might bring into a man a new nature, make him capable of powers and virtues which he did not before possess, unite him in spirit with the higher Powers.

THE DOCTRINE OF THE SPIRIT

In the Old Testament we read of lying spirits as entering into false prophets, so that they led men on to their destruction. And we read of a Divine Spirit, the entry of which into a man gives him superhuman strength or wisdom. When the Divine Spirit came upon Samson, it made him so strong that he could break ropes as if they were burnt flax. It was by the Divine Spirit that Bezalel, the son of Uri,[1] had wisdom to plan all manner of cunning work in gold and silver and stone. In this possession by the Spirit there is nothing ethical; it is an added power and raising of a man's faculties. But in the later times of Israel, when we come to the great prophets and the Psalms, the idea of inspiration by the Divine Spirit, though it might still be thought of as almost physical in character, was yet immensely raised and moralised.

In the Fourth Gospel we find something both of the popular and of the philosophic view when the word spirit is used. While the Evangelist appreciates and adopts the Platonic view of spirit, he yet evidently regards its transmission from man to man, or from God to man, as in a measure physical, or at least as accomplished by some kind of physical contact. Here, as elsewhere, he

[1] *Exodus* xxxv. 30.

fluctuates between the pure spirituality which sometimes attracts him, and the materialism which he feels to be necessary to the existence of the Church in the visible world.

The word *spirit* does not occur in our Gospel so frequently as in the writings of St Paul and even St Luke, but the idea occupies a larger place in the mind and heart of the Evangelist than it does in those of any New Testament writer. He uses the word in three senses, which cannot in all passages be clearly distinguished, but which are at bottom very different.

Firstly, he uses it in a broad and cosmic sense. He is ever contrasting that which is visible and tangible with that which is invisible and eternal. To him the world is but a manifestation in time and place of the spiritual realities which lie above and behind it. The spirit and the flesh are contrasted, and at enmity one with another. Each has its own way of propagation: "That which is born of the flesh is flesh, and that which is born of the spirit is spirit." The matter is summed up in a single sublime phrase, which unfortunately has been the origin of many a metaphysical cobweb: "God is spirit." It is unfortunate that the English version translates the phrase, God is *a* Spirit, which spoils the

THE DOCTRINE OF THE SPIRIT 147

sense.[1] God, the Evangelist insists, is not the God of the Jews, nor of the Samaritans; but wherever men worship in spirit and loyalty, there God is present; and such worship is grateful to Him. It is spirit which is the source of life, he adds in another place,[2] and flesh is of no avail.

This way of regarding the world is that common to all the Platonic schools. Whence the doctrine came to Plato is uncertain: some think that it belongs to his master Socrates; some that he took it from the Oriental mystery religions; some that it follows the lines of early Ionian thought. In any case, he made it his own; and from his day to ours the view that the spiritual is the real and abiding, and the material the evanescent and phantasmal, has been the creed of most of the great teachers of mankind. The Founder of Christianity held the view implicitly; to Him God and the spirit of man were the great realities, in comparison with which nothing mattered; but He did not deal with abstract thought, and never set out His cosmology in philosophic form. In the letters of St Paul the same way

[1] The phrase is parallel to that in the first verse of the Gospel. "The Word was God." Here the English version does not read "The Word was *a* god." I discuss this phrase more fully below.

[2] vi. 63.

of regarding the universe is underlying, and often expressed, as in the phrase, "We look not at the things which are seen, but at the things which are not seen: for the things which are seen are temporal; but the things which are not seen are eternal." But St Paul was above all things a man of action; and he does not attempt to construct a detailed system. The Fourth Evangelist is more contemplative, and it is he who especially brought into the thought of the nascent Church the great ideas of the Platonic philosophy.

Secondly, the Evangelist uses the word spirit in speaking of the experience of the Church. No sooner had Jesus departed, so far as bodily presence went, from the disciples, than they felt among them a continued spiritual power inspiring and guiding them. It was a new experience in the world; and the Society did not hesitate to see and feel in it a continuation of the spiritual life of its Founder. In the Sermon on the Mount, Jesus speaks of the Father as giving the Holy Spirit to those who ask Him. This certainly seems like the original teaching of Christianity. It is, in fact, that of the fifty-first Psalm: "Cast me not away from Thy presence, and take not Thy Holy Spirit from me." In another passage, in *Matthew*, we may discern the impress of a later time. The Saviour speaks of the persecutions of His followers, and bids them, when they are summoned before the tribunals, to take no anxious thought as to what their answer shall be: "It shall be given you in that hour what ye shall speak. For it is not ye that speak, but the Spirit of your Father that speaketh in you."[1] As the disciples were not prosecuted by authority in the lifetime of Jesus, this passage seems to belong to the time after the Crucifixion. Matthew does not add, as the Fourth Evangelist does on a similar occasion, that this must refer to the future: "for the Spirit was not yet given; because Jesus was not yet glorified."[2] But we may best regard it as a gleam reflected back into the life of Jesus from the early Christian consciousness.

According to Luke, St Paul, and other writers of the New Testament, Scripture was revealed to the great teachers of Israel by the Holy Spirit. But in the early Christian Church there was an outpouring of the Divine Spirit, such as the world had never known. Wherever the Apostles and missionaries went, they found a Spirit working not only within them, but for them, removing obstacles, preparing the hearts of men to believe, giving

[1] *Matt.* x. 20. [2] *John* vii. 39.

peace and joy to all who accepted the faith of Christ. The Spirit worked in the Society in its assemblies, and in the hearts of individuals, inspiring, giving courage and wisdom, leading in the way of righteousness and faith.

The great and life-giving impulses which come from time to time from God for the remoulding and raising of mankind take many outward forms,[1] and each leader of men looks at them in a somewhat different way. So we are not surprised to find that the various writers of the New Testament emphasise different sides of the inspiration of the Church. On Luke, who, in spite of his splendid charity, is somewhat materialist, the inspiration makes most impression in its outward and physical forms; to him it is the energy in virtue of which the Apostles heal the sick, and the disciples speak with tongues and exercise the super-physical powers displayed in the *charismata*. The phenomena on which he dwells are closely similar to those familiar to us in recent times in connection with faith-healing and evangelical revival meetings. By the Spirit the Apostles receive the gift of tongues which enables them in a day to convert three thousand hearers. By it Ananias and Sap-

[1] *Exploratio Evangelica*, ch vii.: "The Inspiration of History"

THE DOCTRINE OF THE SPIRIT 151

phira are struck dead, Elymas the Sorcerer is smitten with blindness, Paul and Silas escape from prison, Paul receives frequent directions as to the course of his journeys, and so forth. Luke of course also dwells on the higher manifestations of the Spirit, in preaching, in power to bear persecution, in peace and joy in believing. It is notable that he always speaks of the source of the Christian energy as the Holy Spirit, though the wonders are sometimes spoken of as done in the name of Christ.

St Luke also consistently makes the transmission of the Spirit a result of physical contact. It is by the laying on of the Apostle's hands that the Holy Spirit as a quasi-material essence is given to the converts. Simon Magus thinks that this is done by some secret of magic, and is anxious to purchase the power. Originally, however, the power of the Spirit did not come among the Apostles by the imposition of the hands of their Master, but at the Pentecostal season through flames of fire which descended and rested upon each of them, when at once they began to speak with tongues and to manifest the outward signs of the inward possession by the Spirit. This seems to be the accepted view in the early Church. The Fourth Evangelist, however, has a view of his own as to the original inspiration of the disciples. "On the first day of the week, and when the doors were shut where the disciples were, for fear of the Jews, Jesus came and stood in the midst, . . . and He breathed on them, and saith unto them, Receive ye the Holy Spirit."[1] Thus, in his view, the Spirit was directly imparted by the risen Lord to His disciples as a wind or breath. The direct contradiction between this account and that in *Acts* is commonly passed over by Christians; but it is necessary to say that from the historical point of view the two accounts are not to be reconciled. Another point is that in *Acts* it would seem from the context that it was the twelve Apostles only who received the gift of the Spirit; and the multitude who were gathered into the Church on the day of Pentecost were baptised indeed, but not confirmed by the imposition of hands. According to the Evangelist it was the whole body of the disciples, including apparently some women, who received the gift directly from their Master.

To Jesus Himself the Spirit had come in the form of a dove, to abide with Him. He imparts it to His disciples by breath. But

[1] *John* xx. 19–22.

THE DOCTRINE OF THE SPIRIT 153

these external and visible works of the Spirit are quite eclipsed by the teaching in the last chapters of the Gospel as to the coming of the Holy Spirit to the Church, to be its life and its light. This teaching is essentially Pauline, though the words used are not St Paul's.

St Paul does not speak of the Spirit in the same way as the writer of *Acts*. He speaks of the charismata as the gifts of the Spirit, though he does not value the mere outward manifestations of speaking with tongues and healing so highly as does Luke. It is with far greater force and enthusiasm that he commends the more inward gifts of the Spirit. It is by gift of the Spirit, he says, that one man has the word of wisdom, another faith, another the power to work miracles. But the working of the Spirit is best shown by the blossoming of Christian graces.[1] "The fruit of the Spirit is love, joy, peace, long-suffering, kindness, goodness, faithfulness, meekness, temperance." This, however, is by no means the whole of the Pauline doctrine. All the fruits of the Spirit come from one source only: the life of Christ in the soul. "They that are of Christ Jesus have crucified the flesh with the passions and the lusts thereof." To them sin has become a thing against nature. The

[1] *Gal* v 22.

doctrine of the indwelling Christ is the teaching which is with Paul most fundamental. He is never tired of reverting to it. Not only does Christ dwell within the believer, but in the end the believer's self disappears, his life is hidden with Christ in God. Every Christian is part of the earthly body of Christ, and carries on in the world the obedience of Christ. And Paul makes no attempt to reconcile what seem to a mere prosaic critic the two different views of the source of the Christian enthusiasm. Modern commentators are much exercised to reconcile these views; but St Paul was a pragmatist and cared very little for verbal contradictions. To him, Christ, the Spirit of Christ, the Divine Spirit, are only varied ways of expressing the same experiences and the same facts. It is, in fact, very doubtful whether St Paul himself ever used the rite of laying on of hands. The author of *Acts* says that he did so on various occasions,[1] and one of these occasions is mentioned in the *we* narrative. But since St Paul does not mention the rite in his genuine letters,[2] we may conclude that at all events he did not very highly value it.

The Fourth Evangelist takes a line which is his own, not identical either with that of

[1] *Acts* xix 6; xxviii. 8. [2] Compare 1 *Tim* iv. 14.

Luke or with that of Paul. That he really accepts the Pauline identification appears clearly from two passages, one in his Gospel and one in his Epistle. In his Gospel (xiv. 23) he puts into the mouth of Jesus the words, "If a man love Me, he will keep My word: and my Father will love him, and we will come unto him, and make our abode with him." And in the Epistle he writes (iv. 13), "Hereby know we that we abide in Him and He in us, because He hath given us of His Spirit." And even more clearly, in the wonderful parable of the vine and the branches, he teaches exactly the same doctrine of the indwelling Christ, which St Paul teaches in his similitude of the head and the members. To him, as to Paul, every Christian is a part of the life of Christ.

But the Evangelist is more contemplative, more thoughtful, than St Paul, and we should expect him to take more pains to clarify his thought. He does so by accepting on the whole what seems to have been the usual teaching of the nascent Church. But he presents it to us in a different aspect from that which it bears in *Luke*. He does not dwell on the outward marks of the Spirit, the charismata. But in several passages he speaks of the communion between man and God, by means of the Spirit, as a higher revelation than that which resulted from the bodily presence of the Saviour. In vii. 38 he represents Jesus as saying that the result to believers on Himself shall be a springing of living water within; and he adds, "This spake He of the Spirit which they that believed on Him were to receive." And in the great speech of farewell which occupies chapters xiv. to xvii., the same thought recurs: "I will pray the Father, and He shall give you another Helper, that He may be with you for ever, even the Spirit of truth; . . . He abideth with you, and shall be in you."[1] But the Evangelist guards himself against any misconception to the effect that the Spirit would supersede the Master's own presence, by adding, "I will not leave you desolate: I come unto you; . . . because I live ye shall live also." A little later, in the manner of most great teachers, who put forth first one side of a truth strongly, and then the reverse side, he reverts to his doctrine of the Paraclete:[2] "It is expedient for you that I go away, for if I go not away, the Helper will not come unto you; but if I go I will send Him unto you." Here the real thought in the mind of the writer is clearly that the presence of the spiritual and indwelling Christ is really better

[1] xiv. 16.   [2] xvi. 7.

THE DOCTRINE OF THE SPIRIT 157

for the Church than the bodily presence of the Master. And he puts the same thought into another form later (xx. 29): "Because thou hast seen Me thou hast believed: blessed are they that have not seen, and yet have believed."

At the same time we must observe that this close identification of the Paraclete with the exalted Christ, naturally leading to speaking of Him in the language of personality, had an effect in preparing men's minds for the reception of the doctrine of the Trinity as later formulated in the Church. Elsewhere in the Gospels and the *Acts* the Holy Spirit is spoken of rather as a spiritual influence. And even in the Fourth Gospel, in other passages, this is notably the case. John the Baptist is represented[1] as saying that Jesus baptised with the Holy Spirit. And when, after the resurrection, Christ appeared to the disciples assembled together, He said to them, "Receive ye the Holy Spirit."[2]

Some of the utterances of the Evangelist in regard to the Spirit are strongly characteristic of his point of view. It is notable how closely he connects the working of the Spirit with truth. In some places[3] he uses the phrase, Spirit of truth, and in one he writes,[4] "He

[1] *John* 1. 33.
[2] xx. 22.
[3] xiv. 17; xv. 26.
[4] xvi. 13.

(the Spirit) will guide you into all truth." These words require some comment; and it is to be feared that in the history of Christianity, and especially in its quite modern history, they have given rise to serious misunderstandings. This subject, however, must be reserved for a future chapter.

I think that when some modern critics maintain that in this Gospel the Spirit works not by charismata or gifts, as in the Pauline Epistles, but largely in the field of intellect, they go much too far. In the Pauline Epistles and in the Gospel alike, the place of intellect is a very restricted one. In the introductory verses of the Gospel there is some attempt to sketch a system. But in the body of the work there is little of philosophic system. By one metaphor after another, by signs and wonders and by speeches, the author tries to set forth in manifold ways what the indwelling Christ was to the Church. This idea had so completely occupied and filled his mind, that all the traditions which came to him from the Apostles of actual deeds and words of the Master were fused into new shapes, and built into the fabric of a great spiritual edifice.

What has been said as to *truth* applies also to the other expression, *light*. The light that lights every man who comes into the world, the light which attracts all those who are born of God and whose deeds are good, is also a gift of the Spirit of God, and is no mere intellectual illumination. It does indeed enlighten the mind, but it is from within, by a spiritual influence, not by mere collocation of fact and piling up of reasoning. As Jesus Christ is the life and the way, so also He is the light of the world. In *Matthew*, Jesus says to the disciples, " Ye are the light of the world." After all, there is no contradiction between the two expressions. It was the Christ indwelling in the Church, and shining in the deeds of Christians, who was the light of the world in those days of the early Christian enthusiasm.

Mr Scott has maintained that the doctrine of the Spirit in the Fourth Gospel is superfluous:[1] " The more closely we examine the Johannine doctrine of the Spirit, the more we are compelled to acknowledge that there is no place for it in the theology as a whole." Mr Scott has been attacked for this saying; but I think that it is quite true. In fact, I would go further, and say that, if we except the Synoptic Gospels and *Acts*, the Spirit of God and the Spirit of Christ in the Church are closely identified. In studying the Epistles of

[1] *The Fourth Gospel,* p. 347.

St Paul this came out clearly in my mind;[1] but I did not then realise that what applied to Paul applied also to the Fourth Evangelist. Of course, as the Evangelist is professedly writing a life of Jesus on earth, he cannot use the phrase "Jesus Christ" in the way in which St Paul uses it. But the fundamental belief of the two writers is the same. Even when the Evangelist speaks of the Cosmic Spirit, he identifies that Spirit with the revelation in the flesh by Jesus, just as St Paul writes that it was through Christ that God made the cosmos.

In the third place, I must add a few words as to the mentions in the Gospel of lesser spirits, good and evil. The Evangelist would naturally and necessarily share, to some extent, the opinions universal among his contemporaries as to the agency of spirits in the human world. But he left the speaking of them to others: more important subjects claimed his pen. Angels of light are only spoken of in a distinctive way in one passage (xx. 12), where it is related that when Mary Magdalene looked into the tomb she beheld "two angels in white sitting, one at the head, and one at the feet, where the body of Jesus had lain." Like many of the details in the Johannine account of the last days, this narrative has all the air

[1] *The Religious Experience of St Paul*, p. 259.

THE DOCTRINE OF THE SPIRIT 161

of having come down in tradition. Mary Magdalene, out of whom Jesus had cast seven devils, was quite the sort of sensitive person who might see a vision of angels, and would see them in the forms conventional at the time.

It is well known that the Evangelist passes by those tales of the exorcism of evil spirits which take so large a place among the miracles of healing recorded by the Synoptist writers. There is, however, a passage in his Epistle in which he addresses to the Church a warning: " Believe not every spirit, but prove the spirits, whether they are of God." This advice is strictly practical. As everyone knows, in times and places where a spiritual afflatus is poured out on Christian assemblies, the results are never entirely good. Demons imitate the angels of light. Imposture and greed find occasion to ape spiritual exaltation. But the language of the writer is noteworthy for its gentleness. He does not speak harshly of evil spirits; he merely says that they are not of God, to be avoided rather than combated.

But though the feeling of the Evangelist in regard to demons is for the time wonderfully gentle and enlightened, he has a distinct belief in a great power of evil in the world, as the enemy of all that is Christian and all that is good. If he somewhat disdains evil sprites, he is quite alive to the power of the principle of darkness and wickedness. And it is quite in character that the great condemnation which he utters against this power, Satan, is that he is in continual opposition to the truth: "He is a liar, and the father of lying." He is also spoken of as in his essence (or from the beginning) a murderer. But it is on the first of these condemnations that he most insists. As the whole Gospel presents itself to his mind as truth, and the whole work of the Spirit as the publishing of truth, so the great enemy of mankind seems to him an enemy of the truth. It is to be noted that the writer of the *Apocalypse*, in most respects so different from the Evangelist, has on this point a coincidence with him. Among those who are shut out by the gates of the New Jerusalem, among sorcerers, and impure, and murderers, and idolaters, are especially mentioned those who love and utter lies.

VIII

ESCHATOLOGY: ETERNAL LIFE

It is now generally recognised that the problems and beliefs connected with eschatology lie at the foundation of the teaching of early Christianity, and indeed of all Christianity down to our own days. Every man finds himself a member of a community, a human being of mixed tendencies, born into a world where good and evil, happiness and misery, the material and the spiritual, are strangely mixed together. Every man who reflects finds an infinite number of problems of a moral, intellectual, and spiritual order lying about him; and before he can be at peace or find his place in the vast scheme of creation, he has to take up an attitude, to find some way of relating his own existence, his consciousness and will, to the immense series of external conditions and forces.

The three great questions of eschatology

are: (1) What is the meaning and purpose of the world? Why does it exist, and whither is it tending? How can the individual fall into line to help the world to attain the ends to which it seems to be moving, and to remove the forces of evil which hem it in and hinder it on every side. (2) What is the meaning and purpose of individual existence? Why was I born, and whither am I going? This consciousness of mine—an absolutely unique thing to me, as to all others in their own existence,—will it cease at death, or is it destined for a new life under fresh conditions? (3) I am conscious of belonging at once to two worlds—the world that is seen, the material universe, and the world which is not seen, the realm of the spirit. Which is the more important? Which am I to try to subordinate to the other?

These three questions have perplexed mankind since man became human. All through history, their incidence has grown stronger and stronger. The great and inspired men who have arisen at all times and among all peoples have tried to furnish solutions to one or another of them, sometimes to all of them. Hence arise religions. The great religions of the world may be most readily classified by the attitude which they take up in regard to

ESCHATOLOGY: ETERNAL LIFE 165

these questions. But of course this is no place for such classifications. We can here only consider these questions as far as they refer to the beginnings of Christianity.

And although it is necessary to set out clearly the differences of these questions, yet it would of course be quite absurd to imagine that they have been kept apart in the history of the human mind. Each religion must have some teaching in regard to all of them. But different religions commonly put one or other of them in the foreground and regard the others as subordinate. Nor could we expect that any religious teacher, or any settled religion, would wholly avoid inconsistencies and contradictions in the solutions proposed. The progress of religious belief is not a logical process, but a biological. Thought comes after experience and belief, and only registers and tries to co-ordinate the results of feeling and aspiration. Men live; and thought is little more than a by-product of life. And, life being continuous, there must always be in the intellectual systems of belief a great deal of survival—a survival of ways of feeling and living which really go with an intellectual outlook which has passed away. Thought really follows life at a distance, collects the traces which it has left, and tries to produce from them some not too inconsistent view of the world.

Of course those who think that Christianity came into the world full-grown and complete; that the Bible or the New Testament is the direct word of God, and contains the solution of all difficulties, intellectual and moral, must be left to their belief. But those who understand that religion in all ages is a growing plant, nurtured by the hand of God, but drawing sustenance from the earth and the air which surround it, drawing its principle of life from above, but subject to material and human conditions, must realise that of Christianity, as of all religions, we can never have a complete and final presentation, but only tendencies and approximations. In the New Testament itself we have many very different conceptions of what Christianity really is, of the relations of the individual to the Church, of the Church to its invisible Head, of the world to its Creator. And in no province is there more variety of view in the New Testament than in the province of eschatology. Nor in any other province is there more of incompleteness. We have hints and hopes and aspirations; but nothing even approaching dogmatic teaching.

Early Christian views as to question (1), the

ESCHATOLOGY: ETERNAL LIFE 167

destiny of the world, were mainly taken over from Judaism; views as to question (2), the destiny of the individual, were mainly derived from contemporary Pagan thought; views as to question (3), the relations of the material and the spiritual universe, though in origin Platonic, are the most vital part of Christianity, and the secret of its enduring power and influence.

The first question has been commonly taken as the main subject of Eschatology. And it is now known to scholars how the belief in a future reign of the Saints, and the renovation of the world and material conditions, was the dominant hope of the Jewish race in the age between Alexander the Great and Augustus. The whole apocalyptic literature, which was almost unknown to previous generations of students, has been unrolled before us. And we have learned how many of the phrases which used to seem peculiar to Christianity —the Kingdom of God, the coming Messiah, the final Judgment — were really current phrases in the whole world of Judaism, and had a meaning which must have governed the thought of those who listened to, and those who reported, the first Christian teaching. The different schools of Judaism held various views as to the relations in place and time of the future realm to the present, as to the resurrection of the dead, as to the admission of Gentiles to the benefits of the coming kingdom. Some looked for a merely political restoration; some took a more materialist, some a more spiritual, view of the conditions of the kingdom. But all agreed on three points: first, that the Realm was in the future; second, that it was the Jewish nation, as a nation, not Jews as individuals, who were to partake of it; third, that the scene of it was to be the existing visible universe, though it might be that the universe would have to be prepared for it by unimagined changes.

The second question, as to the future of the individual soul, opens up a far more difficult perspective. Dr Charles, our great authority on the Jewish apocalyptic literature, has maintained that the belief in future bliss for the individual in the realm of spirits was also a product of the apocalyptic beliefs of the Jews of the Hellenistic age. In the Old Testament, Sheol, the place of the spirits of the dead, is, he says, a place where social distinctions persist but not moral differences, a view common in the primitive thought of many peoples. But in apocalyptic literature moral distinctions prevail. In Enoch [1] "three divisions for spirits

---

[1] xxii. 9–13. Charles, *Between the Old and New Testaments*, p. 121.

or souls in the after-world are described: the first for righteous spirits; the second for the spirits of sinners, who died without suffering retribution in this world. To both these classes Sheol will be an intermediate place, from which they shall rise to inherit respectively blessedness and torment at the day of judgment. The third division is for the spirits of sinners who have met with retribution in this life. For them Sheol has become an eternal abode."

Certainly we have here clearly stated a doctrine of Heaven, Hell, and an intermediate state. But, in the first place, it may be doubted whether this doctrine, which first appears after the Jews had been widely dispersed among all peoples, was really of Jewish origin. And, in the second place, it is doubtful how far it affected the Christian origins. In fact, the perspective of the future world which we find in a few passages (and a few passages only) of the Synoptic Gospels is different. The Hellenistic Greeks, who surrounded the Jews on all sides, and mixed with them in the great cities, had almost all advanced from the merely primitive notions as to the future world to a belief in it as a place of retribution, of reward and punishment. It was hardly possible that the Jews should escape the infection. But the other hope, of a national revival and a reign on earth of the Saints, lay at a deeper stratum of their beliefs.

The third question, as to the relations of the spiritual and the material worlds, was scarcely one fitted to the ordinary Jewish intellect, which was very concrete and practical in its tendencies. On their speculative side, such questions belonged rather to the Mages of Persia and the Brahmins of India than to the Semitic peoples. In Greece it was the genius of Plato which set such questions going; after which school after school of philosophy took them up, and provided infinite material for discussion, if not widely accepted solutions. I think that it was in the treatment of this question that Christianity showed its great originality. And in its answer to this question it really answered both the others which I have mentioned before it. The answer perhaps started from Platonism; but it combined with Platonism a profound religiosity such as was not natural to the Greek mind, and is matched only in the utterances of some of the great prophets of Israel.

In the matter of eschatology, as in other matters, the Fourth Evangelist starts from the universal beliefs of his time, which he even shares; but he rises above them through the Spirit into the wide realm of the higher life. There are several passages which prove that the writer, like his contemporaries, Jewish and Christian, was looking for a catastrophic coming of the Messiah and a great judgment of souls. A modern reader is apt to be unaware how profoundly this belief had penetrated the thinkers and writers of Judæa. No one indeed had fully realised this until the recent publication and discussion of the Jewish apocalyptic writings. It was into the Jewish world dominated by these ideas that Jesus was born, and it has been a clear result of recent criticism that they formed part of His habitual thought. However much we may object to the exaggerations and the pedantry of Dr Schweitzer, he has at all events made us more fully realise this fact.

Nevertheless, apocalyptic expectations were only on the surface, and not at the bottom of the teaching of Jesus. The parables in which He set forth the nature of the Kingdom of God, the discourses of which the Sermon on the Mount is the most noteworthy, do not in the main refer to any catastrophic end of the world, but to the inner Kingdom of the Spirit, which was for Jesus the ultimate fact of life, and the dominance of which over what was material and visible was to Him a primary postulate. In the future there will no doubt always be two schools, of which one will regard apocalyptic beliefs as primary in the teaching of the Founder, and the lore of the kingdom within as secondary; while the other school will reverse the order. It is in the latter school that I would unhesitatingly enrol myself.

The Fourth Evangelist in this matter, as in others, carries on the line in which his Master had moved. He makes statements which imply that apocalyptic beliefs were familiar to him and not unacceptable. His contemporary, John the prophet, who wrote the *Apocalypse*, is entirely dominated by them, and strives to read in the book of fate what the nature of the end should be. In a few passages the Evangelist speaks almost in the same strain, notably in the Epistle,[1] "Children, it is the last time; and as ye heard that antichrist is coming, even now there have arisen many antichrists." But here the antichrist is not a hostile power which shall resolutely oppose the coming of the kingdom, but he who rejects the Christian doctrine and despises its communion. To the Evangelist the long apocalyptic passage in Mark's Gospel must have been familiar; and though he does not

[1] ii 18.

ESCHATOLOGY: ETERNAL LIFE

enlarge upon it, he does not repudiate it. Yet he rarely, if ever, makes a statement of an apocalyptic character without adding words which, so to speak, baptise it into the name of the risen Christ, subordinating dreams of the future to experiences of the present. And the hopes and beliefs which were destined in the Church to take the place left vacant by apocalyptic beliefs as they died of inanition, are all to be found in his writings, as perhaps nowhere else.

The earliest of the passages which specially concern us occurs in the discourse of the fifth chapter: "The Father hath committed judgment to the Son." That might seem a translation into the language of the Evangelist of the ordinary Christian apocalyptic belief in the coming of the Son of Man in the clouds. But in the context in which it comes it seems rather to speak of a testing of souls, and an ordaining to eternal life in the present world. This becomes clearer as we proceed: "The hour is coming, and now is, when the dead shall hear the voice of the Son of God, and those that hear shall live." Here again, at the first reading, we seem to hear apocalyptic teaching, but the phrase "and now is" is decisive, and proves that the writer was thinking of present experience, that what was primary in his mind was the call, the voice of Christ offering life to those who were spiritually dead, and lifting them into the realm which is eternal.

In the narrative of the raising of Lazarus, Martha gives utterance to the usual beliefs of the time: "I know that he will rise again in the resurrection at the last day." And the Evangelist, in his usual manner, uses the crass statement of the plain and unimaginative person as a foil to set forth the great doctrines which he has to proclaim: "I am the Resurrection and the Life: he that believeth in Me, though he die, yet shall he live; and he that liveth and believeth in Me shall never die." Owing to their use in the burial service, these words come to us with most solemn associations; but as they stand they are a sublime assertion of the relation of the members of the Church to their invisible Head; conversion is an arising from the dead; and the life which the believer shares with Christ is out of relation to time, is eternal in the heavens.

In the last great discourse, the apocalyptic vision has almost faded, though the destiny of the believer still remains as a starting-point for faith. "I will come again and receive you unto Myself, that where I am, ye may be also."

ESCHATOLOGY: ETERNAL LIFE 175

"In My Father's house are many abodes, I go to prepare a place for you." To much the same effect is a passage in the Epistle,[1] "When He shall appear, we shall be like Him, for we shall see Him as He is."

In one place the function of arbiter in the final judgment is transferred to the *words*, "If any man hear My sayings and keep them not, I judge him not: for I came not to judge the world, but to save the world. He that rejecteth Me, and receiveth not My sayings, hath one that judgeth him: the word that I spake, the same shall judge him in the last day."[2] It will be evident to everyone who reflects that we are here in quite a different atmosphere from that of the Synoptists. The Jesus of history did accept eschatological beliefs; He thought of the course of the existing scheme of things as approaching its end. And He may even have accepted the belief, which certainly was eagerly and tenaciously held in the Society, that He was to come again as judge of mankind, and ruler in a renovated and spiritualised world. But the inspiration of the Fourth Evangelist reached beyond this view. Faith in Christ was eternal life here and now, whether in the present evil world or in a transformed one. By his relation to

[1] III. 2. [2] XII. 47.

Christ and to the earthly Body of Christ a man was absolved or condemned in the judgment of souls, whether present or future. In the Synoptic Gospels we have a certain confusion of tense, spiritual life being spoken of sometimes as present and sometimes as future, although, especially in the Gospel of Matthew, the present tense far outweighs the future. But in the Fourth Gospel the future tense has almost disappeared. Eternal life lies about us here and now. Only occasionally, as in the passage before us, the current beliefs seem to dictate the form of speech.

We know that, in the beliefs of ordinary Christians, as the apocalyptic hope died out, another definite expectation took its place. When men wearied of looking for a Second Coming of the Son of Man in the clouds of heaven, for a judgment before a great white throne, and a millennial reign of the Saints on earth, there arose a belief in the judgment of individual souls at death, and their assignment either to heavenly joys or to eternal pains. In fact, the two beliefs in a general judgment and in an individual judgment, inconsistent as they are one with another, kept their places side by side, the second advancing as the former receded and became more visionary. And so it has remained even to our own days.

ESCHATOLOGY: ETERNAL LIFE

We still repeat in the Creeds a belief in the Second Coming to judgment: but the mass of Christians have had a more potent and practical belief in the joys of heaven and the pains of hell as waiting for the soul when it leaves the body. This latter expectation is so stern and terrible that before long the consciousness of the Church had accepted a belief in an intermediate realm, a purgatory where sins could be by degrees wiped out and atoned for; hell remaining as a threatened fate only for those who died in mortal sin. But the belief in purgatory was one which lent itself to extraordinary corruptions and abuses. The Church practically claimed the power to do as she pleased with the souls in purgatory: to shorten or to protract their punishment. It is obvious what a terrible weapon was thus put into the hands of the rulers of the Church. We cannot wonder that it was a revolt against the abuses of the doctrine of purgatory which precipitated the great Teutonic revolt against Rome in the sixteenth century.

No phrase is more characteristic of the Fourth Gospel than the phrase "eternal life" ($\zeta\omega\grave{\eta}$ $\alpha\grave{\iota}\acute{\omega}\nu\iota o\varsigma$).[1] An examination of the meaning given to the phrase by the Evangelist and

[1] In the English Bible, the word αἰώνιος is sometimes rendered by eternal and sometimes by everlasting.

by his contemporaries will bring into clear relief some of the chief features of his theology. The phrase first meets us in the Septuagint version of *Daniel* in connection with the coming reign of the Messiah. The Kingdom of the Messiah is to be eternal, his dominion everlasting.[1] And it is added that in the great convulsion to come the dead shall awake, "some to everlasting life, and some to shame and everlasting contempt." Here the eternal life of the good Israelite is clearly life in the divine Kingdom of the future.

The phrase occurs in a few passages of the Synoptic Gospels. In one scene recorded by all three writers,[2] Jesus is asked by a wealthy young man what he must do to acquire eternal life. The answer, "Sell all that thou hast," is familiar to us. The same question is said on another occasion[3] to have been asked by a lawyer in order to try Jesus. If these words were actually used by the hearers of Jesus, we must suppose that they had reference, as the phrase has in *Daniel*, to life in the future Kingdom of the Messiah. For the belief in that Kingdom, and the expectation of it, took so large a place in the minds of pious Jews

---

[1] *Daniel* vii. 14
[2] *Matt* xix. 16; *Mark* x. 17; *Luke* xviii. 18
[3] *Luke* x 25.

ESCHATOLOGY: ETERNAL LIFE

at the time, that out of the abundance of the heart the mouth would speak. All the Synoptists add, after the question of the wealthy young man and its answer, a comment by Jesus: "Everyone that hath left houses, or brethren, or sisters, or father, or mother, or children, or lands for My name's sake, shall receive a hundredfold, and shall inherit eternal life." So Matthew (xix. 29). But the variations in the other two Synoptists are striking. Mark[1] writes, "He shall receive a hundredfold now in this time, houses, and brethren, and sisters, and mothers, and children, and lands, with persecutions; and in the age to come eternal life." Luke[2] omits the phrase about houses, and brethren, and sisters, and mothers, which obviously could not be taken literally; but he repeats the contrast between "this time" and "the age to come."

However that be, if we take the passages which I have cited as they stand, it seems clear that those who wrote them meant by "eternal life" what Daniel means by it, life in the Messianic Kingdom. The phrases in Mark and Luke, "this time" and "the age to come," are the regular phrases for a contrast between the world as it was, and the world as it was to be in the Messianic age. It seems

[1] x. 30.   [2] xviii. 30.

clear that whatever was the real thought of the Master, His ordinary hearers supposed Him to refer to their beliefs in a change in the existing world or age, and a future reign of the Saints.

In many passages, however, in the Synoptists, the word life, without the adjective eternal, is used in a lofty and transcendent sense. This was no new thing in Israel. In some of the Psalms the word life does not mean the mere visible life on earth, but something far nobler. "Thou wilt show me the path of life"; "In his favour is life"; "My prayer unto the God of my life." In such phrases as these there is a deeper meaning than that of mere material existence: a reference to the refreshing and upraising of the spirit by contact with God. More inward and more mystic in the best sense of the word are such sayings in the Synoptists as "The way that leadeth unto life"; "He that will save his life shall lose it"; "It is good for thee to enter into life maimed or halt." Such sayings are of the essence of spiritual religion; and if an eschatological shadow occasionally falls across them, it can scarcely mar their brightness.

When we turn to the use of the phrase "eternal life" in the writings of St Paul and the Fourth Gospel, we find ourselves in quite

ESCHATOLOGY: ETERNAL LIFE 181

a new spiritual region. The tense is changed from the future to the present. To St Paul eternal life is the gift of God, and its essence lies in partaking in the life of Christ, in being grafted into Him and being ruled by his spirit. The author of *Acts*, though he often fails to understand the Pauline ideas, puts the "eternal life" in the front of his teaching. He represents Paul and Barnabas as saying to the Jews,[1] "Seeing ye thrust from you the word of God, and judge yourselves unworthy of eternal life, lo, we turn to the Gentiles." In St Paul's own Epistles the idea is set forth with the utmost variety of expression. "The gift of God is eternal life in Jesus Christ our Lord."[2] "He that soweth unto the Spirit shall of the Spirit reap eternal life."[3] "Ye died, and your life is hid with Christ in God."[4] It is unnecessary to multiply quotations, many of which will at once occur to the minds of all who are familiar with the New Testament.

It is certain that, at all events until near the close of his life, St Paul was earnestly looking for a catastrophic return of his Master in glory, to judge mankind, and to set up on earth a Messianic kingdom. But the eternal life of which he speaks does not wait for that

---

[1] *Acts* xiii. 46.   [2] *Romans* vi. 23.
[3] *Gal.* vi. 8.   [4] *Col.* iii. 3.

catastrophe, in order then to be revealed. It is the possession of the Christian from the moment when he turns to Christ and lays hold of the salvation which He has revealed. Thenceforward, it is in him an undying principle, beyond the reach of destruction either by man or by spiritual powers; even the death of the body cannot quench it. "To be spiritually minded is life and peace."[1] As the depths of the sea are untroubled, whatever storms may be raging on its surface, so the Christian can remain calm amid all outward commotions and misfortunes. His heart is in heaven, though he has to live in the visible world. No doubt there is here some inconsistency in the Apostle's teaching. The notions of a visible judgment and a temporal reign of the Saints can scarcely be reconciled with the notion of a present exalted life, unaffected by the outward changes of the world. But it is only the logical modern mind which finds much difficulty in such inconsistencies. It is only the over-trained modern investigator who would think it necessary to try to bring order into the vast and rugged landscape visible to St Paul. Ideas surge up in his mind and find expression, not as parts of an intellectual system,

[1] *Rom.* viii. 6.

ESCHATOLOGY. ETERNAL LIFE

but as the immediate utterance of an internal inspiration.

We have still to consider in what light the Fourth Evangelist regards the eternal life of which he often speaks from many points of view. His thought on the subject is essentially in a line with that of St Paul; but the two great teachers of spiritual Christianity have different ways of setting it forth. In St Paul the idea of eternal life seems to have arisen fully developed at the time of his conversion; he does not explain it, he only tries to express it. The Evangelist is more contemplative; and in his time the necessity of bringing the idea into more definite relations with the actual life of the Church had become apparent. Also he may be said to discard the belief in a Second Coming as an impediment to the course of spiritual religion. He represents his Master as promising to come again to the disciples: "I will not leave you desolate, I will come unto you."[1] But the coming is an inward one, not a catastrophic and visible Parousia; for in the same address to the disciples, Jesus speaks in a perfectly parallel way of the coming of the Paraclete, who will dwell in the Church and inspire it.

In the mind of the Evangelist, eternal life is

[1] *John* xiv 18

not disconnected from the rites of the Church. He writes, "Except a man be born of water and of the Spirit, he cannot enter into the Kingdom of God." It cannot well be doubted that he is here speaking of baptism as the authorised gate of entrance into the Society. And he must be thinking of the Christian Communion when he writes: "The bread of God is that which cometh down out of heaven, and giveth life unto the world." "Except ye eat the flesh of the Son of Man and drink His blood, ye have not life in yourselves. He that eateth My flesh and drinketh My blood hath eternal life." It is curious that after the last saying we have a momentary relapse into the eschatological way of thinking, "I will raise him up at the last day."

In what light the Evangelist looked upon the principle of Life it is hard to say, whether he regarded it as in a sense material or as wholly immaterial. Some of his sayings seem to take Life as a thing which could be transferred from person to person. "As the Father hath life in Himself, even so gave He to the Son to have life in Himself." "The Son giveth life to whom He would."[1] We might even combine these sayings with that in regard to the sacrament, "He that eateth My

[1] *John* v. 21, 26

ESCHATOLOGY: ETERNAL LIFE

flesh and drinketh My blood hath eternal life," and derive a merely magical doctrine of the physical acquirement of eternal life in the sacrament. But in doing so we should do the Evangelist an infinite injustice. Such teaching is utterly out of harmony with his trend of thought. If in one place he speaks thus of the sacrament, in the very same discourse he writes, "The words that I speak unto you are spirit and are life." And in the Epistle he writes, "He that doeth the will of God abideth for ever." We can seldom, in the case of the Evangelist, take one of his phrases as expressing the whole of his view: he expresses various sides of what he regards as the truth in various passages, or even in the same passage.

The notions as to what was material and what was immaterial, what was physical influence and what influence of the spirit, were not clearly defined in the mind of the Evangelist. Is there not very often a similar confusion in the modern mind? Did not Mesmer speak of the influence of mind on mind as animal magnetism? All the words which we apply to the motions of mind and spirit are necessarily taken from the phenomena of sense, and usually carry with them some sense implications.

In the chapter which treats of the Sacraments I will return to this question.

Eternal life is also by the Evangelist regarded as closely related to certain affirmations of doctrine. We see the steps towards this in such a saying as " This is life eternal, that they should know Thee the only true God, and Him whom Thou didst send, Jesus Christ."[1] But here the affirmation of the need of a creed is not emphatic, since the writer often uses the words "to know" in a practical rather than in a theoretical sense. To know is to be in relations with, to grasp. But in other passages the need of right doctrinal views is more strongly emphasised. "He that believeth[2] not the Son shall not see life, but the wrath of God abideth on him." Less severe is another passage: "He that heareth My word, and believeth Him that sent Me, hath eternal life."

In the Epistle, probably written by the Evangelist when old, the failure of his powers and indignation against some heretics who were troubling the Church at Ephesus drive the writer in the direction of dogma. "Who

[1] *John* xvii. 3.
[2] *John* iii 36. The revisers give as an alternative reading "obeyeth not the Son." The meaning is doubtful, and it is possible that the Evangelist's intention was not clear in his mind.

ESCHATOLOGY : ETERNAL LIFE 187

is the liar save him that denieth that Jesus is the Christ? This is the antichrist, even he that denieth the Father and the Son." Such utterances do not very well harmonise with the great theme of the Epistle, "God is love."

It is not, however, very difficult to see the attitude of the Evangelist's mind. Religion to him was at bottom purely spiritual worship. But he could not conceive such worship as existing outside the Society. It was the Church for which Christ died, and which continued on earth the life of Christ, which was the seat of spiritual religion; and eternal life, salvation, belonged only to it. Therefore the rites which shut it off from the world, and the beliefs in which all its members were united, were sacred; and outside the ranks of those who received them eternal life could not be found. The general expressions implying that the Logos enlightened all men, and that Christ died for the world, are concessions, but they cannot compete in the mind of the writer with his intense belief in the Logos Society. And here, as in other matters, he fully develops the views of St Paul.

The second school of Christian teaching, St Paul and the Fourth Evangelist, never preached a doctrine of heaven and hell for individual souls, but a doctrine of eternal life, which was to be partaken of in the present age, but which went beyond the present life into that beyond the grave. Those who were united to Christ by faith had in them this life, and they should never perish, nor should any power be able to pluck them from the hand of God. Those who had not in them the seeds of eternal life must perish and disappear, as all visible things in the world perish and disappear. The Fourth Evangelist regards this life as neither present nor future, but as timeless, as even now hid with Christ in God, while the life which we live in the flesh is little more than illusion.

The liturgy of the English Church fluctuates between the eschatological and the mystic use of the phrase "eternal life." In the collect for the second Sunday in Advent, the phrase is, "the blessed hope of everlasting life." But in the collect for Monday in Easter week, the phrase runs that God in Christ has "overcome death, and opened unto us the gate of everlasting life." The second of these phrases, rather than the first, is in the line of thought of our Evangelist, to whom eternal life was essentially not a hope, but a spiritual experience.

IX

THE SACRAMENTS

I DO not propose here to repeat the exposition by which, in a recent work,[1] I have drawn out the parallel between Pauline Christianity and Pagan Mysteries. I there set forth as the three main features of the Mysteries the following: first, that they had rites of purification and tests on entry into the Society; second, that they had means of communication with some deity to whom they looked up as their head; third, that they extended their view beyond the present life into the world beyond the grave. And I showed that in all these respects there is a parallelism between them and the Pauline churches. In some ways, as in the possession of a regular order of priests or hierophants, and in the attribution of a magical efficacy to the mere external facts of the Sacraments,

[1] *The Religious Experience of St Paul*, pp. 57–101.

the Church of the second century was much nearer to the Mysteries than the Church in the time of St Paul. But in the three respects which I have mentioned there is an undeniable similarity between the first churches and the Greek thiasi; and we cannot be surprised that the Roman magistrates, looking on the religions of the subject peoples with the same calm indifference with which English officials in India regard the popular beliefs, considered the Christian Church to be only another of the many mystic sects to which they were accustomed.

It was the close union which bound together the members of the Church, and their professed adherence to a spiritual Head and source of life, which made them most closely like the Pagan societies. Here we are on safe ground. For whereas the evidence as to the particular tenets and particular rites of this or that Pagan thiasos is of the most fragmentary and fugitive character, so that our knowledge of them must always be very slight, yet on this particular point, the spiritual unity of the thiasos, and its devotion to its chosen deity, the testimony of Apuleius and other writers of the age is quite decisive.

Critics have rebuked me for finding some kinship between the Christianity preached by

THE SACRAMENTS

St Paul and the Mystery Religions of the Greek world. They seem to think that by pointing out this kinship I insult Christianity. There is no insult and no slight in question. If we believe, with the Fourth Evangelist, that the divine Logos enlightens every man who comes into the world; if we hold that the Providence of God is not confined to the Christian Church, but takes within its action all mankind, that God is the God of the whole earth, we shall find nothing repulsive and nothing incongruous in the notion that the light which shines so fully in the Bible and in the history of the Church, shines also in a measure outside the Church. We may hold that not only the religion of the Jews, but also the religions of Isis and of Mithras, had in them some of the elements which went to the nutriment of infant Christianity.

If it can be shown, on historic grounds, that there was no relation and no parallel between the Mysteries and Pauline and Johannine Christianity, so be it. But the critics who take this view content themselves, so far as I have observed, with pointing out the many and clear points of dissimilarity between Christian and Pagan doctrines of salvation; they do not, and cannot, disprove all likeness between them. The differences are obvious enough. The most noteworthy among them is the presence in Christianity, and the absence in the Pagan Mysteries, of a strong historic element. Isis and Mithras were figures of mythology, not of history. The help given by Isis to her votaries, the labours of Mithras in the service of mankind, were to be apprehended only by faith. But Jesus had dwelt on earth, had formed a society in Palestine, had suffered and died under Pontius Pilate. Though the Exalted Christ was the source of the life of the Church, yet the Church was certain that the life in Heaven and in the Church of Christ was a direct continuation of the human life of the Founder. Of course these facts at once draw a broad line of distinction between the Mystery Religions and Christianity. Also the connection of Christianity with the Old Testament and the life of the Jewish people caused it to set forth on a higher ethical level than any sect of Paganism. All our evidence shows that the great teachers of early Christianity would have nothing to do with the Pagan rites, but regarded them as the invention of evil spirits. That they would at all consciously adopt them, or borrow from them, is most unlikely. Yet in any broad view of history it will appear that ideas, when, as it is said, they are in the air, appear at the

THE SACRAMENTS

same time in varied forms in many schools of thought and in many organised societies, when we cannot trace any visible lines of influence. The ideas are, like Virgil's spirits in Hades, waiting eagerly for a body in which they may clothe themselves so as to appear on the stage of mundane affairs; and no one can say whence they come or whither they go.

I do not greatly differ from one of the most learned and most recent writers on the subject, Dr H. A. A. Kennedy.[1] He lays stronger emphasis on the differences between the Mystery Religions and Paulinism, which I fully allow, whereas I have dwelt more on their parallelism, which Dr Kennedy does not really dispute. He speaks strongly as to the ethical superiority of the Pauline faith, as to the loftier view which St Paul takes of salvation, and especially on the difference between faith in a historic person and faith in a mythological personage. But he allows the wide prevalence in the cities in which the Pauline Churches were founded of the mystery ideas, and St Paul's familiarity with them.

The belief in an inspired society and in the eternal life in which that society is rooted, is not only mystic in the best sense, that is,

[1] *St Paul and the Mystery Religions*, London, 1913, last chapter.

related to the higher hidden life which lies at the roots of the visible life, but it is also mystic in a more historic and superficial sense, as an outgrowth, and by far the most noteworthy and valuable outgrowth, of a tendency which at the beginning of the Christian era had been for centuries growing and strengthening in the world, and which had found a temporary and insufficient abiding place in the Pagan Mysteries.

In this main respect there is a close similarity between the views of St Paul and those of the Fourth Evangelist. But when we come to details, and look more closely at what the latter writer has to say in regard to the Christ who is the Head of the Church, the relations of the members one to another, the rite of admission to the Church and the Lord's Supper, the future life, and so forth, we find that the Evangelist has views of his own which are not always identical with the Pauline. And he has a cast of mind very different from that of St Paul, which makes him find very different ways of stating his doctrines from those which we meet in the Pauline Epistles.

In the present chapter we deal with his views in regard to the Christian Sacraments. The Pagan Mystery Religions had their sacraments—sacraments of initiation and sacraments of communion—so constantly, that one might well term them Sacramental Religions. The views of the Fourth Evangelist resemble theirs as a cultivated plum resembles a wild one.

It is by general consent, and by a sort of inspired instinct, that in all the ages of the Church, alike by the great writers of the Church and by the artists who give visible form to popular beliefs, the Evangelist has been regarded as the great teacher on the subject of the Sacraments. In his third chapter, in the discourse to Nicodemus, the doctrine is set forth that it is not only by a spiritual renovation, but also by being born of water, that is, by undergoing the rite of Christian baptism, that a man is brought into the redeemed Society of the Christian Church. And the Fathers of the Church have usually regarded the sublime teaching of the sixth chapter, as to eating the flesh and drinking the blood of the Son of Man, as a clear allusion to the life-giving virtues of the Lord's Supper. Here they have been followed by Christian teachers of all ages. And the sculptors of the mediæval church have adopted their view. In the sculptural decorations of our cathedrals, St John carries the cup, as St Peter holds the keys, and St Paul the sword.

That is one side of the matter. But there is another side which seems in irreconcilable contrast with it. Whereas the Synoptic writers narrate the baptism of Jesus in Jordan by John the Baptist, the Fourth Evangelist omits it; and in a later chapter he observes that Jesus Himself did not baptise, as did His disciples. More remarkable still, strange beyond strangeness, is the fact that in describing the Last Supper the Evangelist does not mention the solemn partaking of bread and wine, with the immortal words, "This is my body" and "This is my blood," which occur in the Gospel of St Mark, nor does he say a word about that institution of the Eucharist as a rite, which is spoken of by St Paul in the Corinthian Epistle. On the contrary, he makes the main feature of the Supper to consist in the washing by the Master of the disciples' feet, and in a command to keep up this custom in future in the Society.

We have here clearly a most difficult problem; and on its solution must largely depend our whole view of the purposes and tendencies of the writer.

If we consider the time and the place of the Evangelist's writing, we cannot doubt that the two rites of baptism and the Eucharist

THE SACRAMENTS 197

were in practice familiar to him. We learn from *Acts* and the Pauline Epistles how early baptism became the entrance gate of the Church. In *Acts* all who profess the simple creed that Jesus is the Son of God are baptised into the name of Christ, and become members of the Society. The Trinitarian formula in baptism belongs to a later time. The command at the end of the First Gospel to baptise the nations in the name of Father, Son, and Holy Spirit certainly belongs to a later date than that to which it is assigned in *Matthew*, since we know that for a considerable time after the crucifixion there was no question of the admission of all nations to baptism, and that baptism was always made in the name of Christ only. St Paul, as he informs us, seldom himself baptised, since he did not regard that as his special mission, but rather preaching. But he fully recognised the importance of the rite, and, in his own fashion, he attached to it a higher and spiritual meaning, "buried with Christ in baptism." And it was from Ephesus that the exact directions of St Paul as to the celebration of the Lord's Supper were sent to the Church at Corinth. Thus in the Church at Ephesus, when the Evangelist wrote, both rites, of baptism into Christ and of the Lord's Supper, must have been in full use, and

St Paul's higher rendering of both must have been familiar. This we must presuppose, in considering what the Evangelist has to say in regard to them.

We shall find that his treatment of them is notable in two respects. First, he seems anxious to detach them from historic antecedents and to attach them to great spiritual facts and laws of the higher life. And, second, though in their case the spirit is everything, yet at the same time the earthly rendering of the spiritual counts for something, and can hardly be dispensed with.

It is noteworthy that in his narrative he does not lay any stress on the historic antecedents of baptism. John the Baptist bears witness to the descent of the Spirit upon Jesus. In the Synoptists this descent is represented as accompanying the baptism of Jesus by John. In the Fourth Gospel, however, nothing is said of such baptism: it is deliberately omitted. Critics give as the reason that the Evangelist thinks of Jesus as too exalted a being to receive baptism from anyone. And in *Matthew* we may see the germ of this notion in the saying of the Baptist, "I have need to be baptised of Thee, and comest Thou to me?" Still, we may observe that this is in fact an example of the

Johannine way of detaching a rite from historic event, and basing it on doctrine or spiritual fact.

In one place, when the Evangelist has made an unguarded statement that Jesus baptised more disciples than John, he goes back on it, and explains that Jesus did not Himself baptise, but the disciples. This is curious, as in the Synoptists we have no record of Christian baptism as a rite until we come to the command, in the very last verses of *Matthew*, to baptise the nations—a passage which, as we have already seen, is certainly by the writer put out of its proper date.

In the Fourth Evangelist's account of the career of John the Baptist we have a clear statement of his way of regarding baptism. John came baptising with water, and he is represented as himself laying stress upon the mere outwardness of the rite: " He that sent me to baptise with water, He said unto me, Upon whomsoever thou shalt see the Spirit descending and abiding upon him, the same is he that baptiseth with the Holy Spirit." Baptism with the Spirit is the work of Jesus Christ, and this is of immeasurably greater value than mere outward baptism, even as the person of Christ is immeasurably greater than that of John. We know that St Paul found at Ephesus a set of persons who were content to be disciples of the Baptist: this gives the more point to the Evangelist's comparison. We infer that the disciples of the Baptist still existed as a society at Ephesus, and that they tried to combine baptism with a faith essentially Jewish. Probably they were among the Jews who grievously disturbed the Church after the departure of St Paul. So the Evangelist contrasts their baptism, which was merely an external rite, with the Christian baptism which accompanied an illumination of the whole being by means of the Spirit.

When we consider the tendency of the Evangelist to the use of symbol and parable, we must allow the probability of the view of several critics that the Evangelist intends to introduce an allusion to it into the miracle of the healing of the man born blind. Jesus anoints his eyes with clay, thus constituting a tactual relation with himself, and then bids him go and wash in the pool of Siloam, after which he receives his sight. One would have thought that the contact with Jesus would be sufficient; but a washing or baptism is also necessary. We may well see here an expression by acted parable of the need for Christians not only that their hearts should be touched by faith in Christ, but that they should go on

THE SACRAMENTS

to the rite of baptism, after which there will come to them full illumination. At the same time, a simpler explanation, that the Evangelist is merely repeating details handed down to him by the separate tradition, is quite maintainable.

Anyone who reads the conversation with Nicodemus will see in what a subordinate place in the mind of the writer a mere outward rite dwells. The Spirit blows where it listeth, in ways which cannot be traced. It is only of Spirit that spirit is born, and it is only by the power of the Spirit that a man can be born again. The idea that baptism by itself could regenerate would be to the writer as monstrous as the notion of Nicodemus that a man must enter again into his mother's womb. Here, as in all parts of the Gospel, it is the Spirit that profiteth. But in the Church of the early second century, baptism held a place of immense importance. It was the open recognition and acceptance of Christianity. It was like the sacramentum of the Roman soldier, when he swore to be loyal to the Emperor. Hence the Evangelist will not depreciate it. A man must be born of water as well as of the Spirit, if he would enter into the redeemed Society.

We must, of course, never lose sight of the

fact that when baptism is spoken of in the New Testament, it is always adult baptism—baptism accompanied by a profession of faith, and a resolve to throw in one's lot with the Society. It does not at all correspond to infant baptism, which, whether right or wrong, stands for something quite different from a conscious acceptance of Christ. Far more nearly does it correspond to confirmation in the Roman and Anglican Churches, and what is called "joining the Church" among Dissenters, or "conversion" in the case of such bodies as the Salvation Army. It accompanied a serious and deliberate decision: people were not baptised in order that they might become Christians, but in order that, having become Christians, they should be admitted to the rites and privileges of the Society. Relapse into sin after baptism was regarded as so deadly an offence, that many men postponed baptism to a late period in their lives to avoid the danger.

The case in regard to the Lord's Supper runs on the same lines, but is still more striking. It seems to us simply astounding that if the Evangelist was acquainted with the rite, he should not attach it to the Last Supper, which he does narrate. M. Loisy [1] says that, having

[1] *Études évangéliques*, p 309.

THE SACRAMENTS

already in his sixth chapter drawn attention to the spiritual value of the Communion, the Evangelist does not think it necessary, when he describes the Last Supper, to narrate its historic foundation, but substitutes the rite of feet-washing, which has really much of the same meaning. This is, however, not a satisfactory explanation of the Evangelist's writing. The washing of the feet of the brethren was to be a practical lesson in the duty of humility and self-abasement. It is parallel to the Pauline exhortation,[1] "in lowliness of mind each counting other better than himself." The beautiful impulse, and the illustration of a moral lesson by a sort of acted parable, are quite in the manner of Jesus; and we can scarcely doubt that we have here a genuine Apostolic tradition of what took place at all events at some meal when the Master and the Apostles were together. But this lesson of humility is quite different from the higher meaning of the Eucharistic feast, rich with the inherited traditions of many generations, which had all felt how a sacramental repast may be a means of bringing together the human and the Divine. Why should not the Evangelist have introduced into his narrative both the washing of feet and the sayings as to the body and the

[1] *Phil.* ii. 3.

blood? It may be said that he does not care to repeat what might at the time be read in the Gospel of Mark. But everyone will feel that this explanation is insufficient. The Gospel of Mark was not then familiar, as the Gospels are now familiar, through the printed version. The Evangelist might surely have enlarged the bare outline of Mark with fuller and more spiritual meaning. It is scarcely possible to find any other reason for his proceeding, except his desire to detach the higher Christian teaching from mere occasion of history, and instead to attach it to the eternal realities of the spiritual world. To the Synoptists the Lord's Supper is a commemorative rite: the Fourth Evangelist seems to foresee its function in the Church of the future, as something much greater than a mere commemorative rite.

That the Evangelist, when he wrote his sixth chapter, had in his mind the Christian rite of Communion seems to be certain. It is in fact made quite clear by his mention both of the body and the blood of the Lord. Body and blood are thus put together in the Pauline and Synoptic version of the Communion, and it is beyond dispute that the Evangelist was familiar with that version. If he had been historically minded, we might

THE SACRAMENTS

regard his account of the Last Supper as intended to deny the historicity of that version. But he is not historically minded: history is to him merely a setting in time and space of the Divine ideas; and he feels quite at liberty to embody them, not in history, but in doctrine.

Thus the rite as it existed in his time suggested to him the spiritual doctrine of eating the flesh and drinking the blood of Christ: that is to say, continuing in the world the divine obedience of Christ. "My meat," the Johannine Jesus says, "is to do the will of Him that sent me." But this doing of the will of God can only come from imbibing the spirit of Christ. "If any man thirst, let him come unto Me and drink." A figurative use of the language as to eating and drinking is found in the book of *Ecclesiasticus* (xxiv. 21), where Wisdom says, "Those who eat me will always hunger for me again; those who drink me will always again thirst for me." It is by being born into the spirit of Christ, and living with His life, that men become branches of the Vine. Then the life of the Vine shall be their life. Their life on earth shall be part of the life of Christ, and shall complete the work which He did in the world, in subordinating His human will to the Divine will.

Because Christians can be helped to do this by the Christian Communion, it is justified: but in itself it is indifferent. This feeling the Evangelist puts in the strongest form in the next paragraph in the words, "It is the spirit that quickeneth; the flesh profiteth nothing: the words that I have spoken to you are spirit and are life." It is his usual plan, when he has said anything which may tend to confirm ritualism, thus to supplement it with an antidote. In the same way, after referring to Baptism, he inserts the verse as to the untraceable action of the Spirit, which may, indeed, come with baptism, of course adult baptism, but may also come in any other way.

On the Jews, who take the words of eating the body and the blood in a literal sense, he pours out the vials of his contempt and ridicule. The Jews find the saying as interpreted to them by Jesus in the later context a hard one: and here the Evangelist is thinking of his own contemporaries, who find a difficulty in comprehending and receiving spiritual teaching in regard to the Eucharist. No doubt many of the converts at Ephesus would carry into Christianity the materialist and ritualist notions to which they were accustomed in the Pagan Mysteries. Those Mysteries were never able completely to sever

THE SACRAMENTS

themselves from magic: that is, the mystæ usually attached a mysterious efficacy to the mere act of partaking, apart from the motion of will and heart which really gave it the possibility of being efficacious. After the Evangelist has shown the Jewish, that is, the materialist way of regarding the Eucharist, he puts in the mouth of St Peter, as the typical Christian, a strong corrective. Jesus said to the twelve, "Would ye also go away?" And Peter answered, "Lord, to whom shall we go? Thou hast the words of eternal life." As I show in another chapter, this phrase "words of eternal life" does not refer merely to teaching by precept or parable, but to the inner teaching of the Divine Spirit, stirring in the hearts of the disciples. It may seem a violent interpretation, when the Evangelist says "The Jews," to interpret him as meaning any literalist, whether Jew or Gentile; but it is clear that he uses the word in this sense in passage after passage. At any rate "the Jews" are opponents of the truth, and not convinced adherents. It is not an explanation of one of the great Christian mysteries to an inner circle that we have in the text, but a broad statement of the Christian attitude towards the Saviour.

There is a very close parallel between the

discourse of the sixth chapter, and the conversation in the fourth with the woman of Samaria. The bread which came down from heaven, in the one discourse, is exactly parallel to the living water, which is a flowing spring of life in a man, in the other discourse. In both, the stupidity and materialism of the auditors is used as a foil to bring out the noble spirituality of the teaching. In both, the moral is exactly the same—the salvation of men through partaking of the life in Christ. But in the discourse to the woman there is no allusion to the Christian Communion. Nor is there any allusion to Baptism, since the water is taken inwardly, and not outwardly, to quench thirst, and not to purify. All this shows the mind of the Evangelist in regard to the Sacraments. They were useful to the Church, and accepted as a matter of course. But their whole validity was spiritual, and there was in fact a great danger that they should be practised simply in obedience to a command of the Founder, or regarded as having any intrinsic or magical value.

In the mind of the Christians of the second and third centuries there was a close connection between the miraculous feeding of the multitude by the sea of Galilee[1] and the

[1] *John*, chap. vi.

THE SACRAMENTS

Christian Communion. This we see alike from early Christian writings and the paintings of the Roman Catacombs. In the case of the latter it is even difficult to tell whether the primary reference of the painting is to the miracle or the Communion. But that this connection was intended by the Fourth Evangelist is not clear. The miracle itself no doubt came down to him by tradition. But in the comment on it which he assigns to Jesus, "Work not for the meat which perisheth, but for the meat which abideth unto eternal life, which the Son of Man shall give unto you," it is very doubtful if there is an allusion to the Sacrament; the meat which abideth is in the context explained to be belief in the divine mission of the Son of Man, or faith. It is true that in the verses which follow there is allusion to the Communion, but it is connected not with the feeding of the multitude, but with the manna which fell on the Israelites from heaven. It was very natural that as the idea of the Communion became more materialist, the comparison of it to the miraculous feeding should arise. But it is more than doubtful whether this was the intention of the Evangelist.

Another point dwelt on by the Evangelist is the contagious character of the spiritual life.[1] "He that believeth on Me, as the Scripture hath said, out of his body shall flow rivers of living water." Any member of the Society who has received the Divine inspiration, and felt within him the impulses of the higher life, becomes a source of inspiration to others. Surely this is in accordance with Christian experience.

Nevertheless, the conscience of the Church has been right in regarding the Evangelist as the advocate and apostle of the Christian Sacraments. There is in him, curiously intertwined with his superb spirituality, a keen recognition that after all man is not pure spirit, and that to have full effect spiritual teaching must be combined with the visible and material.

We may compare the first few verses of the Gospel. In the prologue, where the spiritual doctrine of the Logos is set forth with so much simplicity and nobility, the teaching diverges from that of the spiritual heathen and the Gnostic by the insertion of the strong phrase, "The Word was made flesh." The writer does not say the Word became tenant of a human body, and lived for a while on the earth: the phrase is far stronger—the Word became flesh (*sarx*). In the Epistles of

[1] vii. 38

THE SACRAMENTS

St Paul the word flesh means more than body—it means the materiality of the body. "Flesh and blood," says St Paul, "cannot inherit the Kingdom of God": before that Kingdom comes men must put off the carnal body and assume a spiritual body. "The spirit," he says, "is in constant warfare against the flesh"; and he gives a long list of foul vices which are the natural works of the flesh. According to the teaching of the mystic sects of Asia, the flesh was the principle of evil, and irreconcilably hostile to all goodness. Thus the phrase "the Word became flesh" is a very extreme utterance, and one which must have greatly scandalised the Christians of Ephesus.

This real mixing of the Divine and the human is the Christian doctrine of the Incarnation, as contrasted with the Gnostic doctrine that the Divine and the human could have no direct contact—moved in different spheres. Augustine, after studying the nobler forms of Pagan mysticism, selects this one Christian teaching as that which is not to be found in them. It is the Johannine equivalent of the quasi-historical story of Matthew and Luke of the Virgin Birth. This is quite in accordance with the regular order in the rise of religious teaching. First comes history or myth (for in ancient times the two were scarcely distinguished), and afterwards doctrine.

In the same way, the Christian doctrine of the Sacraments, as set forth by the Evangelist, is pure spirituality humanised. In it there is no trace of the magical: that a mere rite by itself could draw down the Divine power, or lift up the human spirit, the Evangelist would have denied as keenly as St Paul. "It is the spirit that quickeneth; the flesh profiteth nothing." Yet the Word was made flesh: the drama of salvation had to be exhibited on the theatre of time and space. The Divine Spirit must dwell in a mortal body, must suffer and must pass through death, that men also may learn to conquer suffering and death by the power of the Spirit within them. In the same way the baptism with the Holy Ghost may be accompanied by a visible baptism of water; and the imparting to believers of the life and spirit of Christ may be accompanied and symbolised by the rite of the Eucharist. It was the business of the Church, by its organisation, to preserve the outward and visible sign, and to trust to its continued inspiration that the inward and spiritual grace would, when and how it pleased the will of God, accompany the sign. If that grace were taken from the

THE SACRAMENTS

Church, then no doubt the rite would be empty and worthless. That the grace would continue the Church could not guarantee, but she could at least provide a suitable occasion and vehicle. The Church set up the rite as a man may set on his house a lightning-conductor, when he does not know whether the lightning will ever come that way. Such seems to be the sacramental teaching of the Evangelist, remote alike from the materialism of those who regard the rite as in itself efficacious, and the unhealthy spirituality of those who regard the rite as superfluous and indifferent.

In his old age, when he wrote the Epistle, the Evangelist seems to have relied, as was natural to a man with failing powers, somewhat more on the visible rites of the Church. "There are three," he writes,[1] "who bear witness, the Spirit, and the water, and the blood." The Spirit in the Church is always the true source of inspiration and life; but there are associated with the Spirit the water of baptism and the blood of the Christian Communion.

[1] *Epistle* v. 8.

X

JUDAISM AND THE GOSPEL

IN treating of the relation of the Fourth Evangelist to Jewish race and tradition, we must be careful not to confuse different things. First, there is the broad question of universalism, whether those who belonged to other races than the Jewish might, by piety and by following the divine light in their own religions, be acceptable to God, or whether God would accept the Jews only. This question must, in a country of mixed inhabitants such as Galilee, have sometimes arisen in the lifetime of the Founder; and we shall see that according to the Gospels it did sometimes arise. After the crucifixion, when the Church as an organised body was coming into existence, this question was naturally merged in another: whether the Gentiles could be admitted into the Society without becoming proselytes and keeping at least some of the precepts of the

JUDAISM AND THE GOSPEL 215

Law of Moses. This was the question which it was the mission of St Paul to solve.

What makes it as difficult as it is important to keep these two questions apart is the fact that in the Fourth Gospel, and in a less degree in the First and Third, there is a certain confusion of tenses. The life of the Founder is in a measure reconstructed in view of the experiences of the rising Society. That this should be so was inevitable. M. Paul Sabatier has shown how the life of St Francis was, within a few years of his death, rewritten in view of the problems which came before the society which he had founded. In the same way, the controversies of the time of Paul are sometimes reflected in the narrative of the Gospels.

It is by no means easy to determine what was the teaching of Jesus Himself in regard to the racial question. On the one hand, we have His harsh speech to the Syro-Phœnician woman—a speech recorded by Mark, which is regarded as bearing marks of authenticity: "It is not meet to take the children's bread and cast it to the dogs." Matthew in the same connection reports another saying of Jesus: "I was not sent but unto the lost sheep of the house of Israel." I suppose that every Christian reads these words with some pain. Interpreters have many ways of blunting their keenness: but however they be explained, they can scarcely be received with complacency. Nor does the saying stand alone. When Matthew records the calling of the Twelve, he adds[1] that Jesus gave them the direction, "Go not into any way of the Gentiles, and enter not into any city of the Samaritans; but go rather to the lost sheep of the house of Israel." In face of such passages it seems impossible to deny that for some reason, at all events at some time in His life, the Founder of Christianity restricted His mission to the Jews and the Proselytes. But in contrast with these passages we find others of a very different strain. Even John the Baptist is represented as saying to his followers, "God is able of these stones to raise up children unto Abraham."[2] And in the passage which relates to the healing of the Roman Centurion's servant, Jesus praises the faith of the Centurion, and adds, "Many shall come from the east and the west, and shall sit down with Abraham and Isaac and Jacob in the Kingdom of Heaven." As I have observed, it is not easy to reconcile these sayings. It is of course easy to say that in the former of them Jesus is only trying the faith of the woman,

[1] *Matt.* x 5.   [2] *Matt.* iii 9

JUDAISM AND THE GOSPEL 217

believing it to be strong enough to bear the test. And it is not difficult to suppose that the saying to the Centurion is transposed by the Evangelist under the influence of the flow of Greeks into the Society. If so, this saying illustrates the extreme difficulty of discerning between the actual sayings of the Founder of Christianity and the results of the working of His Spirit in the nascent Church.

The truth is that the teaching of Jesus, as recorded by the Synoptic writers, lies so close to the heart of human nature, beneath the externals of nation and training, that it would seem to be quite inconsistent with any exclusive racial feeling. And it is clear that Jesus not only Himself kept the law rather in the spirit than in the letter, but also encouraged His disciples to do the same. The religion bore from the very first obviously the potentiality of becoming a world-religion, although the Apostles seem to have been slow to recognise this fact. Thus St Paul, in insisting on the admission of the Gentiles to the Church on equal terms, was certainly following the line impressed by his Master on the new religion.

But in another way the teaching of St Paul marks a retrogression in liberality. For him the new sacred Society steps into the place of the old racial Church. Jew and Gentile are one in Christ. But it does not seem that St Paul recognised any regular way of salvation apart from incorporation in the Church of Christ. When Luke puts into the mouth of Peter the words, "Of a truth I perceive that God is no respecter of persons; but in every nation he that feareth Him, and worketh righteousness, is acceptable to Him," he gives utterance to a view which goes somewhat beyond what St Paul could have accepted. The teaching is quite in a line with the utterance in *Matthew* xxv., where feeding the hungry and tending the sick is represented as the way of life. St Paul, however, would have maintained that that life can be reached only through the gate of faith, not through that of good works, though we have in *Romans* ii. 1–16 a somewhat different strain.

It may be said that when St Paul says that Abraham was saved by faith, he must have been thinking of faith in the God of Israel, not God as revealed in Christ. It may be so: St Paul often falls into inconsistencies, as do most great theologians, because the particular point which they are considering absorbs their attention and draws it away from all else. In the passage cited he is contrasting faith with works, and not thinking of the object of faith.

JUDAISM AND THE GOSPEL 219

But the inconsistency is only verbal, and did not exist in the mind of St Paul, to whom history was not a mere succession of events in time, but the reflection of spiritual facts. "In Adam," he says, "all die."[1] He would no doubt have agreed with the phrase of the Evangelist, "Your father Abraham rejoiced to see my day; and he saw it, and was glad." So that Abraham also had faith in Christ.

Thus the Pauline teaching continued, in an infinitely loftier and more spiritual way, the teaching of a privileged and chosen people, though the Israel in which he believed was not a race but a society, united to its divine Head, and thence deriving all its power and all its happiness.

In the Fourth Gospel we find in regard to this matter three elements. There is some trace, due no doubt to an Apostolic tradition, of the relations of the Founder of Christianity to Jewish law, and His impatience of it. There is a general acceptance of the Pauline point of view—of salvation through Christ alone. Also there is something of a tendency to spiritual universalism, which belongs to the Evangelist himself, but which is, in fact, a development of the attitude of the Founder.

[1] 1 *Cor.* xv. 22   The tense is *present*.

The Pauline doctrine of salvation by faith lies so deeply at the root of the teaching of the Fourth Gospel, and is so fully implied in all its developments, that we need not dwell in this place on the dependence on it of the Johannine teaching. What is more necessary is to show that, in spite of this fact, the Evangelist stretches out towards universalism with an energy which sometimes leads him into inconsistency. We may begin by citing two passages, "Other sheep I have, which are not of this fold," and " He prophesied that Jesus should die for the nation; and not for the nation only, but that He might also gather together into one the children of God that are scattered abroad," in which there is something of the universalist spirit. But both these passages seem, on a careful examination, to refer only to the admission of Gentiles into the Church, not to the validity of Gentile faith and works outside the Church.

In some passages of the Gospel, however, we have distinct allusions not so much to the admission of Gentiles to the Church as to the reality of religion outside the Church. The event mentioned in xii. 20, the desire of some of the Greeks—Hellenes, not Hellenistic Jews—who were in Jerusalem at a festival to speak to Jesus, seems quite likely to be historic.

The fact is told simply, and it is added that Jesus was pleased at the recognition: He makes the very simple and natural remark, "The time has come for the Son of Man to be held in honour," and recognised not only by his countrymen. The English version, "should be glorified," takes the mind of the reader away, by seeming to refer to some divine exaltation. And it seems very probable that the Evangelist looked on the simple phrase which he had heard from tradition in a symbolic way, for he adds a little discourse, in his usual manner, transposing the simple events of every day into a loftier key. This discourse, beginning, "Except a grain of wheat fall into the earth and die, it abideth by itself alone; but if it die, it beareth much fruit," is one of superb spirituality, but it is in no way appropriate to the context.

The Fourth Evangelist, though he was probably a Jew by race, carries further even than St Paul the emancipation from Judaic nationalism and exclusiveness. To St Paul the Christian Church seemed to step into the place in the Divine favour and purposes held by the Jewish people: the Jewish law was not binding upon Gentile Christians, but they inherited the rich promises made to the Jewish Patriarchs, and became a new and true Israel.

Luke, in the tale of the conversion of Cornelius, shows how by prayer and piety a Roman might come as near to the door of the Kingdom of God as a pious Jew. The writer of the *Epistle to the Hebrews* shows how Jewish belief and ritual was a symbolical anticipation of the faith and the practice of the Christian Church. But the Fourth Evangelist in places goes further than any of these.

Nowhere does his spiritual universalism shine more brightly than in the discourse to the Samaritan woman, which we naturally bring into close contrast with the Matthean saying, "Into any city of the Samaritans enter ye not." He makes a slight concession, "We worship what we know, for salvation is from the Jews." But immediately he is borne away on the flood of a magnificent universalism, "The hour cometh, and now is, when the true worshippers shall worship the Father in spirit and in truth: for such doth the Father seek to be his worshippers." The exclusive privilege of the temple and Jerusalem is at an end: all races may come to God, and worship Him where they please, so long as it is a spiritual worship which they bring. Until one has fully realised what Jerusalem was to the Jews, how completely it represented their national religion, their pride of race, their past history, and their hopes for the future, one cannot fully understand at what a cost of self-suppression and through what painful following of the higher light any Hebrew could reach that utterance. When the author of the *Apocalypse* writes of the future, his highest hope is to see a new Jerusalem: the Evangelist is willing to see Jerusalem for ever eclipsed. No doubt the destruction of Jerusalem by Titus had violently wrenched aside much of the Jewish hope in the city of God; but such a complete carrying on of the tendency of Jesus towards spiritual universalism could only come from His Spirit still working in the Church.

I have spoken of the noble spirituality of this passage as belonging to the Evangelist. In its actual expression, no doubt it does belong to him. The choice of words and the literary style are his. And in the Gospel it is represented as part of a discourse held between two persons only, Jesus and the Samaritan woman, the disciples having gone away into the town to buy food. Who then could report it? The discourse of Jesus gradually slides away from the connection in which it began, and ends with preaching such as the Evangelist may well have uttered in the Synagogue at Ephesus, " God is spirit, and they that worship Him must worship in spirit and truth." One cannot but feel how inappropriate such a sublime utterance would be when addressed to the Samaritan woman, who is represented as a very commonplace and even crass person.

Yet the discourse is but a further projection of the line marked out by the historic Jesus. In the sober and unimaginative record of the trial before the High Priest which Mark gives us, we observe that one of the most telling accusations against Jesus was one brought by witnesses who said, " We heard him say, I will destroy this temple that is made with hands, and in three days I will build another made without hands."[1] But the Evangelist adds that the witnesses did not agree as to what had really been said. It is notable that there is an exactly corresponding want of agreement between our authorities who report these sayings of Jesus. Matthew (xxiv. 1) tells us that when the disciples of Jesus showed Him the splendour of the temple, he replied, " There shall not be left here one stone upon another," alluding doubtless to the destruction of the city which he foresaw. But John reports a saying much nearer to the words of the

[1] Compare 2 *Cor.* v. 1, " We have a building from God, a house not made with hands, eternal in the heavens."

witnesses, "Destroy this temple, and in three days I will raise it up." Evidently the bystanders, or those who repeated these words later, did not understand them. The Fourth Evangelist says that the real meaning was that Jesus "spake of the temple of His body," and that afterwards, when Jesus arose from the dead, the disciples remembered the saying. But there can be little doubt that if on some occasions, as Matthew reports, Jesus spoke only of the coming destruction of the temple, on other occasions he spoke of that temple as having become superfluous owing to the new teaching of the Kingdom of God. Thus the germ of the saying of the Fourth Evangelist, that the true worship of God was independent of place, may be found in the historic teaching of Jesus. Only the phrase "God is spirit" is too metaphysical ever to have been uttered in that teaching.

Also belonging entirely to the Evangelist is the noble passage in the proem, in which the Word is spoken of as a light lighting every man who comes into the world. And elsewhere in the Gospel, Jesus is represented as saying that He is the light of the world, not, be it observed, the light of the Church. In fact, we have here an approximation to the lofty, though too intellectualised, universalism of Justin,[1] in the next generation, who writes: "He is the Word of whom every race of men were partakers; and those who lived reasonably are Christians, even though they have been thought atheists." "Even they who lived before Christ, and lived without reason, were wicked and hostile to Christ."

In speaking of the Sabbath the Evangelist clearly shows his attitude. There is no subject on which his Master's teaching had been clearer and stronger. Each of the Synoptic writers records that teaching. In *Mark* we find the saying, "The Sabbath was made for man, and not man for the Sabbath": one of the most pregnant and far-reaching of all the sayings of Jesus. In *Matthew* and in *Luke* we have the principle, "It is lawful to do well on the Sabbath-day," enforced by the observation that no Israelite was so bigoted in his veneration for the Sabbath as not to attend on that day to the necessities of his domestic animals. There can be no doubt that historically this was the view taken by the Founder of Christianity. In *Acts* and in the Pauline writings we have little in regard to keeping the Sabbath. We observe that the Christian habit of keeping sacred the first day of the week instead of the seventh was

[1] *Apology*, 1. 46

JUDAISM AND THE GOSPEL

already then making its way in the Church. St Paul on the Sabbath goes to the synagogue; but it is scarcely likely that he kept the day at all strictly.

In the time of the Fourth Evangelist, the question of the Sabbath must have become for Christians far less acute. And in a place like Ephesus, where the Jews were in a minority, their non-observance of the day would not be conspicuous. It is therefore somewhat remarkable that in three separate chapters, v., vii., and ix., he should dwell on the offence given to the Jewish people by Jesus' healings on the Sabbath-day. This is a fact for which it is not easy to account, if we do not suppose a strong substratum of tradition in the Gospel. The Apostle on whom the Evangelist relies regarded the breaches of the Sabbath by Jesus as one of the chief reasons of the hatred which the strict Jews felt for Him; and this would be very natural, considering the intense feeling on the subject which dominated Israel at the time. But the Evangelist mixes with the tales of offence because of Sabbath-breaking other elements more closely related to his own point of view. In v. 18 he writes, "For this cause, therefore, the Jews sought the more to kill Him, because He not only brake the Sabbath, but also called God His Father, making Himself equal with God." Jesus, according to the Evangelist, and very probably according to the historic tradition, had justified His activity on the Sabbath by declaring that God did not, as the Fathers had feigned, rest on the seventh day, but worked in sun and rain, in nature and in the hearts of men.[1] To such a saying many parallels may be found in the Synoptics, such as that remarkable passage in *Matthew* in which Jesus bids His disciples radiate kindness on friend and foe alike, as the Heavenly Father " maketh His sun to rise on the evil and the good, and sendeth rain on the just and the unjust." The ending words of the passage I have cited, " making Himself equal with God," belong, of course (if genuine) entirely to the Evangelist; for there is nothing whatever in the saying of Jesus, if I have rightly restored it, to justify such an inference; and it is impossible to imagine that the Jews, seeing before them a being of flesh and blood, could suppose that he made himself " equal to God."

In another passage (ch. ix.) the circumstance that the blind man, whose healing is reported, was made whole on the Sabbath is almost

[1] *John* v 17, "My Father worketh even until now, and I work."

lost sight of in view of the greater question whether such deeds of healing proved the healer to be sent from God, whether they are one of the "signs" of a Divine mission. This latter theme is one to which the Evangelist returns often; and we may suspect that the tale, in passing through his mind, has somewhat altered its centre of gravity. In its original form probably greater stress may have been laid upon the anger of the Pharisees at the breach of the Sabbath. But since that controversy was no longer living, the Evangelist naturally glides on to a subject which was more stirring.

In dealing also with the Jewish Scriptures our Evangelist goes further than St Paul. Paul is quite clear in his determination that the Jewish law was not incumbent on Gentile converts. But nevertheless his rabbinical training, and the habit of bibliolatry which came from it, never quite lose their hold on him. "The law," he says, "is holy, and the commandment holy and righteous and good." To him the tales of the Fall, of the faith of Abraham, of the choosing of Jacob and the rejection of Esau as told in Genesis, are not only true, but they are great events in the deeper history of the world. Paul takes his great doctrine of election and reprobation direct from the Prophets. The Fourth Evangelist never had the rabbinic training. Time and space had removed him far from the worship of Scripture, which had so close a relation to the religious life of Jerusalem. To him the whole value of the Scriptures lies in the one fact that they contain prophecies, which have been fulfilled in the life of Jesus Christ. Over and over again he cites passages of Scripture as foretelling the doings and the sufferings of his Master. In the nineteenth chapter, which records the events of the crucifixion, the phrase "that the Scripture might be fulfilled" recurs as a refrain. It was that the Scripture might be fulfilled that the soldiers parted the garments of Jesus by lot; that He said "I thirst"; that the Roman soldiers did not break His limbs, but pierced His side with a spear.

The matter is summed up in a phrase contributed by the Evangelist himself, "Ye search the Scriptures, because in them ye think ye have eternal life; and these are they which bear witness of Me." But apart from their prophecies of Christ, the Scriptures scarcely come into the Fourth Gospel at all. The old battle as to the independence of Gentiles in regard to the law had been fought by Paul and won. For the cosmology of Genesis the Evangelist substitutes a new and more philo-

JUDAISM AND THE GOSPEL 231

sophic cosmology, holding that the world was made through the Logos for mankind. He has, in fact, abandoned the Old Testament for Plato more completely than did Philo, and far more completely than did the early Church.

I have observed that in the universalism of his religious faith the Fourth Evangelist goes beyond St Paul. This will clearly appear if we compare the utterances of the two writers in regard to Israel. St Paul earnestly believed the Jews to be the people of God, having a special calling and relation to Him. Israel by no means ceases to exist at the coming of Christ, but is extended and spiritualised. In *Romans* (ch. ix) he argues that although the adoption by God and the promises belong to Israel, yet they appertain not to the physical descendants of Abraham, but to those who are the children of his spirit, the children of faith. Thus from the true Israel many of Jewish blood are shut out; while many Gentiles become in Christ the children of Abraham. But as he works out the consequences of this doctrine, his tribal conscience sometimes revolts. God, he says, has not cast off His people. The Israelites have the inestimable privilege of being the custodians of the oracles of God. St Paul hopes that in the end all of them will be saved. But it is clear to him that henceforth they must share their privileges as the people of God with the Gentile converts; and that if they reject the faith of Christ they will be cut off and wither. Always the distinction between Jew and Gentile is present to his mind. And it seems from *Acts* that it was only the repeated experience that the Gentiles were more ripe for faith in Christ than the Jews which by degrees drove him further and further from his racial prejudices.

The Fourth Evangelist, living at a time when the Christian Church was more clearly separated from Judaism, and in a city which was thoroughly cosmopolitan, had not the same force of national feeling to hold him back; and so with freer and bolder steps he advances towards the universalism which was from the first implicitly present in his Master's teaching. He can scarcely go further than the moral taught in the story of the Good Samaritan; but he can develop that moral in an intellectual direction. The theme of the whole of his eighth chapter is that spiritual likeness, which is the same thing as spiritual descent, is of far more account than mere physical race. John the Baptist, as reported in *Matthew*, had said," " God is able of these stones to raise up children unto Abraham "; but

JUDAISM AND THE GOSPEL 233

that writer does not report of Jesus any saying quite so strong. But the Fourth Evangelist represents his Master as declaring that the Jews who bitterly oppose Him are the children rather of Satan than of Abraham, since their deeds show their spiritual kinship.

It is noteworthy that the opposition to Jesus, the persistent misunderstanding of His teaching, and the plots against His life, which are in the Synoptists ascribed to the Pharisees, the Lawyers, and the Sadducees, are by the Fourth Evangelist attributed to "the Jews." An explanation of this very remarkable fact has to be sought. It is clear that such an use cannot come from the Apostle John, nor any of the Apostles. It can only come from a source far remote from Palestine. For during the life of Jesus the whole of His following consisted of Jews, whether of Judæa or Galilee, and the people as a whole do not seem until the very last days to have been hostile to Him. According to both Matthew and Mark, the enemies of Jesus did not dare to arrest Him publicly, for fear of a tumult in His favour. And if the Jews had been consistently hostile, could Pilate have placed on the cross the title "This is the King of the Jews"?

A clue may perhaps be found in the speech

of St Paul at Miletus. As we know from *Acts*, in most places which St Paul visited it was the Jews who were his bitterest persecutors and opponents; and they succeeded in inflicting on him five distinct scourgings. He declares in the speech at Miletus that his great difficulties at Ephesus had arisen from the hostile plots of the Jews. It would therefore seem that at Ephesus the Jews were especially hostile to Christianity. How strong they were even within the Church we can judge from the *Apocalypse*.[1] But the Jews outside the Church were doubtless still more bitterly opposed to anything which was dangerous to their national feeling, and incapable of understanding the lofty spiritual teaching of the Evangelist. He might naturally think that the Jews of Jerusalem, in the fanatical days which preceded the destruction of the city, would be still more bigoted in their hostility.

Although the hostility of the Jews to Christianity was specially keen at Ephesus, we know that it was everywhere prevalent. Family quarrels are notoriously among the most bitter. And it is well observed by Mr Scott[2] that many of the objections brought forward by the Jews to the teaching and person of Jesus are just those which we find

[1] See above, p 36 [2] *The Fourth Gospel*, p. 73.

in the Talmud and in the work of Celsus, who derived his arguments from Jewish sources. There is therefore a dramatic propriety in the Evangelist's constant reference of cavilling to the Jews. But it is dramatic rather than historic propriety, since the objections which the Jews raise are usually such as belong to the end and not to the earlier part of the first century.

XI

THE CHURCH AND THE WORLD

THERE is no point in which the teaching of the Fourth Evangelist is closer to that of St Paul than in his doctrine of the Church. This is very natural. The feeling that the Church was the body of Christ, and that Christ was the life alike of the Church as a whole, and of the individuals who composed it, so filled the horizon of what we may call the first spiritual school of Christianity, that it tended to shut out what lay beyond.

In the view of the Evangelist, every Christian became, through the inward grace which accompanied baptism, a part of the Christ on earth. The parable in which he most clearly formulates this view is that of the vine and the branches. It is interesting to compare this parable with the closely similar and yet in some ways different comparison of St Paul, that of the limbs and head of the body. Of course it does not do to take a metaphor as if it were a scientific statement, nor to analyse a poetic figure as if it were mere prose, yet, bearing this in mind, we may well briefly dwell on the two figures. Put together, they make up a better representation of the inspiration of the Church than either makes separately.

The comparison of St Paul is one side of the truth. It sets in a clear light the superiority and the continued rule of the Founder. The same blood flows through body and head; but whereas in the body it is useful only for the natural processes concerned with our life on earth, breathing and digesting and the rest, in the head it subserves the noblest of the purposes for which man exists, thought, feeling, and imagination. The highest duty of the limbs is to move as the head directs them, to fulfil the purposes in life which the head judges worthy, to obey and to serve. And the head may be regarded as having a life of its own, almost independent of that of the body; at least it is the earthly seat of a spirit which dwells in it but is not essentially confined to it, which through it acts upon the world, but yet sits above it; which may even, as psychologists are beginning to see clearly, act directly upon other spirits without being restricted by merely physical conditions.

It is perhaps not fanciful to think that in St Paul's mind, when he made the comparison, the infinitely greater spiritual eminence of the Head of the Church than that of the members, and their duty to follow in all things the will of their Lord, was on the surface. But there was certainly also present to his mind the community which their common relation to the head sets up in the limbs and parts of the body. For on this point he in fact dwells at length, speaking of the functions of the more and the less comely parts of the body, of the eyes, and hands, and feet. They are parts of a whole and related one to the other mainly because they are all alike servants of the head. In the same way it is their relation to their exalted Lord which binds Christians into a society.

The parable of the Evangelist in which he speaks of the vine and the branches is in some ways truer and more telling. I may say at once that I deem it in the highest degree improbable, if not impossible, that the comparison could have come from Jesus Himself. Not only is the character of the comparison quite different from the character of the parables given in the Synoptists, more reflective and far-fetched, less simple and direct, but also the relation of the Master to His Church which it illustrates is the relation which subsisted in the Church at the end of the first century, not the relation which held while Jesus was on earth. As applied to the relations of a wandering teacher, at the head of a band of devoted followers, the comparison would lack point. But it is suggestive beyond suggestiveness if we think of it as dawning upon an inspired Evangelist half a century later.

One difference between this comparison and that of St Paul strikes us at first glance. Though head and limbs have a common life, yet the head is not the limbs. But not only do the vine and the branches have a common life, but the branches *are* the vine, as much as is the stem or the root. Another difference is not less clear: if the head be cut off from the limbs, it dies; if the branches be cut away from the vine, it does not die, but throws out fresh shoots. Indeed, as the Evangelist himself points out, the cutting in (not cutting away) of the branches is necessary to their full productiveness. We must not, however, strain the differences between the two parables. Only we may note that the complete identification of the vine with the branches is valuable in the thought of the Evangelist; and it brings out in relief that complete identity of the Ruler of the Church and the members of the Church on which he does not tire in insisting.

There are two other comparisons prominent in the Gospel which throw light upon the Evangelist's conception of the Church. One is that of the sheepfold. The fold is the visible society, and the sheep are the Christians, like sheep, according to that most exquisite Psalm which begins " The Lord is my Shepherd, I shall not want," but also separated from other flocks and having a close relation one to another. The relation of Christ to the sheepfold is expressed in two ways.[1] He is first spoken of as the door of the fold, through whom alone any man can enter into it. It is only by being united to Christ that Christians become united to one another; through spiritual community with their Master they are made members of His flock. Next, Christ, in a more pleasing and enduring metaphor, is spoken of as the Good Shepherd. Here we have the very language of the Psalm adopted and transfigured with Christian meaning. None of the Parables of the New Testament gained greater vogue among the early Christians than this: on the walls of the Catacombs the Good Shepherd carrying the lamb on His shoulders is one of the most frequent and best beloved emblems.

[1] x. 7–11.

THE CHURCH AND THE WORLD 241

And in the carving of the marble sarcophagi of Rome, which are a little later than the earliest paintings of the Catacombs, the same charming figure makes its constant appearance.

It has been suggested that the frequency of the figure may be partly accounted for by the fact that it was a mystery, that is to say, that its meaning was only understood by the Society; and so even Pagan sculptors might be set to produce it without offence. Shepherds in rural scenes are of frequent occurrence on Pagan sarcophagi of the period. There may be something in the suggestion; but the real reason for the frequent choice of the emblem lies deeper, and belongs to the Christian consciousness. It is frequent because it was favourite and beloved. Perhaps some may think that we have here a proof that the comparison was actually used by Jesus in His teaching. But this does not follow. Other scenes which especially belong to the Fourth Gospel are notable favourites with the painters of the Catacombs, especially the healing of the paralytic man at the pool of Bethesda, who is represented as carrying his bed,[1] and the scene of the raising of Lazarus. It is clear that the "spiritual" Gospel had among the early Christians of the city of

[1] v. 9.

Rome a vogue even greater than that of the other Gospels. In those days the people, whatever may have been the case with the few men of higher education who came into the Church, did not value the current tales from the great biography in proportion to their historic authority, but in proportion to the echo which they called forth in their own spirits.

The other figure, which is more familiar to us in the Synoptists, is that of a kingdom. But the Evangelist does not use the figure often, perhaps because the eschatological views to which it especially belongs are absent from his Gospel. And when he does use it, it is in a peculiar sense. "My kingdom is not of this world." While the mass of Christians were eagerly expecting the return of their Master in the clouds of heaven, accompanied by legions of angels, to set up in the world a visible realm of righteousness, the Evangelist recognises his Master, not as an earthly sovereign, set up as ruler and judge by a great cataclysm, but as king of an inner and invisible realm, of the divine kingdom which is within us. "Jesus answered, Thou sayest that I am a king. To this end have I been born, and for this came I into the world, that I should bear witness unto the truth. Every-

THE CHURCH AND THE WORLD 243

one that is of the truth heareth My voice." The King as a witness of the truth at first strikes us as an incongruity. This might seem the province of the Prophet and the Teacher rather than of the King. But the Evangelist does not use the word truth in the ordinary sense. Here he uses it obviously not in the sense of truth to fact, scarcely even in the sense of ideal or spiritual truth. He means rather, those who are faithful and listen loyally to the voice of God make up a spiritual realm of which Christ is Lord. It is a less direct and simple way of putting the matter than is the parable of the shepherd and the sheep; but at bottom there is the same meaning.

That the writer has in his mind, in this as in other parts of his Gospel, the Christ of the Christian experience rather than the Jesus of history is clear enough. This fact comes out, almost naïvely, in many passages, especially in the last great discourse. "Because I *was* with you, I said not these things unto you."[1] Of course this implies that the Master was no longer with His disciples in the free daily intercourse of a common life. "These things" are the wonderful instructions and consolations which have gone before, and which relate altogether to the conditions of

[1] xvi 4.

the inspired Church, not to those of the witnesses of the life. It is quite true that in the context we have an explanation. "These things have I spoken unto you, that when their hour is come, ye may remember them, how that I told you." No doubt many minds will prefer to take this explanation literally, and to suppose that Jesus gave secret instructions to His Apostles to be stored up for future use. But if my view of the character of the Gospel be right, such a hypothesis is excluded. I do not believe that it can be reconciled with modern views of history. It would imply that Jesus spoke in the manner of the Evangelist, and not in the manner recorded in the Synoptists. It would imply that He gave His instruction not in short and pregnant sayings and parables, but in long discourses. It would imply that an Apostle committed these discourses to writing or to memory, and reproduced them after many years. And, above all, it would prove that the accounts of the doings of the Apostles after the Crucifixion in the Synoptic writings are quite without foundation. Were or were not the Apostles surprised and disconcerted at the death of their Master? The Synoptics affirm that they were; but how could they have been, if their minds had been carefully prepared for this very eventuality? History affirms that it was the resurrection, and the conviction of the Apostles that their Master still lived, which was the starting-point of the faith: if He had told them that He was going from them and returning, would they have shown the joyous surprise at his reappearance which is so vividly portrayed in the Synoptic Gospels? The fact is that the discourse given by the Evangelist is a literary convention, accepted by writers of the time as quite allowable, though to us distasteful, because we live in a different intellectual world, and take a view of the necessity of accuracy in history which not only was not accepted by the Evangelist, but which he could never have been brought to understand. He cared for truth as much as we do; but his conception of what constituted truth is, as I have shown elsewhere in this book, utterly different from ours.

Perhaps the mixture of tenses in the Evangelist's mind comes out still more clearly in another passage:[1] "While I *was* with them, I kept them in Thy name." Would anyone, even if he regarded death as near, speak thus of the life which was still strong within him? Many Christians are so accustomed to regard their Master, not as "perfect man," but as a

[1] xvii. 12.

supernatural being merely condescending to human conditions, that they regard nothing that He might say or do as to be judged by the canons of reason and probability. But this view seems to me not a higher, but a lower one.

It is consonant with the root-idea of the Evangelist that the life of Christians on earth is a continuation of the life of Christ on earth, that he should represent the Founder as promising that the same privileges which had belonged to Him, as Son of God, should be extended also to them. This is one of the main features of the Gospel, and it is one which is often insufficiently regarded. Every reader sees how in the Gospel Jesus is exalted as the Son of God and the manifestation of the Father. But not every reader sees that what is affirmed of the Founder is in most matters affirmed also of the followers. "The glory," Jesus says, "which Thou hast given Me I have given them." And there is another still more striking passage: "He that believeth on Me, the works that I do shall he do also; and greater works than these shall he do, because I go unto the Father." The Founder has been speaking of the notable works which He has done by the power of the Father; and He adds that these works shall still be done in the

THE CHURCH AND THE WORLD 247

Church, which is as inseparably part of Himself as He is part of the Father; and that even greater works shall mark the progress of the Society, because it is united not to the visible, but to the exalted Christ. One could not, of course, hold that any of the followers of Jesus has ever come within measurable distance of Him, not even St Paul or St Francis, but yet the community, in virtue of the indwelling Spirit of Christ, has had a greater and wider effect in the world than had the Founder.

And the result of this indwelling Spirit is, or should be, Christian unity and love of the brethren. "That they may be all one; even as Thou, Father, art in Me and I in Thee, that they also may be in us."[1] A glorious ideal indeed, which has never in the course of history been attained, but which remains before the Church as a beacon. We know very well from *Acts* and the Pauline Epistles, that though at moments it seemed as if "the multitude of them that believed were of one heart and soul,"[2] those moments were few and fleeting, and that there were from the first jealousies, strife, envyings, and all the troubles which spring from the worldly temper. But nevertheless, there was in the Church a closer unity than that which was a feature of all the

[1] xvii. 21. [2] *Acts* iv. 32.

mystic societies which abounded on the shores of the Mediterranean, and which angered the conservative Romans as being anti-social. As the tone of the Christian community was higher than that of the Pagan societies, so was the mutual love of the members greater, and the devotion of all to the interests of the Society and to the service of its Head more complete; and it was in fact this devotion which made the Christian Church become in time the most powerful force in the Roman Empire, and induced the time-serving Emperor Constantine to throw in his lot with it.

The Church not only is an unity in itself, but it stands in strong opposition to its medium, the World. The other-worldliness, which has from the first been at once the honour and the reproach of Christianity, is strongly emphasised in the Fourth Gospel. In the presence of the Roman power the Church was constantly repeating the words addressed to Pilate, "My kingdom is not of this world." It is natural that the Evangelist should not always use the word *the world* in the same sense. In some places he uses it in the simple and natural way, as when he speaks of the light which lighteth every man who cometh into the world, or of the Saviour as sent to save the world. But often, as was

THE CHURCH AND THE WORLD 249

natural to one who felt that he belonged to a little society which was in constant hostility to the world which it opposed and despised, the Evangelist thinks of the world as an enemy, as *the* enemy with which the Church has ever to grapple. The disciples are called out of the world into a supermundane organisation. "If ye were of the world, the world would love its own; but because ye are not of the world, but I chose you out of the world, therefore the world hateth you." But the contest between the Society and the hostile environment, although it visibly goes on all around, is yet really in the spiritual world, which is the real world, already determined. "In the world ye have tribulation; but be of good cheer, I have overcome the world."

It is hard to define the exact thought of the Evangelist, when he speaks thus of "the world." Ancient thinking was far less exact and definite than modern. And a mystic like the Evangelist will use words not in the concrete way of a historian, but with all their atmosphere of meaning which appeals to the imagination and the emotions rather than to the intelligence. He would not be thinking primarily of the Roman Empire, which in Asia Minor interfered but little with the early proceedings of the Christians: outside Judæa anything like an organised persecution of the new sect did not exist. As it is clear from *Acts*, it was the irreconcilable hatred of the Jews, stirring up popular tumults, which the early missioners of the faith had to encounter. The Roman officials were far more likely to protect than to harass them. But when we consider the Ephesian background of the Gospel, the character of "the world" will be clear. A busy thriving city, in the very highways of trade, and in the main channel through which Asiatic influences spread into Europe, and European into Asia, comes up to our imagination. There were the quays and the markets of commerce; there were the resorts of pleasure and dissipation; there were the halls and porticoes where the philosophers discoursed all day; there were the frequent processions and shows of the votaries of Isis and Cybele, with their trains of shaven priests and self-mutilators; above all, there was the organised worship of the great goddess Artemis, "whom all Asia and the world worshippeth," by whose cult Ephesus had grown rich, and whose image was copied in scores of cities of Asia Minor. It was a world not at all like the severe crowds of Jerusalem: more like the Vanity

Fair of the imagination of Bunyan, wholly given to pleasure and to gain.

Such a world must always be in opposition to the seriousness of religious reformers, who regard the amusements of the frivolous, and the search after wealth and visible honours, as unworthy of the attention of men whose hearts are set on the things which are invisible, who make the doing of the Divine Will the one worthy purpose of life. But while most reformers struggle against it like men who try to swim across a swift stream, the early Christians regarded it as a thing already overcome by the cross of Christ. The world had been conquered by the devotion of the Son of God; what remained to His followers was only to keep what He had won, and not to allow the conquered foe to rise from the ground.

As to those who came into and composed the Church, the Evangelist is quite explicit. They were the children of the light, not of darkness; they were those who had nothing in common with the world, and so were hated by the world. Their coming into the Church was a result of Divine grace and favour; but they could not have come if they had not loved truth and sought the light. They were scattered through the world like the grains of gold in quartz rock; and when Jesus Christ was lifted up, they were drawn to the Society which inherited the Spirit of Christ. They were God's, and God gave them to Christ, and with them all who should believe through them.

Mr Scott, with other good authorities, has tried to show that the Evangelist contemplated with favour the organisation of the Church under leaders, that he regarded a fixed constitution of it as good and necessary.[1] In my opinion he scarcely proves his point. I should allow that, considering the view which the Evangelist took of the Sacraments and of miracles, he would not be disposed to undervalue the need of a visible church with a fixed organisation, and it is easy to understand that later times might find in such sayings as "As Thou didst send Me into the world, even so sent I them into the world," a justification of such teaching as that of the Apostolic succession. But this seems to be stretching the meaning of phrases which have really a simpler and more natural interpretation. Early as the notion of ruling bishops made its entrance into the Churches of Asia, it can scarcely have been accepted when the Gospel was written.

∨ As the Evangelist deals so largely in allusion

[1] *The Fourth Gospel*, p. 111.

and in symbol, it is not difficult to find in his words reference to any of the early Christian views. But it is much safer to take a broader and more literal view of them. When the Evangelist wishes to avoid an unpractically spiritual view at any point, he does not hesitate to say so clearly. ⌁He regards the greatest value of miracles as symbolical, yet he does not throw doubt on their actual occurrence. ⌁He thinks that it is degrading to attach an excessive or magical significance to the Sacraments, yet he declares them essential to the Church. But he does not clearly suggest that Church discipline and the Episcopal order are essential.

Let us turn again to the figures under which he presents the relation of the Church to her Head. He might easily have modified the figure of the vine and the branches by teaching that while Christ was the stem of the vine, the Apostles and their delegates were the branches connecting the stem with the leaves and twigs which might stand for ordinary believers. But he does not say this: he puts all Christians into a similar relation towards the inner life of the Church. No doubt the figure of the vine and the branches occurs in the last great discourse; and some critics might hold it to be addressed only to the Apostles; but such an interpretation would be at variance with the whole character of the Gospel. Similarly, in the parable of the sheepfold, the Evangelist might have spoken of under-shepherds or of sheep-dogs, but he does not do so: there is only one shepherd, and only one door to the sheepfold; and the sheep stand on one level. So again, when the Kingdom of Christ is mentioned, the Kingdom has but one ruler. He speaks of one Lord and Master, and of all others as brethren. Even in the Epistle we have no mention of Apostolic authority, or of subordination of one Christian to another, such as we find in the pseudo-Pauline Epistles to Timothy and Titus.

We need not take these facts as proving that the Evangelist was a convinced democrat in matters of Church government. Such matters do not seem to have occupied his mind. I should be quite ready to allow that there are passages in the Gospel which could be used, and were at a later time used, in the interests of ecclesiastical discipline and subordination. By a prophetic instinct working beneath the surface of consciousness, the Evangelist may have been dimly aware of the dangers which threatened the Church from such movements as that of the Montanists at the end of the second century. He may have

THE CHURCH AND THE WORLD

obscurely felt that by doctrine, by sacrament, and by organisation, the Church must before long assert herself in the face of a hostile world. But we are bound to go by the facts. And in fact we cannot find that the Evangelist asserts the necessity of Church discipline as he asserts the necessity of doctrine and of sacrament.

Had St Paul been alive when the Gospel was written, he, with his genius for organisation, would probably have seen the necessity for, so to speak, hardening the shell of the Church. It was in the Pauline Churches that Episcopacy originated. But the Fourth Evangelist was a saint and a mystic, and not concerned at heart as to the outward organisation of the Christian Society.

XII

TEACHING AND ETHICS

In the present chapter, as much as in any other, we shall be called on to combat current conventional views, while we try to set forth the character of the words and the teaching of the Saviour as understood by the Evangelist, and the relations of this teaching to Christian faith.

We are familiar with a literal and unimaginative interpretation of *word* and *work*, which is widely current. It is supposed that Jesus set forth truths (not truth) as to the being of God, as to His own relation to the Father, as to the nature of spiritual things; and that in order to show that He had the right to proclaim these truths, He did certain mighty works, gave supernatural signs that He was authorised thus to expound the nature of the supersensible. As in all views of the Divine which are honestly held, there is a

TEACHING AND ETHICS

certain kernel of truth in this way of taking the Gospel. But it is only the lower and more materialist side of the truth, the same kind of truth which some Jews grasped when they realised that Jesus was the Messiah whom they had expected, and whom they wanted to make a king, or which the crowd at Jerusalem accepted when it welcomed Him as the Son of David. But it is not a view which really appreciates the teaching of the Evangelist.

It is necessary briefly to distinguish the senses in which the word truth is used. These are three, which we may term (1) the scientific, (2) the metaphysical, (3) the ethical or spiritual.

The first of these is in our days the most usual. We regard a statement as true if it conforms to the facts of experience, whether material or psychological. A true witness is a witness who states appearances exactly as they were. A true theory is one which conforms to experience, and explains the facts. A true picture is one which gives the outer world as it is presented to our sight. This use of the word is so usual with us that we do not realise its essential modernity. It was Greece which first trained the world to it, Greece, the country in which science was born. And modern progress in science and devotion to science has accustomed us to it more and more, until it has become almost an effort to us to think of truth in another light.

The second sense, the metaphysical, contrasts the obvious views of things, the presentations of sense, with the truth or reality which lies behind them. It regards the visible and audible world as full of illusion, and the world of reality as lying beyond and above it in the supersensible world, or in the Divine thought. Such a view is perhaps most fully developed by the sages of the East, of India and Persia. But it was introduced into the West and naturalised there, first by the philosophers of Ionia, who sought the real and permanent among passing phenomena. Anaxagoras of Clazomenæ taught that it was only intelligence or the idea which brought order into the chaos of phenomena. Heracleitus of Ephesus said that wisdom is one thing: it is to know the thought by which all things are steered. But it was Plato who superseded all earlier and dominated all later philosophers by his theory of ideas, by his view that all material things were but imperfect copies of the types laid up in heaven. After Plato the search for what is real, for the one

TEACHING AND ETHICS

among the many, and for being through illusion, was carried on by all the philosophic schools. In our days metaphysics has fallen into disrepute. Philosophers continue their discussions at the universities; but the public knows little of them, and does not greatly concern itself with their disputes. But we must remember that at the beginning of the Christian era philosophy held the place in the mental atmosphere which is now taken by science; and that every man of education concerned himself with those metaphysical problems which we are apt to regard as indifferent, or at all events insoluble.

These renderings of truth, *alêtheia*, come down to us from Hellas. They are intellectual renderings. But in mankind, and especially among primitive peoples, other conceptions of truth are prevalent. The intellectual faculties after all are by no means the whole of man. The Hebrew word *'emeth*, rendered by *alêtheia* in the Septuagint, and by truth in our version of the Old Testament, has a more ethical meaning.

In Asia generally, and notably among the Jews, when truth is spoken of or a true person commended, it is seldom that the word bears the restricted scientific sense. Truth in man is sincerity and transparency of soul, loyalty in word and action. Its essence is set forth in the speech of the chivalrous Achilles of Homer:[1] "He is to me as hateful as the gates of death, who utters one thing with his lips and hides another in his heart." And since man can only speak and think of God in ways borrowed from his experience of his fellowmen, the truth of God also is at bottom a kind of loyalty to man, a uniformity, a steadfastness in mercy and in justice, which is revealed in a measure to experience, but can only be fully apprehended and realised by an exercise of faith.

Those who are familiar with the *Psalms*, that noble gift of Israel to mankind, must be well aware of the way in which the word *truth* is used in our English versions of them. I need but recall a few familiar phrases. "Lead me in Thy truth and teach me." "The paths of the Lord are mercy and truth." "O send out Thy light and Thy truth; let them lead me." "Thou desirest truth in the inward parts." "Hear me in the truth of thy salvation." "Mercy and truth are met together." "The truth of the Lord endureth for ever." Similar phrases are to be found in *Proverbs*, and in *Isaiah* and the other prophets: I need not add to my citations. It must occur to

[1] *Iliad*, ix. 312.

every thoughtful reader that the sense or senses attaching to the word truth in the *Psalms* is quite different from that usual in modern life. We use the word predominantly to signify correspondence between statements and actual experience. This is a natural result of our immersion in the facts of science and observation and the material world. We also speak of a true friend or a true heart, signifying steadiness and loyalty. But the other meaning is altogether predominant.

If we turn to the Fourth Gospel, we find indeed traces of both the scientific and the metaphysical uses of the word truth; but the word is predominantly used in the ethical and spiritual sense. We will begin with a few examples in which the Evangelist dwells on what may be called facts, though mainly facts not of material but of spiritual experience.

In the colloquy with Nicodemus, the Evangelist expressly declares that a part of the truth which Jesus taught was not new, but such as an Israelite should easily recognise. Jesus sets forth one of the grandest laws of the spiritual world, the unforeseen and spontaneous action of the Divine Spirit in the world. "The wind bloweth where it listeth, and thou hearest the voice thereof, but knowest not whence it cometh and whither it goeth:

so is everyone that is born of the Spirit." (The last sentence might be more intelligibly rendered if we wrote "such is the action of the Spirit on all those who are born of it"). Immediately Jesus goes on to say with surprise, "Art thou a teacher of Israel, and understandest not these things?" And indeed "these things" are taught in a fashion which is inimitable in the Hebrew *Psalms*. "Whither shall I go from Thy Spirit, or whither shall I flee from Thy presence?" "Cast me not away from Thy presence, and take not Thy Holy Spirit from me." Such utterances are frequent in the *Psalms*. And the eternal type of the man obsessed by the Divine Spirit which he cannot escape is Amos the herdsman of Tekoa, to whom the voice of God came while he followed his calling, and burned like a fire within him, until he gave utterance to the inward passion.

The Gospel teaching in such matters as these is continuous with that committed to Israel; not a new doctrine, but an old doctrine made fresh by the life of Him who uttered it. It was a part, no doubt, of the Truth which Jesus had to proclaim to the world. It is, in a lofty region, strictly scientific truth, or truth of observation and experience.

The modern mind, however, is very apt to

regard as assertions of scientific truth, or matter of fact, what was not really in ancient literature meant as such. For example, in the prophecies of the Bible we are apt to find exact descriptions of events in the future, when what the prophet really discerned and meant to set forth were underlying tendencies which were working their way towards the world of sight, but might never reach it. We may illustrate this from a passage in the Fourth Gospel.

In xvi. 13 it is written, " He (the Spirit) will show you things to come." And no doubt the inspired utterances in the early Church did sometimes speak of the future. But the Greek word used is in the present, *erchomena*, things that are on the way towards us. And it is the character of the noblest prophecy not to specify the exact time or manner of events in the future, but to dwell on tendencies, what is striving out into existence. Through all history the prophets who have tried to detail future history have failed; but the great ones among them, who have seen into the heart of things and declared in what direction they were moving, have succeeded. The truth of prophecy is not truth to fact but truth to idea. Again, it is written (xiv. 26), " He shall bring to your remembrance all that I said unto you." This is just the sort of saying which the modern mind, when untrained, misinterprets. The whole character of the Gospel shows clearly that when the author thus writes he does not mean that the Spirit shall recall to the memory of the disciples the exact words of their Lord: that is not the result of inspiration, but rather the function of an exact and retentive memory. What he clearly means is that the Spirit shall reveal the higher meaning of the utterances of the Master, in their relation to the life of the Church. The function of the Spirit is to guide to the higher truth, to take the impulses of the indwelling Christ and reveal them to the disciples.

Surely no view of the mission of Jesus could be more false than that which would regard Him, who was the way, the truth, and the life, as a mere proclaimer of truths in the usual current sense of the word. The kind of truth which our great researchers are ever striving after, and which is embodied in our manuals of science and of history, is of a kind to which the Founder and His Apostles alike were indifferent. It is concerned with the world visible and tangible and audible. Our senses and our intelligence were given us that we might acquire for ourselves this kind of truth;

TEACHING AND ETHICS

and if it were revealed to us by any kind of inner inspiration, it would be almost worthless to us. It is the search for it which is the great discipline of the intellectual life; and whether we find or fail to find it, we grow by the search. But the field of this truth is not the world of spirit. Those who think that because Jesus was the Son of God He could not be wrong in attributing a particular Psalm to David or a particular saying to Moses show a crassness of imagination which is exactly like that of the Woman of Samaria, when she said, "Sir, Thou hast nothing to draw with, and the well is deep: from whence then hast Thou that living water?" or like that of Nicodemus when he objected, "How can a man be born when he is old? can he enter a second time into his mother's womb, and be born?" It was indignation at such want of spiritual comprehension which stirred up the Evangelist to write his "spiritual gospel"; and those who are the children of the truth in the higher sense of the word will always repudiate such materialist limitation of outlook.

But for a higher rendering of the moral and religious doctrine of Israel, we naturally go rather to the first three Gospels than to the Fourth. The summary which is commonly called the Sermon on the Mount has far greater contents in this line than have the writings of our Evangelist. There is another kind of teaching which seems to him at once more novel and more spiritual, and which he is apt to call " My words " or " the truth."

There is a lofty Platonic sense which may in some cases influence the expression of the Evangelist. To Plato the world of ideas, the invisible and eternal world in which were laid up the patterns of earthly things, is the real or true world, and the reflections of that world in the visible universe are little more than illusion. Even St Paul, though he reaches this idealist position by a road of his own, yet seems sometimes to reach it, as when he writes, " Let God be found true and every man a liar,"[1] or again, " The things which are seen are temporal; but the things which are not seen are eternal."[2] But the detached philosophic thought of Plato is in complete contrast to St Paul's practical ways of regarding things. And the Fourth Evangelist is nearer in this matter to St Paul than to Plato. After all, the garb of a Platonic philosopher will not fit him. In his Preface he uses the term Logos, borrowed from the schools of philosophy; but he does not write his Gospel in that key.

[1] *Romans* III. 4   [2] 2 *Cor.* IV 18

The truth, as taught by the Evangelist, does not consist of mere truths. It does not include the facts of the visible world, which are matter of observation. Nor does it consist in an intellectual illumination, which sees the permanent in the temporary and the reality lying behind the mere phenomenon. Of course it is not wholly independent of intellect, but it is not primarily intellectual. It is not, indeed, any connected or reasoned system of belief. It is what St Paul sometimes calls a *mystery*, not that it is an abstruse matter demanding thought and investigation, but that it embodies the secret principle of life of a sacred society, and must not be lightly spoken of to unbelievers. If we begin by quoting a few passages from the Evangelist, this will become clearer.

The higher kind of truth found by the Evangelist in the teaching of his Lord is often called by him words or sayings, *logoi* and *rêmata*. "The words which I speak unto you, they are spirit and they are life."[1] "If ye abide in me, and my words abide in you, ask whatsoever ye will, and it shall be done unto you." To the same effect is the speech of St Peter: "Lord, to whom shall we go? Thou hast the words of eternal life." The

[1] *John* vi 63.

connection of the words with life is insisted on in another passage: "If a man keep My saying, he shall never see death."[1] In some passages the Evangelist seems even to equate two things which to a superficial view seem most opposed, words and works: "The words that I say unto you I speak not from Myself: but the Father abiding in Me doeth the works."[2] In other passages, instead of words or sayings, we find the expression truth: "Ye shall know the truth, and the truth shall make you free."[3] "To this end have I been born, and to this end am I come into the world, that I should bear witness unto the truth."[4] In the same way the Paraclete or Comforter is called "the Spirit of truth"; and of the Saviour Himself it is said, "I am the way, the truth, and the life."

It is clear that in such passages as these the reference is not to any verbal teaching, however lofty, but to the faith which unites the disciples to the Master, and makes of the two one mystical body, in which impulses come to the members from the Head, and the members reflect on earth the Divine life. "This is life eternal, that they should know Thee, the only true God, and Him whom

[1] *John* viii 51
[2] *John* xiv. 10, compare xv 22–24.
[3] viii 32
[4] xviii. 37.

TEACHING AND ETHICS 269

thou didst send, even Jesus Christ." *To know* in this passage is clearly not to be aware of, or to be convinced of, the existence of God and Christ, but to have communion with them through the Spirit. It is contrasted with mere intellectual gnôsis, such as the Gnostics relied on. It is, in fact, the "truth" of the *Psalms*, but adapted to new conditions, and become almost a technical word in the new religion.

Nevertheless, those are in the right who regard the Evangelist as the first originator of a creed. As he sees the need of sacraments, so he is aware that some basis of common belief and common expression of belief is necessary to every religious body which will maintain itself apart from the world. When St Paul has to state the common beliefs to Christians, he falls back on the main facts of the life and death of his Master, as he received them from tradition, more especially on the Resurrection from the grave. The Fourth Evangelist, true to his general principle of detaching belief from fact of sense and attaching it to Christian experience, takes a somewhat different line.

There is this about the Evangelist, which indeed adapts his work far better to the building up of the Church, that he does not confine himself to the setting forth of the highest truth in an abstract form, but realises that for ordinary humanity it must embody itself in forms, whether speculative or practical. He cannot think of a loyal spiritual union with the Society unless it be united with a minimum of consent to doctrine. Before a convert can be received into the Society, he must accept the rudiments of a creed. He must believe that Jesus is the Christ, that He is the Son of God, that He came in the flesh, and not merely, as the Gnostics held, as a sort of spiritual apparition. This outline of a creed seems to the Evangelist indispensable, and in the Epistle he dwells on it; but even there it is the practical results of the creed, rather than its mere expression, of which he thinks. "Who is he that overcometh the world, but he that believeth that Jesus is the Son of God?" And more strongly still, "This is the antichrist, even he that denieth the Father and the Son." This is probably the earliest form of the Christian creed. From the first the creed was a baptismal confession, and when the Ethiopian was baptised by Philip, the instructor was content with the simple confession, "I believe that Jesus Christ is the Son of God."[1] Sometimes it

[1] *Acts* viii. 37. This verse is omitted in the R.V.

is such words as these that the Evangelist means when he speaks of *rêmata*, rather than of any moral and spiritual teaching. Such words are the natural and almost inseparable accompaniment of membership of the Society and faith in its spiritual Head. And the truth of these words is their consonance with the experienced relation of the exalted Christ to the Church. If this pragmatist view of doctrine had always been preserved in the Church, if the mere logical intellect had been warned off the sacred ground of belief, many of the evils from which the Church at a later time suffered would have been avoided.

There are certain aspects in which religious and spiritual truth presents itself to the Evangelist, of which I must briefly speak. In the first place, the acceptance of truth seems to him an escape from bondage into a glorious liberty. "The truth shall make you free": that is, union with Christ shall set you free from the bondage of sin and death. St Paul also is very fond of speaking of the freedom which comes from faith in Christ, "the glorious liberty of the children of God." There can be no doubt that while to many modern Christians the faith of Christ seems a kind of discipline and self-restraint, it was another aspect of it, the escape from a smaller to a larger and more glorious life, which most impressed the first disciples.

To St Paul the escape was primarily from slavery to the Jewish Law, with its exacting materialism. But in the time of the Evangelist Jewish Law had been left behind in the progress of the Church. To him the freedom was from sin, and Satan, the source of sin. "He that committeth sin is the slave of sin." And the Son of God was made manifest on earth that He might destroy the power of sin, and set its captives free.

Another of the aspects in which truth appears to the Evangelist is as a touchstone to discern those who have in them the seeds of eternal life. "He that rejecteth Me, and receiveth not My sayings, hath one that judgeth him: the Word that I spake, the same shall judge him in the last day." Of course the Evangelist does not put this forward as rounded doctrine. He more often speaks of judgment as committed to the Son. But we see his meaning. The mere utterance of the higher truth tests men: if they accept it and carry it into their lives, they become heirs of eternal life; if they reject it, they are by the mere rejection condemned.

The Gospel of the Evangelist is not only a gospel of freedom, but also a gospel of love.

TEACHING AND ETHICS

"If ye love Me, keep My commandments," comes in the Gospel. In the Epistle we have the same idea worked out with an iteration which never tires. Love is the bond which connects all the factors in the spiritual world, as (to use a modern comparison) gravitation is the bond which connects together things material. The founder of Christianity, in a well-known passage in all the Synoptists, bases love to man on love to God, and puts the latter in the first place. But to the Fourth Evangelist the love of the brethren for one another, which is part and parcel of their love for Christ, is so insistent that he is inclined to give it first place. "If a man," he writes, "say, I love God, and hateth his brother, he is a liar: for he that loveth not his brother whom he hath seen, cannot love God whom he hath not seen."[1] This is part of the wonderful lovingness of the Evangelist; and it reflects the spirit of the Church; for it was the mutual love of Christians which overcame the world.

Another teaching of the Evangelist, which is common to him and the Synoptists, and indeed all New Testament writers, which runs, indeed, like a golden thread through all early Christian teaching, is devotion to the

[1] *Epistle* iv. 20.

Divine Will. "I came not to do mine own will, but the will of Him that sent Me" is an expression of the spirit of the Master's life which is seen not only in the acts of the historic Jesus, but in the lives of all His true followers, from that day to this. It is love for the Divine Will which connects the successive generations of Christians, and forms them, as has been well said, into a "logos society." Here, at least, there is no discrepancy between the earlier and the later views of the Founder. The most marked and essential feature of the human life of Jesus Christ continues to be the most marked and essential feature of the Church. Devotion to the Divine Will is the blood which circulates alike through head and limbs, the sap which flows through the stem and branches of the vine. To do that will was to the Master meat and drink; and the same Divine sustenance has never failed His Church.

When we have spoken of the love of God, which leads men gladly to devote their lives to His service, and love for the brethren, which binds the whole society into an unity, we have practically finished with the ethics of the Fourth Evangelist. In this respect he presents a strong contrast to St Paul, whose Epistles are full of maxims of conduct, who tells his converts how they are to bear themselves towards the surrounding heathen and the political authorities, what are the mutual duties of husbands and wives, parents and children, and the like. As the Evangelist gives us a spiritual version of his Master's life, so he transforms morality by a spiritual principle. St Paul says that love is the fulfilling of the law, and the key to all Christian virtue. But to the Evangelist love seems to take the place of every sense of duty. Hence we cannot expect from him that deep sense of sin which is so conspicuous in the Pauline writings, and which was, no doubt, produced in the mind of the Apostle by the facts of his own life, and his spiritual wrestlings. "Perfect love," the Evangelist says, "casts out fear"—among other fears, the fear of punishment for sin. But, in his view, sin was impossible to the true disciple: "Whosoever abideth in Him sinneth not." "Whosoever is begotten of God doeth no sin: he cannot sin." All sin belongs to the world: "the lust of the flesh, and the lust of the eyes, and the vainglory of life." And as the Society stands in radical opposition to the world, these things have no hold on it. Yet in another passage he allows that in practice even Christians fall into sin: "If we say that we have no sin, we deceive ourselves." But the blood of Christ, union with the Divine Head, cleanses from sin, and imparts the principle of eternal life. In the fervour of the early Church the notion that men could fall into sin through ignorance and want of self-control naturally occupied a small place in the hearts of believers. But in fact, as in the doctrine of the Evangelist as to salvation by faith, we must presuppose a Pauline stratum, so we must suppose that the Church of Ephesus maintained the Pauline ethics.

XIII

MIRACLE

Next to the relation of Christian faith to the words, we have to speak of its relation to the works, of the Founder. We have the same story to tell again. As the Evangelist soars above the literal value of the words of his Master, so he regards His mighty works as valuable indeed to impress the people in their natural form, but far more valuable in the higher meaning which shines through them.

Those who have to do with the Moslem population of such countries as Syria and North Africa tell us that there no teacher attains to influence and credit unless he becomes renowned as a worker of marvels. M. Doutté, who had a long experience in Algeria,[1] tells us that he made the acquaintance of many local saints, but of none who had not this faculty. The working of marvels

[1] *Revue de l'hist. des religions,* xl. p. 355.

was the seal of their vocation, without which it would not have been accepted as authentic. The Fourth Evangelist takes this view as natural and universal. He thinks that those who cannot rise to the height of pure spiritual teaching may well be drawn to the faith by the evidence of miracles. This view indeed he expresses clearly enough: "Though ye believe not Me, believe the works." In another place he writes: "Many believed on His name, beholding the signs which He did. But Jesus did not trust Himself unto them, for that He knew all men," and so knew that men who were thus impressed by mere visible wonders would not be a high type of disciple. Jesus expresses impatience at the demand for miracle, saying sadly, "Except ye see signs and wonders, ye will not believe." Quite in the same line is the saying to Thomas, "Because thou hast seen Me, thou hast believed: blessed are they that have not seen, and yet have believed."

But though persuasion through visible signs and wonders may be the mark of a low level of spiritual development, yet the signs and wonders themselves may be the expression and the vehicle of "the word." The mere wonders may be *signs*; they may be of such a character as to show unity of nature be-

MIRACLE 279

tween the Christ and the Heavenly Father: "My Father worketh even until now; and I work." This was said when Jesus was reproached for healing on the Sabbath-day. The phrase is too brief to be clear; but it seems to mean that as God does not suspend His beneficent action in the world on the Sabbath, so His Son on earth should not cease on that day to do to men such good as falls naturally in His way. The unity of will of the Father and the Son is shown in action as well as in thought. Another passage is even more remarkable: "The Father, abiding in Me, doeth His works." The Evangelist felt that the works of the Church were the result of her union with the exalted Christ, and his mind goes on to the view that the actions of Jesus in the world were the result of His union with the Father. He works back from the experience of the Church, as he so often does, to the history of the Founder.

We have traces of the same line of thought in *Matthew*; but there it seems more appropriate to the actual teaching of Jesus: "That ye may be the children of your Father which is in heaven, for He maketh His sun to rise on the evil and the good, and sendeth rain on the just and the unjust."[1] Here the

[1] *Matt.* v 45

direct relation of men to God is spoken of rather than the relation of the Church to Christ: the spirit is broader and more universalist; but the Fourth Evangelist was in his way not less in the line of the highest religious thought than the First.

The Fourth Evangelist looks at miracles notably in a different way from the Synoptists. As critics have observed, the place which they take in relation to faith is inverted. In the Synoptists faith is, in some cases at least, a necessary condition in the person who is healed before the healing can take place. To the Fourth Evangelist faith is not represented as the condition of miracle, but as its result. The miracle is wrought that men may believe. Again, whereas the miracles of healing in the Synoptists are miracles of mercy and compassion, wrought because Jesus had sympathy with the sufferers, the miracles recorded by the Fourth Evangelist tend to the glory of Him who wrought them. They are proofs, not of His humanity, but of His divinity.

And further, particular wonders hide beneath their surface some thesis of the higher Christian teaching. Indeed, the description of a miracle is often followed by an exposition of its higher or spiritual meaning. We may give a few examples. The feeding of the five

MIRACLE

thousand with loaves and fishes is used as a parable not once only but twice over, in a lower and in a higher sense. First, Jesus says to the multitude which followed Him across the sea, "Ye seek Me, not because ye saw signs, but because ye ate of the loaves, and were filled. Labour not for the meat which perisheth, but for the meat which abideth unto eternal life." Those who came after Jesus merely for what they could get were at a lower level even than those who were taken with visible signs. But the miracle was more than a mere sign or proof of a Divine mission. The multiplication of loaves and fishes was a sign of the wonderful satisfying virtue of the bread which came down from heaven for the feeding of the Church. It was early believed that the Evangelist here refers either primarily or secondarily to the Christian sacrament; and we treat of the passage more fully in that connection.

When Jesus heals the blind, the inner meaning is that He came into the world to remove the blindness of sin and of ignorance, "that they which see not may see, and that they which see may become blind."[1] The Synoptic writers see in these sudden cures the result of mere kindness and love for

[1] ix 39.

mankind; but to the Fourth Evangelist that seems a superficial view, which by no means exhausts the significance of the event. In the same way, the raising of Lazarus is no mere action of kindness and friendship: its main importance is that it introduces the Christian sentence, "I am the Resurrection and the Life." And when we think of the vast, the inestimable service to the Church which the phrase has rendered, we shall keenly feel that the allegorising of our Evangelist was the result of a profound Christian inspiration.

In the case of another noteworthy miracle, the turning of the water into wine, we are on less safe ground, since the Evangelist does not in this case himself give the interpretation. Modern commentators find a natural contrast between the mere water of the Jewish dispensation and the wine of the Gospel. And this interpretation may serve, since at the time there was no ascetic aversion to wine, but it was regarded as one of the kindest of God's gifts to men. But as it stands the miracle is closely like those mere marvels which abound in the Apocryphal Gospels, and the tales in regard to which sprang out of the mere desire to magnify the supernatural powers of the Founder.

It is well known that other classes of

MIRACLE

miracles, especially exorcisms of evil spirits, are not recited in this Gospel. It is a very remarkable instance of omission, which must be purposeful. Possibly the explanation may be a simple one, that the Evangelist intended only to bring in a small number of miracles, in fact seven, to illustrate spiritual truths, and the tales of exorcism did not seem suited to his purpose.

The story of the raising of Lazarus has been the subject of infinite discussion. Some critics have given a very elaborate account of the method of its composition, and the reasons for the insertion of every detail. It can scarcely be doubted that the emphasis laid by the Evangelist on the fact that Lazarus had been dead for some days shows that he meant to insist on the supernatural power of Jesus. But it is easy to be led away by fancy when we try to discover hidden and symbolical meanings in the details of a story. Other critics are disposed to think that there was some actual historic foundation for the narrative; and I am ready to agree with them. It has been said that so remarkable a miracle could not, if it had really taken place, have been omitted by the Synoptists. But the Synoptic narrative really only touches a few detached points of the life of Jesus; and it may be that the Fourth Evangelist has worked up the tale from his own point of view, and made it loom very large in the prospect. To us, as to him, the main value of the episode is in the spiritual meaning which it conveys.

It is, of course, quite impossible to recover the exact facts which, supposing the event to have a historic basis, constituted that basis. The view of Renan, that something like a pious fraud was arranged between Jesus and His friends at Bethany, is of course most repulsive to all Christians. And it is quite gratuitous, for the Evangelist deals so freely with his sources of information that we cannot press this or that detail of the narrative into evidence of collusion. We must be content to say that the story is probably a transposition into a higher key of something which really happened, but which probably did not take the great place in the imagination of the people of Jerusalem which the Evangelist supposes.

It remains to speak of the two great miracles of the Gospels, which were not signs of something beyond them, but which were regarded as primary events in the history of Jesus Christ: His birth and His resurrection. Of course, when the Evangelist wrote, the tale of the Virgin Birth was current in the Church. It would have been hard *à priori* to tell what line he would take in regard to it. On the one hand, it might well seem that the appearance of the Word in flesh might be the occasion of a special miracle. There is certainly no actual contradiction between the tale as told in the First and Third Gospels and the first verses of the Fourth. But if we look beyond mere words and statements to ideas, we may see that the Virgin Birth on the one hand, and the coming of the Word on the other, might well be regarded as alternatives. In *Matthew* and *Luke* there is no notion of pre-existence: the Jesus whose life they tell begins to exist at the Annunciation. And, as M. Réville points out, there is an incongruity between the idea of a divine son born by a special interposition of God at a particular place and time, and the idea of an ever-existing Word, revealed to sense and in time. It would be simpler and more natural that the Word should be united to humanity at the Baptism by John rather than before birth. Holding a very definite view that what was born of the flesh was flesh, and what was born of the Spirit was spirit, the Evangelist would have no occasion to seek for a miraculous origin of the body of Jesus.

And I think that a careful reader of the narrative of the meeting of John and Jesus will see that such notions were in the mind of the writer. It is true that, by one of those curious omissions which surprise the student of the Gospel, he does not actually mention the fact of baptism. This may well be because it was beneath the dignity of Jesus to be baptised by anyone. But he lays extreme stress on the testimony of John, that he disclaimed for himself the Messiahship, but declared that he had seen the Spirit descending as a dove out of heaven, and abiding on Jesus. One reason for thus dwelling on the self-subordination of the Baptist to his successor probably was that there still existed, in the time of St Paul, a sect at Ephesus who acknowledged the baptism of John and looked up to him as its founder; and it was important to meet the views of this sect. But however that be, it is simple and natural to suppose that for the Evangelist this descent of the Spirit and its abiding on Jesus was the occasion on which the Divine Logos was united to the human Jesus, and thereafter took the place of His natural soul. This view would of course be similar to that of the Docetists, who regarded the human life of the Founder as a sort of mirage, and thought that the Divine Spirit

MIRACLE

which had come to Him at baptism deserted Him again on the cross. It cannot, in fact, be denied that if the narrative of the Evangelist be regarded as a biography, recording actual doings and teaching, it is closely akin to Docetism. It is only by looking at it in the light of the idea, not of the fact, that it gains its true position.

These, however, are speculations. What is quite clear and certain for all serious students is that the Evangelist does not value the tale of the Virgin Birth, that he bases on it no teaching, and never appeals to it as evidence of the supernatural character of the Founder. No doubt his mere passing over of the tale would not in itself be conclusive, for the Evangelist assumes as known many things which were part of the recognised biography. But it does have some significance when, in more than one place,[1] he speaks of Jesus as the son of Joseph. For it is his habit, when he finds any account or statement in the earlier biographies which seems to him unworthy of the Son of God, to alter it to make it more appropriate. If he had objected to the statement of the paternity of Joseph, it is almost certain that he would have found a way of avoiding such statement.

[1] i. 45 ; vi. 42.

The other great miracle, that of the Resurrection, with the appearances to the disciples, is prominent in the Gospel. The story is told so simply, and so circumstantially, that it is hard to accept any view in regard to its origin except that it came to the Evangelist on the authority of one of the Apostles. And the graphic touches in regard to the disciple whom Jesus loved are noteworthy. When he heard from Mary Magdalene in the early morning of the third day that the stone which closed the tomb had been rolled away, he at once set out for the spot, he and Peter running together; and being no doubt the younger man, he ran the faster, and, coming first to the tomb, looked in, and saw the linen cloths lying. When Peter came up, and went into the tomb, he followed, and saw "the napkin which was upon His head not lying with the linen cloths, but rolled up in a place by itself." "And he saw and believed." It is no doubt very difficult ever to judge from the naturalness and vividness of a story that it is really historic. But it is very hard for any reader not to think that we have here a simple piece of testimony, an uncoloured narrative of fact. The authority would naturally be St John: this is perhaps the passage in the Gospel where his personality most clearly shows through. When, in the same passage, we read that Mary Magdalene mistook the risen Christ for the gardener, we have another point in which the eye-witness is clear. I feel sure that the Evangelist is reporting testimony which had come to him by direct authority; only the phrase "the disciple whom Jesus loved" speaks of the admiring pupil who put the tale upon paper, not of the Apostle.

The further narrative of the appearances of Jesus to the disciples is less vivid; but that also must be based on the statements of an eye-witness. The main fact to which it testifies, that the Apostles believed that they saw their risen Lord, is beyond dispute historic. But how far this vision must be regarded as miraculous is a difficult question. To answer it, a man should have a very complete knowledge of the results of the psychical studies of recent years.[1] The only properly miraculous element in it is the physical: that it was the actual body which had hung on the cross which appeared to the disciples. Luke, who has a great love of miracle, and introduces it whenever he can, dwells most decidedly on the physical reality of the Lord's body, which ate and drank in the presence

[1] On this subject see a remarkable paper by C W. Emmet, in the *Modern Churchman*, iv. p. 188.

of the Apostles. The Fourth Evangelist, though he says nothing of this, mentions the doubt of Thomas as to the physical reality of the body, and how that doubt was satisfied. Even if that story is taken from Apostolic testimony, we need not, in view of the beliefs of the time, and our author's comparative disregard of fact, take it too seriously. In any case, here, as elsewhere, when he has trespassed on the verge of materialism, he redeems the situation with one of his immortal sentences, " Blessed are they that have not seen, and yet have believed," a sentence torn fresh from the life of the early Church.

XIV

CHRISTOLOGY

AFTER the statement given above of my views as to the authorship and origin of the Fourth Gospel, it is evident that I cannot regard the Christologic views enshrined in the wonderful discourses of the Gospel as proceeding direct from the Jesus of history. That indeed is a view commonly assumed in the pulpit and in devotional literature; but it is not a view which is held by most competent authorities. Even conservative theologians are ready to allow that in those discourses we must recognise not merely the literary style of a great theologian, but also his turn of thought. The only question—and it is one of great difficulty and complexity—is how far the discourses are based on the actual tradition of the Apostles, and how far they contain elements which can only have come into them in the time of the first growth of Christianity, after the crucifixion.

I

It is unnecessary to say much in this place as to the basis of the Johannine Christology in the experience of the Church, because the exposition of this relation has been our main theme throughout. One chapter we have already devoted to the subject; and it is impossible to speak of the Christian Church and the Christian sacraments without continual reversion to it. We must now content ourselves with assuming that the translation into a biography of the experience of the Christ who was the Head of the Church and the constant source of its life was the one great purpose of the Evangelist.

One cannot doubt that, as the Evangelist often inserts in his narrative, on the ground of a special tradition, events and details which do not appear in the Synoptic Gospels, so he may from time to time record for us sayings which really come from the Founder, but have been in the transmission somewhat modified. But to recover these original sayings is a well-nigh impossible task. The writer's mind is so steeped in religious experience that all tradition has become transposed, and we have always to regard his repetition of traditional speeches as a compound of various elements. If we compare the traditions contained in all the Gospels to sticks partly immersed in water, so that they are seen refracted, then we shall say that the Marcan, and part at least of the Matthean and Lucan, reports bring before us that tradition but slightly refracted, but the Fourth Gospel brings it before us widely removed from its actual position. Thus when we pass from the explication of the elements in his Christology which the Evangelist adopts from the experience of the Church to the investigation of the elements which have a root in tradition, but are transformed in the mind of the writer, we pass from a comparatively easy to a far more difficult task. The history of thought in the Church for the first three centuries is largely the history of Christologic doctrine. This doctrine began to form immediately after the crucifixion, so soon indeed that it is scarcely possible to see unmodified the naked facts of history. Perhaps the readiest way to trace the development is to set aside, as far as may be, the Pauline views, which are less based on tradition, and to look at the text of the Gospels, which are more so based. In particular the phrase " My Father" in the mouth of Jesus is significant; and its use shows a rapid development. The phrase is distinctive, as Jesus never says to His disciples "our Father," but always "My Father and your Father."

In the Gospel of Mark, Jesus does not use the phrase "My Father." But in eschatological passages there is something similar. In viii. 38 Jesus says, "Whosoever shall be ashamed of Me and of My words, . . . the Son of Man shall be ashamed of him, when He cometh in the glory of His Father with the holy angels." So again in xiii. 32 we read, "Of that day and hour knoweth no one, not even the angels in heaven, neither the Son, but the Father." The judge of mankind, who is to come in the clouds of heaven, is necessarily a supernatural person. Most modern writers regard the eschatological element in the Gospels as primitive, and think that Jesus did speak of His speedy return in glory. I am not altogether convinced that this is the case. However this be, it is noteworthy that the Jesus of *Mark* does not in the course of His teaching proclaim Himself as the Son of God, except when, in the eschatological passages, He also calls Himself the Son of Man.

The tone of *Luke* is in this matter similar; but there are a few passages where one hears a different note. Some of these again are eschatological. Thus in xxii. 29 we read, " I appoint unto you a kingdom, even as My Father appointed unto Me, that ye may eat and drink at My table in My kingdom." And in xxiv. 49, "Behold, I send forth the promise of My Father upon you." Such at least is our English version; but the meaning of the phrase is in my opinion very doubtful. There is, however, one far more important passage, which *Luke* (x. 22) has in common with *Matthew* (xi. 27): "All things have been delivered to Me of My Father: and no one knoweth who the Son is save the Father; and who the Father is save the Son, and he to whomsoever the Son willeth to reveal Him." In other places in *Matthew* the phrase "My Father" recurs, as in xvi. 17, "My Father which is in heaven," and especially in the very striking passage, xxvi. 53, "Thinkest thou that I cannot beseech My Father, and He shall even now send Me more than twelve legions of angels?"

The only passage among these which calls for special comment is that common to *Matthew* and *Luke*. It is the only passage in the Synoptic Gospels which bears a close resemblance to a large number of passages as to the relations of the Father and the Son to be found in the Fourth Gospel. Naturally it has been much discussed. Every careful reader will feel that it is curiously different from all that goes before and all that follows it in the two Gospels. And in *Luke* it distinctly comes in in such a way as to interrupt the connection—Jesus is thanking the Heavenly Father that He has hidden the coming of the Kingdom from the wise and understanding, and revealed it to babes. He continues, "Blessed are the eyes which see the things that ye see: for I say unto you that many prophets and kings desired to see the things which ye see, and saw them not; and to hear the things which ye hear, and heard them not." The sense runs on with perfect clearness. But in our text of *Luke* the passage I have quoted as to the Father and the Son comes in between the saying that God has been pleased to reveal great things to babes and the saying that the disciples had been greatly privileged to hear such things. It seems to me that, according to all principles of literary criticism, we must suppose that the inserted words come from some other source, and are badly dovetailed in, or rather thrust in without dovetailing. In *Matthew*, in the same way, this saying is an intrusion. But of course this criticism does not touch the further question whether the source from which the words are taken is one which records genuine sayings of Jesus, or whether it is a document which develops those sayings in the direction in which Christian thought was steadily drifting in the second half of the first century.

For myself, I freely accept the second view. We know from recent discovery in Egypt of collections of fragmentary sayings of Jesus that such documents circulated at quite an early period; and we also know that from the very first they were subject to the influence of the contemporary thought of the Church. Nor do I believe that during His earthly ministry our Lord gave utterance to metaphysical views such as that in our text. All His teaching for which we have satisfactory evidence is of quite another character. And there would be something extraordinary, not to say paradoxical, in thanking God, at one moment, that the Gospel is revealed to babes, and at the next moment giving utterance to views which the simple disciples of Galilee could not understand. Those who regard the life and the words of our Lord as quite supernatural and abnormal will not be shocked by such incongruities; but those who hold the doctrine which has always been maintained by the Church, that Jesus Christ was not only divine, but also perfect man, will expect to find in His words that sweet reasonableness which one of the greatest of modern critics has singled out as their most marked characteristic. In any case, we may maintain, with no fear of contradiction by any competent critic, that the text may quite well have come into the two Gospels from some other source than exact and unmodified tradition.

One thing, however, is quite clear. Whether Jesus spoke much or little of His relation to the Father, such a relation, close and perpetual, lies under the whole Synoptic narrative. In all the events of life, and in all teaching, Jesus felt that His mission was to be of one will with the Father in Heaven, and to carry out the work among men which He came to do. "Not My will but Thine be done" is the burden of His whole life. The constant presence and support of the Spirit of God is to Him a perpetual inspiration. This it is which placed Him on an entirely different level from all His contemporaries. What has been called the God-consciousness, an unbroken communion with Divine goodness and power, is exemplified in His life.

II

It is precisely this constant consciousness of a Divine presence, this earnest acceptance of a Divine purpose, which is expressed in a

CHRISTOLOGY

great part of the Fourth Gospel. We may feel that ever to be conscious of this inspiration, yet to speak of it but seldom, according to the Synoptic portrait, is really a more sublime way. But the Fourth Evangelist could not be content with this. In his spirit that which he felt to be the truth and the real meaning of the Master's life burned its way into utterance. The unity of spirit with the Father, of which Jesus was conscious, must, he thought, have been clear and conspicuous to every true disciple. It was the dominant fact of the whole situation, occupying in regard to the mere visible incidents of life the same relation which in the kosmos spirit bears to flesh. It was quite in the manner of the time that, when he began to write down an account of the sayings and doings of the Master, he should bring to the surface what he regarded as the underlying ideas, represent Jesus as openly proclaiming the relation to the Father which was really implicit, and even in the narrative of actions rather embody their higher meaning than their more obvious circumstances. He forgets that in living as a man among men, subject to the most ordinary human needs, with limited knowledge and human relationships, the Word must have been limited by the conditions of the flesh.

St Paul had been faced by the same difficulty, how the Spirit which was the life and inspiration of the Church could have been in a real sense human. He meets it by the doctrine of the Kenosis; he teaches that when the Lord came down to dwell on earth, He deliberately emptied Himself of His Divine attributes, and accepted the limits of ordinary humanity, becoming submissive to pain and death. The Fourth Evangelist does not accept this view: he thinks that from Jesus as He lived on earth rays of Divine glory frequently shone out. Thus in general he rules out of the life all that in his view was unworthy of the Son of God. Yet he was still often under the influence of tradition, and inserts human traits, sometimes explaining them away, sometimes leaving them in contrast with the general tone of his narrative.

To take a few examples. When Nathanael first comes to Jesus, He says to the newcomer, "When thou wast under the fig-tree I saw thee." Evidently we have here a little fragment of a story preserved like a shell in chalk. The story itself is not told, and what it may have been we cannot conjecture. But the Evangelist uses it as an example of a more than human knowledge of the hearts

CHRISTOLOGY

and thoughts of men, a *sign* of Divinity. On a later occasion,[1] Andrew and Philip brought to Jesus certain Greeks who were at Jerusalem at the time of the feast. Jesus naturally welcomed their homage; to Him the friendship of no human heart was indifferent or worthless. But the Evangelist cannot bring himself to regard so simple an occurrence as trivial; he leads on from mere recognition of his Master by strangers to His glorification and future exaltation. On the day when Jesus was betrayed,[2] the officers who came out to arrest Him, when He said calmly, "I am He," went backward and fell to the ground. This looks very much like an exaggeration into the supernatural sphere of a natural feeling of respect and compunction which the officers may well have felt in the presence of Jesus, but which, according to the Evangelist, they soon changed for one of hatred and spite.

The Jesus of the Evangelist, like the child in Wordsworth, comes trailing clouds of glory from heaven, which is His home. All through the writer's history of the last days, though he seems to preserve many details of true tradition, he is on the watch to keep out any phrases which would seem to him to degrade his Lord.

[1] xii. 20.   [2] xviii 6.

We cannot have a more striking contrast between the Jesus of the Synoptists — the Jesus of history — and the Jesus of the Fourth Evangelist, than is shown in the sayings of Jesus as to His own death recorded in the two biographies. In Mark's account of the agony in Gethsemane, Jesus says, "Father, all things are possible unto Thee; remove this cup from Me: howbeit, not what I will, but what Thou wilt." What could be more touchingly, more piercingly human? Jesus is represented as shrinking, as any one of His followers might shrink, from the pain of martyrdom. Opponents of Christianity have found these words weak and effeminate; and they have had no difficulty in finding hundreds of heroes who have gone to pain and death not with shrinking, but with exultation. But which course is the higher? The height of unchristian heroism may be found in the Red Indian brave, who sang joyously as he was tortured at the stake. In his way he was splendid. But the Christian martyr, with more highly developed consciousness, and therefore with more acute sensitiveness, feels intensely the prospect of pain and death, but yet is willing to undergo them because it is the will of his Father; and probably in the actual suffering finds the trial to which he

CHRISTOLOGY

had looked forward after all easy to bear. He meets pain not with the heroism of a dauntless will, but with the certainty of Divine aid. If there be any truth in Christianity, and any meaning in history, his is the nobler line.

In the account of the Fourth Evangelist Jesus takes quite another view :[1] " I lay down My life that I may take it again. No one taketh it away from Me, but I lay it down of Myself. I have power to lay it down, and I have power to take it again." The Evangelist felt so keenly the divine nature of his Master, that he could not endure the notion of His suffering at the hands of men, otherwise than voluntarily. But it is obvious that by taking this view, he has deprived his Master, not only of all humanity, but of all heroism. His Jesus is not made perfect by suffering, but raised above all suffering by the power of the divinity within Him.

Had the Evangelist worked out this view with consistency, he would have produced a purely Docetic doctrine, and reduced the life of his Master to a mere mirage. From this bottomless swamp he is rescued by a happy inconsistency. When he comes to narrate the actual facts of the crucifixion, which he had heard at first or second hand from actual

[1] *John* x. 18.

witnesses, he does not altogether take the Docetic view. Yet his narrative is very different from that of the Synoptics, in that he does not dwell on the agony of the cross, and omits the piercing sayings which have made the story of the cross one of the greatest powers over the human spirit which the world has known. The only utterances which, in his version, come from the Saviour on the cross, besides the commendation of His mother to the beloved disciple (probably a historic detail), consist of the words "I thirst" and "It is finished." As everyone knows, a terrible and burning thirst is one of the most poignant sufferings of those who are wounded and tortured. But the Fourth Evangelist does not represent that thirst as a natural one. "Jesus, that the scripture might be accomplished, saith, I thirst."

Yet, after all, he preserves the main thing, that it was the historic Jesus who sat wearied with the journey by the well of Samaria, wept by the grave of Lazarus, and perished on the cross. The Word, after all, became flesh, though the Evangelist, after accepting this bold statement, does a great deal in the course of his narrative to empty it of meaning.

So in a multitude of passages the Evangelist puts into words that consciousness of a close

CHRISTOLOGY

relation to God which Jesus seems, as a matter of history, to have expressed seldom and guardedly. Where he is nearest to actual history is in the passages which speak of Jesus in relation to the Divine will. These passages are many: "My meat is to do the will of Him that sent Me, and to accomplish His work"; "I seek not Mine own will, but the will of Him that sent Me." Such sayings as these are entirely in line with others in the Synoptists. All three of them[1] record a saying of Jesus, when His mother and brethren came, intending to put Him under restraint: "Whosoever shall do the will of God, the same is My brother and sister and mother." In the Lord's prayer the phrase "Thy will be done" is very prominent. And in the scene in Gethsemane we have the same refrain, "Not My will but Thine be done." Only the notion of a possibility of opposition between the will of the earthly Jesus and the will of the Father, which is hinted at in the scene at Gethsemane, is naturally set aside in the Fourth Gospel.

In the Synoptic Gospels the unity of will and purpose between Jesus and the Father in Heaven is much more often assumed than asserted. Jesus spoke, men felt, as one having a direct commission from above, and not like

[1] *Mark* iii. 35, and parallels.

the Scribes. In His miracles of healing He does not say "God wills thy healing," but "I will; be thou clean." Though His discourses are constantly revolving around the Father in Heaven, He speaks of "My words" as of direct authority.

The Jesus of the Fourth Evangelist, on the contrary, is always proclaiming His close relation to the Father. It is not only that the Son is like the Father, "My Father worketh until now, and I work"; "The Son can do nothing of Himself, but what He sees the Father doing"; but a more intimate relation still is set forth. The Son fully represents the Father on earth. "The Father loveth the Son, and showeth Him all things that Himself doeth." " If ye had known Me, ye should have known My Father also." " As the Father knoweth Me, even so know I the Father." In the passage which deals with the raising of Lazarus, Jesus is represented as saying, "Father, I thank Thee that Thou heardest Me." This may well be a fragment of tradition; it is thus that the Jesus of the Synoptists prays. But the Fourth Evangelist cannot leave the phrase without comment; he adds, " I knew that Thou hearest Me always: but because of the multitude which standeth around I said it, that they may believe that

Thou didst send Me." Finally, we have the passage in which, in his own manner, the Evangelist sums up the situation in a single pregnant phrase, " I and the Father are one," a phrase on which the later discourses in the Gospel are a commentary. " The glory which Thou hast given Me I have given unto them; that they may be one, even as we are one: I in them and Thou in Me, that they may be perfected into one." Here the Evangelist has passed from the tradition altogether; he is thinking of the inspiration of the Church, in which to him, as to St Paul, there dwells the Christ who is the same as the Spirit of God. The glory which was given to the earthly Jesus has been given also to the Society which continues on earth the life of Christ, and by that life rises into unity with God. But this unity does not belong only to earth, it stretches also to the heaven, which, to the writer, is at once future and present: " Father, I will that they also whom Thou hast given Me be with Me where I am."

The Fourth Evangelist not only accepts from tradition accounts of the deeds of his Master; but he naturally also accepts some of the phrases in regard to Him current in the Society. He accepts and vindicates his Master's claim to the title Christ or Messiah.

This he seems to do especially in opposition to the Jews. He brings forward the current objections of the Jews to the Messiahship of Jesus, such as His plebeian origin and His Galilean birth-place, His neglect of the Sabbath, and the like, and furnishes replies. It is, however, noteworthy that the Evangelist does not counter the Galilean objection by the assertion that Jesus was really born in Bethlehem. This controversial element, however, is only subordinate, a sort of by-play in the Gospel. One feels that the question of the Messiahship has with time become less acute. The title Son of Man, so frequently applied to Himself by Jesus in the earliest tradition, does occur in the Fourth Gospel, but not with any striking novelty of meaning. On the other hand, the term Son of God, which Jesus does not directly apply to Himself in the Synoptic Gospels, plays a far greater part in the Fourth Gospel, as is indeed natural after what has been above said.

III

So far we have little but the immediate interpretation of experience and tradition. But the tendency to speculative thought which is clearly marked in the first verses of the Gospel comes to the surface in it from

CHRISTOLOGY

time to time. Even St Paul, immersed as he was in practical life, had theories as to the pre-existence of Christ; the Evangelist naturally speaks of the glory which He had with the Father before the world was. He came from the Father, and went back to the Father. "As the Father hath life in Himself, even so gave He to the Son also to have life in Himself." In these phrases, which are not prominent in the Gospel, we may find the germs of much theological speculation which was already beginning to spring out of the fruitful soil of Ephesus. We may regret that the Evangelist did much to spoil his rich contribution to theology by the narrowness—a frequent accompaniment of a fervent spirit— which denies a share in the Christian Church to any who do not hold the right theological views. "He that hath the Son hath the life; he that hath not the Son of God hath not the life."[1] We might pass this as a mere statement of experience: the writer saw that the life which is eternal in Christ belonged only to the Christian Society. But when he writes, "This is the antichrist, even he that denieth the Father and the Son," we begin to hear the rumbling of the distant thunder of clashing creeds, and of the intolerance which would not

[1] *Epistle* v 12.

allow that any speculative views which are not authorised by the majority can be in the way of salvation.

Of the three great Christian doctrines which centre in the person of the Saviour, the doctrines of the Incarnation, the Atonement, and the Exaltation, the first and third are of the essence of the Evangelist's teaching, and we have already sufficiently considered them. The doctrine of the Atonement is far less prominent. In a few phrases, and especially in a verse in the Epistle, "the blood of Jesus His Son cleanseth us from all sin,"[1] we seem to have a definite statement of the doctrine. Probably both St Paul and the Evangelist accepted that belief,[2] though with neither of them is it fundamental, and neither would have adopted the doctrine of the Atonement as it grew to be before very long in the Church. Salvation with both of them consisted in sharing the life of Christ, not in appropriating the merit of His death.

Yet we must not forget the degree to which the Isaian picture of the suffering servant of God dwelt in the minds of the early Christians, so as to tinge the Synoptist

[1] *Epistle* i 7, R.V.
[2] This statement modifies the view I had expressed in *The Religious Experience of St Paul*, p. 194.

CHRISTOLOGY 311

Gospels. We have even reason to think that it was accepted as referring to Himself by the Saviour. And in the Isaian description the doctrine is clearly set forth that the suffering of the just has a vicarious efficacy, and tends to do away with the sins of the erring. In such a sense and so far, the doctrine of the Atonement was clearly a part of the earliest teaching of the community. It was only when the thought of the Church broke away from its feeling and experience that the doctrine became unreal and pedantic, as it is in the writings of Irenæus and Tertullian.[1]

In the entrance into the Church of Platonic philosophic thought we must certainly see the influence of the Ionian cities. At Ephesus the Christian Gospel is fairly launched on the sea of theosophical speculation. What we call doctrine and the Roman Church calls dogma is quite without roots in Jewish soil. It never occurred to Hebrew priest or prophet to set forth a series of statements as to the God of Israel which every Hebrew must subscribe under penalty of rejection from the community. It was the keeping of the law, the observation of ritual and festival which

[1] See the *Bampton Lectures* of Dr Rashdall (not yet published)

constituted Jewish orthodoxy. But Greek philosophy had long before the Christian era broken up into a number of schools, each of which had formulæ of its own on the most important subjects, and was ready to defend them in controversy. Greek philosophers did not persecute one another, perhaps because they had no power over the civil authorities, but they regarded one another as deluded.

Of course the most important contribution of the Fourth Evangelist to the foundation of Christian doctrine lies in his adoption of the doctrine of the Logos. I do not propose to go with any thoroughness into the history of this doctrine. That would require a knowledge of the history of philosophic thought, and, I may add, a taste for philosophic speculation, to which I can lay no claim. The literature on the subject is almost inexhaustible.[1] It seems, however, to me, that those who have written on the subject have seldom taken sufficiently into account the very fragmentary state of our knowledge of the currents of philosophic thought in the Hellenistic age, which makes any treatment

---

[1] I remember, as an undergraduate, attending a course of lectures by (the then) Professor Lightfoot, on the Fourth Gospel. By the end of the term he had barely gone beyond the first few verses.

of the subject imperfect. We know that Heracleitus of Ephesus had a doctrine of the Logos; and that there was a school of Heracleitan philosophy which flourished for centuries, probably as much at Ephesus as anywhere. We know that the Stoics had a Logos doctrine which was of great importance in their system. And we know that in the teaching of Philo, the Alexandrian contemporary of St Paul, teaching in regard to the nature and the functions of the Divine Logos holds a great place. We know also that in the Book of Proverbs and in the Jewish Apocrypha the Word or the Wisdom of God is much spoken of. But these are patches of light in a sea of darkness. Our knowledge of the philosophy of the Hellenistic age is very imperfect. I may be allowed to cite an archæological parallel. We can identify the works of one or two centres of Hellenistic art: Athens, Pergamon, Alexandria, Rhodes, Stratonicea. But probably many great cities at the time had a school of art differing in some respects from those of their neighbours. And in the case of the great mass of works of sculpture of the period B.C. 300-1 we cannot definitely give them to one school or another. In particular we know of one or two important pieces of sculpture signed by

Ephesian artists: one by Agasias, son of Dositheus; another by Agasias, son of Menophilus. Both are admirable figures of combatant warriors. They prove clearly the existence of an important school of sculpture at Ephesus in the second century B.C. But, apart from their inscriptions, we should certainly have attributed them to the great school of Hellenistic sculpture in Pergamon. In the same way, there were no doubt in the great cities schools of philosophy of which we have quite insufficient knowledge. It is notable that the Evangelist brings in his sentences about the Logos as if he were stating something very simple and undisputed. Very probably he takes for granted some scheme of philosophy at the time current at Ephesus, but to us unknown.

Thus to suppose that it was necessarily from Philo that the Evangelist took the Logos doctrine seems to me quite unnecessary. I do not think we can even venture to say that the doctrine is definitely Alexandrian, among all the lines of Hellenistic thought.

It is the more difficult to determine the relation which the Logos doctrine of the Fourth Evangelist holds to some or all of the views known to us, because he does not go into any detail. In the first few verses of the

CHRISTOLOGY

Gospel he slightly sketches a doctrine of the Divine Word as existing in the beginning with God, and as the agent through whom all things were made. He says that the Logos was the source of light to men, and that the Logos was divine: not that he was, as our version has it, "God."[1] He adds that the Word became flesh, and was so manifested to the world in the person of Jesus Christ. Then he passes on to his biography.

It is much to be regretted that the English version of the first few verses of the Gospel is very misleading. It is a defect which could hardly have been avoided, except by the use of a long paraphrase, since it is impossible to render each Greek word by an English equivalent. But two phrases in particular certainly tend to mislead. "The Word was God." Here the Greek, θεὸς ἦν ὁ λόγος, means something much more indefinite: it is not ὁ λόγος ἦν ὁ θεός. It might well be rendered "The Word was of the nature of the Divine"; just as in a later passage (iv. 24) πνεῦμα ὁ θεός may well be rendered "God is of the nature of spirit." Still more perverse is the rendering, "All things were made by Him": a far nearer translation would be, "All things came into being through Him,"

[1] See above, p. 147.

πάντα δι' αὐτοῦ ἐγένετο; and this is almost a repetition of the view in *Proverbs* (viii. 22–31), where the Divine Wisdom is spoken of as present at the creation of the world: "Then was I with Him as a master-workman, and I was daily His delight." Of course in the subsequent verse, "The Word was made flesh, and dwelt among us," the Evangelist greatly adds to the old doctrine; but that does not justify the translation of the earlier verse.

The originality of the Evangelist lies, not in a new theory of the Logos, but in his conception of the embodiment of the eternal Word or the eternal Wisdom in the person of the Founder of Christianity. His rendering of the biography which he had to write did not depend, in fact, on any philosophic views, but on the Pauline doctrine of the immanent Christ, which was a direct rendering of the experience of the Church. But on one point probably a philosophic tradition influenced him. He could not bear to think of the Divine Word in the flesh as limited in knowledge or liable to human error. "He needed not that anyone should bear witness concerning a man, for he knew what was in man."[1] In the Garden of Gethsemane, "Jesus knew all the things that

---

[1] *John* ii 25.

CHRISTOLOGY

were coming upon Him."[1] When Nathanael came to Him, Jesus showed such a knowledge of his history as appeared to Nathanael supernatural.[2] And so on in other cases. Peter indeed says simply, "Thou knowest all things."[3] It is quite true that the highest Divine inspiration does impart to the person who is inspired a wisdom which comes from above, and is often of a most striking kind. But we have no reason to think that it imparts true and exact knowledge in regard to facts of sense which are out of the range of sense. No doubt one must speak cautiously, for modern psychical research seems to show that there may be thought-transference apart from sense-knowledge. But, on the other hand, psychical research does not show that such means of knowledge belong to the best and noblest of mankind, but rather to people of backward races and those who are nervously unstable.

Perhaps all that we can say, in the present state of our knowledge, is that if our Lord was tempted like as we are, if the life He lived on earth was a really human life, we must regard Him as limited in knowledge, just as limited in space, and limited to the ordinary senses, just as capable of pain and of sorrow.

[1] *John* xviii. 4.   [2] *John* i. 48.   [3] *John* xxi. 17

Unmeasured knowledge would raise Him out of our reach, as much as would insensibility to pain, which also seems to be attained in abnormal psychical conditions. If we must choose between the Pauline doctrine of the kenosis and the Johannine attempt to raise the Founder while on earth above earthly conditions, we should certainly choose the former. The modern mind will, one hopes, find a more excellent way than either. But that question I must reserve to the next chapter.

XV

THE GOSPEL AND MODERNITY

THE teachings which the world has learned from the Fourth Gospel are so many and so great that the Evangelist stands in the very first rank of those whose voices echo down the ages. So spiritual is his doctrine that those who walk after the spirit in all ages will be drawn to him and follow his leading, to the great health of their souls. There is much less that belongs merely to the time and the place than there is even in the Pauline Epistles, less of supposed science, less of speculative philosophy, less of views based on the temporary necessities of the Church. And if the notions of the Evangelist in regard to history are, like those of St Paul, little in accordance with modern methodic ways, yet it is easy to make allowance for this.

There is a luminous distinction, which is developed and insisted on by William James in his remarkable work on *Varieties of Religious Experience*, between the classes of men whom he calls the once-born and the twice-born. The once-born are the healthy-minded optimists, who regard good as naturally stronger than evil, to whom faith in the Divine leading is easy, who escape the severe crises of life. The twice-born are the naturally pessimistic, to whom evil seems dominant in the world, and who can only escape into the region of a secure faith through terrible mental struggles and sufferings. The Gospel of Matthew, in its earlier part, with its unclouded confidence in the Divine Father and in Providence, with its delight in the beauty of the two worlds of nature and of spirit, is naturally akin to the former of these classes. St Paul, with his crises and mental struggles, must for all time be the classic example of the faith of the twice-born. The Fourth Evangelist cannot be summarily assigned to either class. He insists strongly on the need of a second birth. Yet we do not find in his writings the traces of constant warfare between flesh and spirit which so deeply tinge the works of Paul and of Augustine. Faith in Christ is not reached by him through struggle and tribulation; it attracts him by its natural beauty. He is led to it by love, not driven to it as a means

THE GOSPEL AND MODERNITY

of escape. In the Fourth Evangelist both the once-born and the twice-born may find the greatest satisfaction and the sweetest consolation.

In the preceding pages I have tried to mark the position of the Fourth Evangelist in relation to the writings of early Christianity and the life of which they are an embodiment. At present I propose briefly to reconsider his main tenets in relation to modern conditions and the existing mental and spiritual horizon. This I will do under five heads, considering the Evangelist's attitude in relation to

I. Christian faith and eternal life,
II. The history of the Founder of Christianity,
III. The sacraments,
IV. The Church, visible and invisible,
V. The formulation of doctrine.

I

It will be well to go straight to what is the fundamental point in the teaching of the Fourth Gospel, that the belief, the presence of which makes a Christian, and the absence of which leaves no basis for Christianity, is the consciousness of a living Power, a Spirit ever working in the Church, and tending to the promotion in the world of a spiritual kingdom, the Kingdom of Heaven that is within us.

If we try scientifically to classify beliefs we shall say that this belief is a species of the genus of religions which are rooted in the faith in an indwelling or immanent Deity. The teaching of the First Gospel is primarily a doctrine of the divine transcendence; the teaching of the Fourth Gospel is essentially a doctrine of the divine immanence. What, however, are the marks which distinguish the Christianity of the Fourth Evangelist from other religions of this genus? They are mainly two. In the first place, the divine immanence taught by this great leader of the Church is one exhibited upon earth in the person of the Founder. It is God as revealed in the life and death of Jesus Christ, as seen on earth for a time under human conditions, who is the Christian inspiration. Whether God thus brought home and revealed to men be termed the exalted Christ or the Holy Spirit is a matter of less importance, and in fact as regards that point the various writers of the New Testament are not at one among themselves. It is the power, the working of the Spirit of which they are intensely conscious; the intellectual apprehension of it is comparatively immaterial.

In the second place, though the Spirit may reveal Himself to individuals, generally speaking the Christian does not stand as one who approaches God as an individual, but as a member of a society, whose life in the world is a continuance of the life of Christ. The essence of Pauline and Johannine Christianity is that the Christian is a partaker of a common life which is divine and eternal. This is their idea of spiritual Christianity.

To the Evangelist the Christian communion with the Divine appears to lead direct to salvation, to the eternal life which Jesus came to reveal to men, the life which is timeless. It dawns upon those who become members of the Christian Society; they feel that it is a possession of the community in which each individual has a part. And they feel that it abides also with the Founder in the heavenly places. They hope that at death, whatever passes and is destroyed, this eternal life will not pass away, but that they will more fully enjoy it in the presence of their risen Lord. To the Evangelist, filled with this confidence, the questions of eschatology pass into the background, and become of little importance; whether the scene of this higher life be a glorified and changed material world or an unknown spiritual universe he does not determine. What entirely contents him is the view expressed in the Colossian Epistle,[1] "When Christ, who is our life, shall be manifested, then shall ye also with Him be manifested in glory"; or, as the Evangelist himself puts it, "Where I am, there shall ye be also."[2]

In the chapter dealing with eschatology we have seen how, in the history of Christianity, there are three ways in which the better hope, the hope of life and immortality, has been embodied.

In the very early age the Jewish hope of a Messianic rule, of a visible divine kingdom set up on earth, was baptised into Christianity. When early Christianity adopted it, it transformed it in two ways: first, by accepting Jesus as the Christ, the Messiah who was to bring in the new age and to be king of the new kingdom; and, second, by removing the hope from a merely racial basis, and extending it to all who accepted the Christian Messiah.

This was the earliest eschatologic belief of Christianity. And as extremes meet, we need not be surprised to find that the belief in a divine rule, a Christian community on earth, is also the most modern. We hear on all sides that the people are turning more and more to a determination that a kingdom of righteousness

[1] iii. 4.   [2] *John* xiv. 3.

THE GOSPEL AND MODERNITY

and justice must be possible here on earth, and to a conviction that those who give their lives to the endeavour to bring in such a kingdom are the truest followers of Jesus Christ. Among ourselves, as among the ancient Jews, this enthusiasm is greatly mixed with materialism, with an exaggerated belief in the value of things which can be seen and enjoyed. Often a mere improvement in the physical condition of the masses of the people is spoken of as if it would ensure happiness and spiritual health. There is here a great deal of illusion; yet one would not wish to say a word against a hope which inspires thousands of men and women to endure suffering and death in the hope of preparing for their children and their countrymen a brighter and more serene life. Instead of protesting against such belief it is best to try to supplement it, in the spirit of the Master's saying, "Man shall not live on bread alone, but by every word that proceedeth out of the mouth of God."

The second way in which the aspiration after a higher life was embodied in early Christianity was in a belief in a great judgment of souls and their assignment to a spiritual realm of happiness or misery, according as their life on earth had been one of beneficence or of evil doing. The germ of this view must be sought in the Far East; it was brought to the West from Egypt and Babylon by the mystery religions of the Hellenistic age, by which Judaism itself was largely influenced. In formed Christianity the ideas of Heaven, Hell, and Purgatory as places for departed souls were dominant; but their gates were guarded by the forces of the Church, and opened not necessarily in accordance with the ethical character of the dead, but with reference also to his beliefs, and his obedience to the Church. It is very hard to say how far a belief in the rewards and penalties of a future life dominate the thoughts of English people at the present day, or, what is more important, regulate their conduct. The tradition is strong, and among the less highly educated parts of the community it probably acts subconsciously, rising to the surface in hours of stress or in prospect of death. But I think it is, in the mass of the people, certainly decaying, with effects for good and for evil which it is hard to measure. Among more thoughtful people the belief is much refined and etiolated: probably few believe that the soul dies with the body; but of the future beyond death men seldom speak, and seldom have a clearly formulated belief.

No doubt in a rude and unbridled age

THE GOSPEL AND MODERNITY 327

crude and vivid beliefs as to future rewards and punishments are of immense value in curbing the passions of men, and leading them, if not to repentance, at least to penitence and restitution. But such beliefs are not at a high ethical level, and when once they have fallen into decay their materialism is apt to be treated even with ridicule.

In particular some of the leaders of the proletariate are strongly convinced that the traditional doctrine of Heaven and Hell tends to thwart and maim those attempts at the improvement of social and material conditions from which they hope everything. They are persuaded that the Churches foster this doctrine in order that the well-to-do may enjoy the things of this life, and hold up before the poor the hope, which they deem illusory, of retribution in a future state. Hence the teaching of Heaven and Hell seems to them anti-social, and they condemn it in no measured terms. They may be partly right; but they are certainly largely wrong. Let us by all means do what we can to improve the distribution of wealth and to redress social inequalities, but the whole history of the world proves that the peoples who content themselves with aiming at worldly prosperity and do not trouble about the infinite possibilities and eternal destinies of the soul do not find what they seek. All true progress must have a spiritual side. As Mrs Browning has written, "It needs a high-souled man to move the masses even to a cleaner stye." And the high-souled man will not and cannot think the health of the spirit and its high hopes beyond the present life a matter of indifference. If we discard the too crude notions of the Middle Ages as to the doom of souls, we must in some way preserve the high spiritual truths which found incorporation in those beliefs, or we shall revert to barbarism. No higher or greater thing is produced on the earth than a noble personality; and that this personality should at death simply disappear is not to be thought; though in what way it survives is a matter not of knowledge but of hope.

The third way in which Christianity received the higher hope is the mystic way of a belief in a higher spiritual life, not only lying in the future, but around us here and now. When thought began to realise the superiority of the spiritual element in life to the material elements, and to recognise the transitory and evanescent character of the latter, it fled for a refuge to the belief in a great spiritual realm of which all the visible and tangible is but a faint and vanishing reflex. Such views, developed in full force among the sages of India and Persia, were inculcated in Greece by the Platonic schools of philosophy. Meantime, the psalmists and prophets of Judæa had received parallel beliefs, altered in accordance with the far more definite and powerful theology of Judæa. The great thinkers of early Christianity, Paul and the Fourth Evangelist, baptised these spiritual ideas into Christianity, chiefly by means of their conviction that the source of all life and light was the Exalted Christ.

They also, in a sense, narrowed these ideas by holding, as they certainly did, that only by a conscious acceptance of the Exalted Saviour could a man enter into the higher life. It is open to us to think that, like the great thinkers of all ages, they were right in what they affirmed rather than in their denials. History has given us unnumbered instances which show how, through Christian faith, Christians have attained to the highest life. But there is no need to deny that for those outside Christianity God may, in His mercy, provide other ways for attaining that life, though in a less perfect degree.

In all ages of Christianity spiritual idealism has been the dominant note in the writings of the great teachers of the Church. But it would be a mistake to think that it is peculiar to the highly educated, that it can only be reached by profound thought. It can also be attained by a kind of religious intuition. Men and women of quite ordinary intellectual attainments, but endowed with a deep spiritual sense, live constantly in communion with the unseen; their thoughts and hopes are set on things not attainable by bodily sense, but revealed to the heart. Amid the buffetings of fortune and the losses which come to all of us, they can realise that these calamities are but an outward show, and that a peace which is beyond their reach rests upon those who live in harmony with the Divine will, and in practice of love to God. Nor do such souls fear that death will have power to tear them away from such higher communion; it can only remove them to another province of the spiritual world.

II

But the Fourth Gospel, as we have abundantly seen in the course of this work, is not merely spiritual. It fully recognises that since man has a body as well as a spirit, it was necessary that the Word should become flesh. The Evangelist believed that his Master had done mighty works, had opened the eyes of the blind, and even raised the dead. He held the belief, in his time universal, that a Saviour sent into the world must be able to work miracles, and that if He had not done so, the disbelief of the Jews would have been, in a measure, justified; at all events, inevitable. Those who were not attracted by His spiritual teaching might well believe in Him for the works' sake.

Judging from the practical point of view, it must be reckoned as a great merit in the Evangelist that he did not allow spiritual passion to carry him entirely away. Defective as, from the modern point of view, his notion of history is, yet he was right in insisting on the historic character of the great events in the life of the Founder. The reality of the revelation of the Divine Word under the forms of space and time was felt by the teachers of the early Church to be a matter of life and death. Those who regarded that life as a mere appearance or mirage preserved the possibility of a philosophic religion, but not of a Christian Church. Ignatius, writing to the Church at Tralles[1] early in the second century, puts the matter clearly: "Be ye deaf, therefore, when anyone speaketh unto you

[1] Ch ix.

apart from Jesus Christ, who was of the race of David, who was born of Mary, who was truly born, ate and drank, was truly persecuted under Pontius Pilate, was truly crucified and died, in the sight of the things that are in heaven and on earth and under the earth; and was truly raised from the dead, His Father having raised Him up."

So much of historic fact the Evangelist saw to be indispensable to Christian belief. And so had St Paul judged before him:[1] "I delivered unto you first of all that which also I received," and he goes on to mention the death and resurrection of his Master. And in our own day it is impossible that the Church should survive as an institution if she gave up the historic reality of her Founder,—though in regard to the details of His life every modern mind is obliged to take a more critical view than was possible in the early ages of Christianity—or abandoned her conviction as to the general character of His deeds and words.

The scientific view of history, as an evolution manifested in time and showing a regular succession of cause and effect rather than as a series of unconnected views picturesque but irrational,—this view has come to stay. In all the universities of Europe and America

[1] 1 *Cor.* xv 3.

THE GOSPEL AND MODERNITY 333

it has made steady progress, until now it has hardly any serious opposition to encounter from those who reflect.

In the wake of physical science history has turned towards research, towards the investigation of document and of monument, towards the ranging of facts. Historians give their lives to the study of original authorities, to the weighing of evidence, to an earnest and prolonged endeavour to ascertain what really happened in the periods of which they treat. History, of course, must always have another side: the side of ideas. The historian is not, like the investigator in natural science, a man without bias, aiming only at the ascertainment of fact. History is closely connected with practical life; and the historian is commonly inspired for his task by the hope of throwing from the past a light upon the present. While he is a historian, he is at the same time a politician, or a person belonging to a particular school in religion, in sociology, or in ethnology. Subjective and *a priori* tendencies can never be shut out of the writing of history: it is essentially an ethical task.[1]

[1] In view of the terrible events now taking place in Europe, I cannot help saying that false and unworthy views as to idea in history may so far prevail, even in the case of those well exercised in historic method, as to pollute the whole of historic study with disease

THE EPHESIAN GOSPEL

We have to consider what are the results upon modern conceptions of Christianity which flow from both these historic tendencies: the tendency to an exact and realistic study of the sequence of events in the past, and the tendency to regard all human history in an ethical or dynamic way, as the manifestation of spiritual tendency and divine idea.

There[1] has been of late a strongly marked tendency among writers in Germany and England to concentrate attention on the human life of the Founder of Christianity, and the Synoptic Gospels in which it is reported in the most objective and simple way. The attempt was to throw a strong historic light on the Christian origins; to exhibit the drama as it actually took place with the walls of Jerusalem and hills of Galilee for a background. That process has gone on and is still going on.

It has been a work of great intellectual enterprise and force. Some writers declare it to be the greatest intellectual achievement of our time. The background against which the drama of salvation was played out, Palestine and the Græco-Roman world, has come out most vividly, and the gracious figure of

[1] The following paragraphs are from the *Modern Churchman*, July 1914.

the Master who taught as never man taught, and lived as never man lived, stands out more clearly. But of course it would be absurd to represent the process as one only of gain. The result has been that the super-normal and miraculous element in that life has dwindled. And to many excellent Christians this must seem a loss. Such often say with Mary, "They have taken away my Lord, and I know not where they have laid Him." And yet, after all, Mary came to realise that it was really a step in her Master's exaltation which had taken Him away. Only what was material had disappeared; and the reply of the angels comes down the ages: "He is not here, He is risen."

The greatest of our losses, which may however in the long run be for the good of the Church, lies in our changed view of the Fourth Gospel. I do not wish to speak too dogmatically, since I know that many good critics still hold to the Johannine origin, and the historic exactness, of this Gospel. I am convinced, however, that we shall have to give up this view, that we shall be obliged to allow that though the Fourth Gospel contains valuable historic material, yet what is its main treasure, the speeches of our Lord contained in it, belongs not to the lifetime of the

Founder, but to the early experience of the Church. And I am also convinced that when once we have made up our minds to this change of view, we shall in the end more fully realise the value of the writings of the first and greatest of the Christian mystics.

Yes, there has been loss as well as gain. We live in a country of business men. When one of them makes a loss what does he do? He faces the facts, refuses to deceive himself, writes off bad debts, introduces better machinery, and often more than regains what he has lost. May not the Church do the same?

Thus we need not despair if our gain in historic outlook has been in some of us accompanied by a certain amount of disillusion and disappointment. It seems that we cannot from mere outward and visible fact gain a clear perception of the vast spiritual revolution which was taking place in the world. While we realise that if we had been in bodily presence in Jerusalem or Galilee at the time we should have seen and heard many of the things which the Synoptists report, we also realise that it was not by the senses only that the true inwardness of Christianity could be grasped. It seems to me that, as the first apostles of Christianity were defective through

THE GOSPEL AND MODERNITY 337

the narrowness of their horizon, and because they saw Christianity too exclusively under material conditions, and in a Jewish setting, so it has been with Christianity, and not least with the Reformed Churches, in the last centuries.

Their conception of Christianity also has been too much coloured with Judaism; they have regarded Christianity too exclusively as a religion which sprang up at a particular time and in a definite place, and not as the consummation of the religion of the world. To Catholics Christianity presents itself too much as a supernatural system introduced into the world by a supernatural person, who, by miracle, proved Himself to be divine, and to have a right to set forth for all time the conditions of salvation, which are enforced by a church of which the clergy have supernatural powers. And most Protestants, though they profess the belief that the Spirit of Christ still dwells in and guides the Church, yet are closely bound to the letter of the New Testament, which they in practice regard as an infallible guide.

A way of escape from our difficulties may perhaps lie in following a line like that taken in the first century by St Paul and the Fourth Evangelist. These great writers did things for nascent Christianity without which the Christianity we know of could not have come into existence. They reduced the materialist element in Christianity and increased the spiritual element. St Paul, as he himself is careful to tell us, knew but little of the earthly life of his Master, nor did he, when he had opportunities, curiously inquire about it. He knew in fact little more of it than a frankly sceptical school of German criticism would leave us. The two facts of it which seemed to him of supreme importance were the death on the cross and the resurrection, or continued life in the Church, two facts of the most objective history. The Fourth Evangelist deliberately sets himself, all through his Gospel, to correct the historic tradition of his Master's life, and to bring out its spiritual and inner meaning. If, as a historian, he sets before us a being who could never have walked the soil of Palestine, he, as a theologian, laid the foundations of mystic Christianity for all time. For the teaching of the Virgin-birth he substitutes the doctrine of the Logos. Like St Paul, it is Christ exalted and Christ the life of the Church that fills his mind and heart.

A great part of what are taken by modern uninstructed Christians for necessary sides of Christian belief—assertions as to events in the life of the Founder—are not really at all of the essence of Christianity, and are only supposed to be so in consequence of perverted education. According to the old proverb, a little knowledge is a dangerous thing. And the result of a superficial training in science and history in a modern school is often to produce in the mind of the learner an extremely shallow conviction of the all-importance of literal accuracy in the statement of fact, and a want of comprehension of the extremely modern character of this tone of mind. To a mind thus attuned the Gospel history is either literally true or a congeries of falsehoods: the phrases of the Creed express literally a number of facts as to the Divine nature, or they are a dreadful delusion. Most of us are so wrapped up in the things of sense that we take spiritual truths to be not symbolic statements, but prosaic assertions of fact.

Such a frame of mind is very hard to modify. And while many men are in it, any attempt to throw the early Christian teaching into true historic perspective, and to show how much more important are ideas and tendencies than visible facts, must have great danger. It is hard to persuade such literalists that what we are criticising is not any necessary part of Christianity, but only a modern mirage of it.

The best that one can hope is that the mirage is by degrees becoming more dim, while the reality which it so delusively reflects is growing clearer.

III

The Evangelist attaches great value to the Christian sacraments of Baptism and the Lord's Supper. Such outward and visible means of appropriating the grace ever flowing from the Head of the Church into her body, he saw to be necessary, if the Church was to persist in the world as a visible organisation. Against their abuse, against any notion that they had a magical value, he warns his disciples. The notion that men can by the mere performance of certain rites draw down to themselves the grace of God finds no place with him. Such a notion in his time only belonged to the more retrograde and materialist; in the Pauline Churches it could find no place. The Evangelist counters it with his immortal saying, "The wind bloweth where it listeth." But he saw that to any organised Church some sacraments were necessary. He would see at Ephesus how in every one of the pagan religious societies, the thiasi of Isis and Kybele and Mithras, such sacraments naturally grew up. So he avoids alike the materialism which soon began to invade the Christian sacraments, and the ultra-spiritualism which was destined soon to mislead the Montanists, and to drive them into wild and unregulated excesses.

Human nature being what it is, had the Evangelist entirely overlooked the need of sacraments, his Gospel would have been a far poorer gift to mankind. There will always be many in the Christian society to whom such rites are quite necessary, who without them would feel that Christianity was evanescent and would fall away. The study of history establishes in the clearest way the need of outward ordinances. And spiritual Christianity, while looking beyond the mere outward rite, will never dare to despise it. On the contrary, the deeper study of psychology in our day has proved to what an extent outward rites may react on inward feeling, may serve as a means of stimulating and preserving spiritual enthusiasms. If there arises among more sensuous natures a tendency to overvalue these "means of grace," the Christian to whom they are less attractive and less necessary will view this tendency, unless carried to the extreme of materialism and magic, with a respectful sympathy. When we consider what the great sacraments have been in the history of the Church, we must, in spite of their great liability to abuse, allow their Divine origin and sanction. The solitary thinker and writer is naturally drawn towards the doctrine of the Spirit, and is apt to overlook the corporate needs of the Church. But those who have the practical guidance of the Christian Society will set a higher and a juster value upon the visible and tangible means of grace. It is one of the clearest proofs of the inspiration of the Evangelist that his book gives satisfaction to both of these tendencies.

IV

In another matter, the outward organisation of the Church, we cannot expect much definite teaching from the Evangelist. In his time the first fervour of the Christian movement was not exhausted. The local Churches were scarcely organised; they were small democracies or theocracies under the immediate governance of the Spirit. A vivid picture of their constitution and their proceedings is given by St Paul in his first Corinthian Epistle (chap. v.). The faithful are to assemble together, and to expel from the community by a popular vote any person who degrades the Church by an evil life. If there

THE GOSPEL AND MODERNITY 343

were at the time Bishops, which is possible, but not certain, they were only executive officials chosen from among the Elders. I do not think that we can find anywhere in the Fourth Gospel any hints in regard to the external organisation of the Church. Had St Paul been writing at the time, he could not, with his genius for organising, have entirely passed by the questions of Church officials, of the relation to the surrounding heathen, and the like. But the Evangelist, even in his Epistle, does not concern himself with such questions.

It cannot be denied that as the Church took up a more defined position in relation to the State, and in relation to the surrounding heathen society, some hardening of her crust was necessary; some organisation inevitably took place. And for such organisation abundant models existed in the cities of Asia Minor, which were accustomed to manage their own affairs in all smaller matters, as well as in Jewish Synagogues and Pagan thiasi. There is no need to say anything here as regards this development, for it is posterior to the age with which we deal. It has been in most respects justified by success. But the question what organisation is best for various branches of the Church is a large one.

What St Paul and the Fourth Evangelist had at heart was the internal unity of the Church as the body of Christ on earth, every member of which was in close relation to every other member. The only unity which they recognise is a unity of spirit.

Like so many of the spiritual teachings of St Paul and St John, the doctrine of the Church has been accepted by those of a materialist turn of mind in a materialist sense, and for unity of spirit they have read unity of government. As a matter of history, the outer unity of the Church has never been complete. From the first, small sections of the Church preferred autonomy, and broke away from the main body. And before the power of the Roman Popes was fully established there came alienation between East and West, which destroyed all possibility of external unity. Since the Reformation there has not been, even in Western Europe, unity of Church Government; nor, so far as anyone can see, is there the least probability that such unity can ever be established. It is more than doubtful whether such unity of government would be a thing desirable, even if it could be settled on reasonable grounds. The nations of Europe, east and west, north and south, so differ in character and political

THE GOSPEL AND MODERNITY 345

genius that different kinds of government, alike in Church and State, are necessary, if each is to remain true to the national bent, and to do in the world the work committed to it by the Divine Ruler. But what can be aimed at is a federation of Church with Church, a federation by which each may retain its special character, and yet be on friendly and tolerant relations with the rest. And the spiritual ideal of universal sympathy and love of Christian for Christian stands before us as clearly as ever since the first days, while the more easy and rapid communications of modern times make the expression of the feeling, if the feeling exist, more easy. Could there have arisen before our times such a movement as that of the Christian Students' Union? Could mutual friendship of the Churches in the mission-field have been so clearly forced upon us?

V

We come finally to the vexed and difficult question of Christian doctrine and the Creeds. It results from the discussion in the last chapter that the creed of the Evangelist is nothing like so definite as popular theology supposes. Hasty readers take detached phrases of the

English version, "The Word was God," "I and the Father are one," and, reading them in the light of the familiar Creed, think that the whole matter is simple. But these phrases in Greek to the people of the time would have had a far more vague meaning. The first, as I observed in the last chapter, is of very indefinite meaning, and may perhaps best be rendered by "The Word was of divine nature." And the second phrase may be rendered, "I and the Father are indissolubly united" (ἓν ἐσμεν). To suppose that such phrases can be used as clear-cut propositions in a logical construction is absurd. We have to approach them not from the platform of the Creed, but from the ground of the earliest Christian teaching.

The Synoptic Gospels,[1] invaluable as they are, the sources of our knowledge of the life and teachings of our Founder, do not greatly help us in dealing with the philosophical and doctrinal aspects of Christianity. It is true that here and there in these narratives we catch a glimpse of something more than human, a broken light of the eternal shining in a mundane setting. But so long as their Master was with them in the flesh, the problems of Christology could scarcely arise for the Apostles. It

[1] The following paragraphs are from *The Modern Churchman*, July 1914.

THE GOSPEL AND MODERNITY 347

was after His departure, in the middle of the first century, that they began to press. The first writer to give to them any definite answer was St Paul. St Paul must not be held responsible for the schemes of doctrine which subsequent writers have grafted upon his words. But he was a deep thinker; and he lived in the full stress of the religious awakening to which he tried to furnish ways of thought. If his mental training was in a measure perverted by rabbinic subtleties and logomachies, he yet lived in places where the light of Greek culture was shed abroad, and he had a great sensitiveness to what was best in his religious surroundings.

To the twelve their Master must have appeared at first as a Jewish prophet; later they came to think of Him as the Messiah; and after the crucifixion they began to realise that what they had witnessed was really the crowning revelation of God to man. But they still clung to the belief in their Master's speedy return in the clouds of heaven; they thought that He had come for the sake of the Jewish race only. The horizon of St Paul and the Fourth Evangelist is quite different. It is enlarged by baptising into Christ much that was best in the religions of the world at the time. Greek monotheism, the Hellenic doctrine of the Word, the mysticism of Egypt and the East, were all absorbed into the expanding life of the society, and were all transmuted by the ever-working Spirit of Christ into forms suited for His own dwelling-place. Christ as the heavenly life of the Church, and the Church as the earthly body of Christ, grew together and expanded until they became the supreme religious phenomenon of the age; and after the last rival of Christianity, Mithraism, had been overthrown, they absorbed all the springs of religion into one great river of God.

Formulæ may, from certain points of view, be desirable or necessary. But we must be careful not to overestimate them. At best they are approximations, relative truths in relation to experience and action, not the embodiment of any absolute or scientific truth.

If we compare the writings of St Paul and St Luke we shall at once see how unconscious those writers were of any formal doctrinal views on the subject of the Trinity. In *Acts* the striking religious phenomena which marked the first age of Christianity, and the spiritual powers exercised by the Apostles, of course Divine in origin, are repeatedly spoken of as gifts of the Holy Spirit. St Paul sometimes speaks of them in the same phraseology. But when he is writing of the peace and joy, the salvation, which belongs to believers, he often regards them as the result of the working of the Spirit of Christ, or of the exalted Christ in the Church. And in some passages he identifies the Holy Spirit with the Spirit of Christ. It is abundantly clear that he does not try to make any metaphysical distinctions in regard to the Trinity. He is speaking of the facts of Christian experience, and the words which he uses are not the expression of any developed theological system, but come fresh from the heart. I do not say that such merely approximate ways of speaking should or could have been kept up in the Church. But at least we have a warning not to regard exact theology as necessary to Christianity.

The Fourth Evangelist's attitude in regard to Creed differs somewhat from that of St Paul. Whereas the intellectual element in his creed is less developed, he clings to it with more passion. He does not see the need of such a theory of kenôsis as we find in St Paul, a theory intended to explain the relation of the historic to the spiritual Christ, though it must be added that St Paul merely states the view in one passage, and does not work it out in any detail. The Evangelist, after stating his *logos* doctrine, does not analyse it; and although he represents Jesus in a supernatural aspect, he does not try closely to connect that aspect with points of the logos doctrine as held by those with whom he was conversant. The complete freedom of self-determination, and the miraculous powers which he attributes to his Master, are not the fruits of wisdom so much as of character and spiritual supremacy. Yet he is very severe on those who throw any doubt on the divine sonship; and in the divine sonship he includes a complete monopoly of the way of approach to God. If the Epistle be by the Evangelist, he goes so far as to say that denial of the divine sonship of his Master is antichrist, and an utter rejection of saving truth. Yet there is a great difference between his intolerance, if we must so call it, and the intolerance of the Church at a later time, inasmuch as the denials which he views with horror are not denials of any mere intellectual statement, but denials of the principle of Christian life, as he understands it.

St Paul and the Fourth Evangelist clearly saw that the doctrine of an indwelling Christ in the Church needed guarding. They held that if an exalted Christ was the light of the Church, it was Christ arisen and glorified who was thus exalted, not a human Jesus translated into heavenly places. St Paul is quite clear on this point. Christ, he says, when He came on earth, emptied Himself of His divine prerogative, took upon Him the form of a slave (for that is the real meaning of the word *doulos*), and submitted to human conditions, even to death, whereupon God highly exalted Him. The Fourth Evangelist more closely identifies the Jesus of history with the exalted Christ, but he does so by constructing for Jesus on earth an ideal life, from which weakness and human limitations are excluded, although here and there a touch of naturalism comes in.

It would take us too far if I tried at this point to collate these views with those prevalent in modern Christianity and those which appear to belong to the future. Certainly in modern England the teaching of the Living Christ has been far more strongly dwelt on than the doctrine of the Holy Spirit. Christian experience has been interpreted rather in the light of the former teaching than in that of the latter. All that need be said here is to insist that both teachings alike have Apostolic authority; both alike have a great place in the history of the Church. Every Christian has the right to interpret his experience in the light of either, accordingly as nature and intellectual tendency may dictate. If a man choose to speak of the Christian life, with its aspirations, its hopes, and its beliefs, as the result of the inner working of the Holy Spirit, he speaks with St Paul and with St Paul's Master. If a man prefer to regard it as the outward result of the life of Christ in the soul, he again speaks with St Paul and the Fourth Evangelist, to whom we owe the eternal parables of the body and the members, and the vine with its branches.

Offshoots of the logos doctrine have constantly arisen during the history of Christianity. But so long as the Jewish cosmogony was regarded as history, they could only take a very imperfect form. When the doctrine of evolution came to hold the field, an immense future was opened for them. When two points are accepted, first that the Universe is the result of Divine reason and goodness, and second, that Christianity is the consummation of human progress, to which the process of the ages leads up, then we have a scheme to which only some form of the logos doctrine corresponds. In H. Drummond's *Ascent of Man* we have a Christian logos doctrine put in popular form. In the philosophy of Bergson, for instance, we have the basis of what may be a logos doctrine adapted to modern intellectual conditions. When the old view of a series of special creations was given up, its place could only be taken either

THE GOSPEL AND MODERNITY 353

by a materialistic theory like that of Haeckel, or by some form of logos theory, since it is impossible that Christianity should be left on one side in any idealist view of creation.

VI

The times in which we live are in some respects singularly like the time of early Christianity. Then the Roman Empire had spread over all the Mediterranean lands a veneer of material civilisation, travelling had become easy, and life ran on smooth wheels. The same result has been produced in modern days by our discoveries and inventions, the use of steam and electricity, the cult of hygiene, the general spread of comfort. Then the wide use of the Greek language, and with it of Greek science and philosophy, had produced a high general intellectual level among the more leisured classes: all who thought, thought under Greek conditions. A similar intellectual condition has now arisen from the dominance of science alike in our knowledge of the material world, and in our study of man and his history. From England and America to India and Japan, a common intellectual groundwork is laid down; and men from farthest East and farthest West can meet in conference and congress, and find themselves in thorough understanding with one another, making the same assumptions and pursuing the same investigations.

Even in the matter of religion the resemblance between the age of the Cæsars and ours is striking. Then in all countries the ancestral religions, consecrated by long use and adorned with pomp and riches, were giving way, and their place was being taken by new enthusiasms, starting from the body of the people, but looked on with sympathy by such of the cultured people as were not satisfied with Greek religious philosophy. In the same way, now, in Europe, in India, in China, popular religion, in spite of occasional recrudescence, is slowly being sapped and vanishing, while all kinds of new enthusiasms and forms of belief are rising and claiming their place. The gap between the beliefs of the highly educated and the populace is growing, and has grown until it is an obvious danger to society. The rise and spread of new sects —the Christian Scientists, the Mormons, the Futurists, and so forth—is notable in England and America; and though few of these sects can offer any serious reasonable defence of their tenets, they are by multitudes accepted, and accepted with enthusiasm.

But, it will be said, granting a similarity in conditions between the age of the Cæsars and ours, where shall we look for a start for the revival of faith? We cannot expect a St Paul to arise; and the intellectual conditions which made the Fourth Gospel possible no longer exist. It is quite true that the age does not seem to encourage the rise of great personalities. We cannot hope that one man will arise to adapt Christianity to new conditions. But how if the place of great personalities may be taken in a measure by movements, by great currents in the moral and intellectual worlds?

In the first place, I would suggest that modern historic criticism, in destroying our confidence in the literary records of early Christianity, has done a work in some ways parallel to the work of St Paul and his school. Even sceptical criticism leaves us with a more definite information as to the life, the words and deeds of the Founder of Christianity than was possessed by St Paul. If the miraculous halo round His figure is fading, the severest investigation leaves us with a conviction that our Master claimed a unique relationship to the Father in Heaven, that never man spake as He spake, that in His life the will of God was more fully revealed than in all the rest of history. But still, the fading of material knowledge throws us back on the life of the spirit; and we realise with St Paul that it is the Spirit in the Church which is the great gift of Jesus Christ to mankind. We are driven, like our Evangelist, from letter to spirit, from reliance on a life lived in space and time to a reliance on a life which is eternal in heaven.

And though no one in our day would venture to write a life of Christ according to the spirit, yet has not the study of nature and of man shown us in recent years more and more clearly the truth of the Johannine teaching that the material is unreal and evanescent, and the spiritual is the truly abiding, and the source of the life which is eternal? I will not speak of the growing spirituality of the study of matter. What more concerns us is the result of the study of the unconscious in man, and the spiritual world in which he dwells like a fish in the ocean. The trickery and imposture which have accompanied the experiments of the professed spiritualists, the low level of the morality of their lives, have disgusted many earnest students, and made them turn away from such experiments as revealing rather diabolic than divine influences. With this revulsion I sympathise; yet surely some of the well-established facts of spiritualism, the transference of thought from person to person, or the remarkable dominance of will and belief over what is merely material, are of the utmost importance to our views on the subject of religion. We are gaining a conception of a realm beyond and above the visible world, which seems to make impossible in the future any merely material or magical conception of religion.

I cannot but think that this great widening of our horizon will have a strong and stimulating effect on many of our religious beliefs. It will raise our belief in the spiritual basis of life, and show us that it is the spirit that quickeneth, the flesh profiteth nothing. It will make a revolution in our notion of death, and bring life and immortality to light. Whatever we may think of spiritualism, *spirituality* has become a more reasonable explanation of the world, and a kind of Christian mysticism more possible. In mysticism in the past there has been as much dregs as in other forms of religion; it has been allied with astrology, with magic, with self-hypnotism, with hysteria; but there is in it a deep well of truth, and a certain strain of it is as essential to all higher religion as a certain proportion of oxygen is to the air we breathe.

Everyone must feel that there is a new stir

in Christianity. Activity in the mission-field, and the rise of such important movements as that of the Christian Students, compel Christianity to modify its formulæ, and to take on new aspects. The last decades of the nineteenth century were a time of comparative inertia in Christianity: with the new century fresh life has begun to come into the Christian Churches. Those who attended the remarkable meeting at Edinburgh a few years ago speak of it almost with awe, as of a time when the Spirit of God was sensibly present, and an outpouring like that at the first Whitsuntide took place. The Church has to live up to that standard.

But movements like the Christian Student movement, the new spirit in our missions, the Christian Social Union, are all at present in the making. And the necessary intellectual basis has not been thought out. This is a work which naturally falls on Broad Churchmen, and it is one of the most imperative needs of the age. None of us can hope to do more than contribute a few elements to the necessary reconstruction of Christian theology; but light is coming in from many sides; and the attitude of earnest welcome to any light, however broken, is the one which best becomes us.

INDEX

Acts of the Apostles, 21, 27 *seq.*, 33, 65, 135, 157, 159, 197, 226, 232, 247, 250, 348
Alexander the Great, 10, 11, 17.
Alexandria, its influence, overrated compared to that of other Greek cities, 59, 75, 313.
Amazons, in relation to worship of Artemis, 4
Androclus, mythical founder of Ephesus, 3.
Antioch, relation to Ephesus, 37, 47.
Antony (Mark) enlarges sanctuary of Artemis, 5
Apocalypse, the, 28, 34 *seq.*, 40, 43 *seq* , 172, 223, 234
Apuleius, 190
Aquila in Ephesus, 20, 32.
Artemis of Ephesus, worship of, 3, 8, 25, 34, 250
Asiarchs, 23.
Atonement, doctrine of, not fundamental in St Paul or in Fourth Gospel, 310.

Babylon, influence of, 4, 7
Bacon, B W., 53.
Baptism, *see* Sacraments.
Baur on Paulinism, 38.
"Beloved Disciple," the, 40, 69 *seq* , 84, 288.
Bezalel, 145

Cæsar (Julius), deified by Ephesians, 18.

Caiaphas, 77
Capernaum, Jews of, 114.
Catacombs paintings of the, 209, 240 *seq*
Celsus, 235.
Cerinthus, 49, 80
Charles, Dr R. H., 168
Christ, Pauline teaching of, 25, 115, 128, and Church in Fourth Gospel, 129 *seq* , indwelling, 154 *seq* , 316, 322, exalted, 192 *seq* , 243 *seq* , 329. *See* also Jesus and Christology
Christology of Fourth Gospel, 291–318, 322 *seq*
Church, the, Pauline doctrine of, 128, 221, in Fourth Gospel, 129 *seq* , as distinguished from the world, 236–255, organisation of, 342 *seq* *See* also Sacraments
Clementine Recognitions, the, 88
Coinage of Ephesus, 11.
Colossians, Epistle to the, 31.
Corinth, differences from Ephesus, 30.
Corinthians, First Epistle to, 26, 127, 196, 342
Corinthians, Second Epistle to, 26, 29, 127
Cornelius, 222
Council of Ephesus, 49.
Creeds, the, 345 *seq*. *See* also Christology.
Crœsus, King of Lydia, 2, 8.
Cumont, 45

Dale, Dr A. W., 85.
Daniel, 188
Demetrius of Ephesus, 24
Docetism, 286, 303. *See* Gnosticism
Doutté, 277.
Drummond, H., 352.

Ecclesiasticus, 205
Ephesians, Epistle to the, 31
Ephesus, early history and character, 1-18; St Paul in, 19-33; after St Paul, 34-81, St Paul writes from, 197, 200, 314.
Eschatology, 167 *seq*, 324 *seq*
Eternal life, 138 *seq*., 177-188, 323 *seq*.
Ethics of Fourth Gospel, 256 *seq*.
Eucharist, *see* Sacraments.
Eusebius (historian), 141.
Evil spirits in Fourth Gospel, 161.

Forgiveness of Sin, 130 *seq*.

Galatians, Epistle to the, 127
Gnosticism, 49, 80 *seq*., 90, 270.
Gospel, the Fourth, relation to Ephesus, 53 *seq*.; authorship, 54 *seq*; character of composition, 56 *seq*.; allegory in, 57 *seq*., sources of, 66 *seq*; spirituality of, 75 *seq*, 91; materialist element in, 80 *seq*., 146; origin and purpose of, 86 *seq*., its writer's idea of biography, 92-123; its basis in Christian experience, 124-140; use of the term *spirit* in, 146 *seq*.; eschatology and doctrine of eternal life in, 163, 188, sacraments in, 194, 213, in relation to Judaism, 219-235; on the Church and the world, 236-255; ethics of, 256 *seq*.; miracle in, 271 *seq*, its Christology, 291, 322 *seq*.; lack of historicity, 335 *seq*.

Hebrews, Epistle to, 58, 79.
Heracleitus of Ephesus, his philosophy, 9, 10, 258, 313.
Holtzmann, H., 67.
Homer on Truth, 260

Ignatius, St, on fighting with wild beasts, 27; his letter to Ephesians, 47 *seq*, 331

Jackson, Dr H Latimer, quoted, 73.
James, William, 319 *seq*.
Jesus, faith of, 19, name of, 21, 22, 62, sayings of, 62 *seq*, 73, 82 *seq*., 96 *seq*, 147; His eschatology, 171 *seq*, 192, 197; baptism of, 198; restriction of mission, 216, 219 *seq*., 238 *seq*., 261, 265, 296 *seq*., 332 *seq*, 358. *See* also Christ.
Jews and Judaism, 17, 19, 20 *seq*, 33 *seq*, 45, 61, 65, 114 *seq*., 126, 167, 206; relation of Judaism to Gospel, 214-235, 337.
John the Baptist, his disciples in Ephesus, 19, 87, 198, 200, 216, 232, 285 *seq*., 286.
John the Presbyter, 16, 42
John the Prophet, author of the Apocalypse, 16, 41
John, St, First Epistle of, 40, 42, 65, 155 172, 186 *seq*, 13, 310
John, St, Second and Third Epistles of, 42 *seq*.
John the son of Zebedee, 16, 39 *seq*, 41 *seq*., 49, 69 *seq*., 84, 141.
Jülicher quoted, 39.
Judaism, *see* Jews.
Justin, 226.

Kennedy, Dr H. A. A., 193.
Kenosis, Pauline doctrine of, 300.

Lazarus, resurrection of, 174, 282 *seq*, 304.
Liberty in relation to truth, 271 *seq*.
Lightfoot, Bishop, 62.

INDEX

Logos, doctrine of the, 33, 44, 82, 187, 210 *seq*, 225, 285, 304, 312 *seq*, 346 *seq*.
Loisy, Dr Alfred, 53, 202
Love, Christian, 136 *seq*, 272 *seq*
Luke, St, on Paul in Ephesus, 20, on laying on of hands, 21, his account of riot at Ephesus, 25, his purpose in writing Gospel, 95, relation to Mark, 95, and Q, 96 *seq*, on Scripture, 149, on the Spirit, 150 *seq.*, 179, 211, 218, 222, 285, 289, 295 *seq*
Lysander, worship of, by Ionians, 17.
Lysimachus, Ephesus enlarged by, 3.

Magic, 22, 47, 151.
Marcion, 38.
Mark, St, 68, 84, 95, 117, 172 *seq.*, 179, 196, 204, 215, 224, 294, 302, 305.
Mary Magdalene, 160 *seq.*, 288.
Matthew, St, 65, 95 *seq.*, 149, 179, 197 *seq*, 211, 215, 216, 224, 228, 232, 279, 285, 295 *seq*, 320.
Megabyzus, leader in worship of Artemis, 4.
Miletus, 10, St Paul's speech in, 25, 27, 29, 34, 128, 234
Miracles, 135 *seq.*, 253; in Fourth Gospel, 277 – 290 *passim*, 306.
Mithras, *see* Mystery religions.
Modernity, 319–361 *passim*
Moffatt, Dr Jas., quoted, 39, 45, 52, 58, 67
Montanism, 48, 341.
Mystery religions, 14, 45, 126, 189 *seq*, 206, 241, 348

Nestorius, 49.
Nicodemus, 112 *seq.*, 121 *seq.*, 195, 201, 261, 265
Nicolaitans, 35 *seq*.
Nicolas of Antioch, 37.

Onesimus, Bishop of Ephesus, 48.
Origen, allegorising of, 76

Papias and John the Presbyter, 43.
Paul (St), his visit to Ephesus, 19 *seq*; stay and work in Ephesus, 19–35; on Orders in Church, 41, relation to author of Fourth Gospel, 54, 75, 78, 88 *seq*, 99, 309, and *passim*; mystic doctrine of, 127 *seq*, 193; on forgiveness, 130 *seq*; view of the Universe, 148, of Scripture, 149, of the Spirit, 153 *seq*; eschatology of, 181 *seq.*, on sacraments, 183–198, on flesh, 211; on Judaism, 217 *seq.*, 229 *seq.*, on Church and World, 237 *seq*, on truth, 266; on facts, 269, 332, on liberty, 271; on kenosis, 300; "twice-born," 320
Persian invasions, 2, 8, 10.
Peter, St, 71 *seq*, 84, 207, 267, 288.
Philo, 57, 59, 314.
Phocæa, early importance of, 2
Plato (Platonic teaching), 89 *seq*, 101 *seq.*, 147 *seq.*, 170, 258, 266, 311, 329.
Plutarch, 17, 94, 125.
Polycarp, St, 48 *seq*
Prayer, 132 *seq.*
Priscilla (Prisca) in Ephesus, 20, greeting to, 32
Psalms, the, 145, 148, 189, 260, 262, 269.
Purgatory, 177.

"Q," 96 *seq*

Ramsay, Sir W., quoted, 16.
Renan, 284.
Réville, Albert, 285.
Roman Empire, rule of, in Asia Minor, 12, 125, 249, 353.
Romans, Epistle to the, 32, 231

Sabbath, the, 226 *seq*
Sacraments, the, in St Paul and in Fourth Gospel, 189-213 *passim*, 281, 340 *seq*
Samaria, the woman of, 113 *seq.*, 208, 222, 265, 304
Samson, 145
Sanday, Canon, 53
Schleiermacher, 100
Schweitzer, Dr, 171
Scott, E F., quoted, 59, 88, 159, 234, 252.
Scriptures, interpretation of, 149, 229 *seq*.
Sheol, 159 *seq*
Smyrna, 36, 48.
Socrates, 100 *seq.*, 147.
Spirit, the, in Pauline theology, 82, in Fourth Gospel, 141-162, 261 *seq*, 321 *seq.*, 348 *seq.*

Synoptists, *see* Matthew, Mark, Luke
Syro-Phœnician woman, 215.

Thomas, St, 290
Timothy, Epistles to, 254.
Titus, Epistle to, 254.
Truth, doctrine of, 158 *seq.*, 243 *seq*, meanings of, 257 *seq*
Tylor, his *Primitive Culture*, 142.

Virgin Mother, the, 33, 50, 211, 285.

Wendt, H. H, 67.
Westcott, Dr B F, 96
Will of God, devotion to, 274 *seq.*, 298 *seq.*

Xenophon, 101 *seq*

www.ingramcontent.com/pod-product-compliance
Lightning Source LLC
Chambersburg PA
CBHW072132220426
43664CB00013B/2217